PROGRAMMING
LANGUAGE CONCEPTS

PROGRAMMING LANGUAGE CONCEPTS

Carlo Ghezzi
Politecnico di Milano

Mehdi Jazayeri
Synapse Computer Corporation

175 YEARS OF PUBLISHING
1807 1982

John Wiley & Sons, Inc.
New York   Chichester   Brisbane   Toronto   Singapore

Library of Congress Cataloging in Publication Data:

Ghezzi, Carlo.
  Programming language concepts.

  Bibliography: p.
  Includes index.
  1. Programming languages (Electronic computers)
I. Jazayeri, Mehdi. II. Title.

QA76.7.G48   001.64'24   81-16032
ISBN 0-471-08755-6   AACR2

Printed in the United States of America

10 9 8 7 6 5

To Anny and Mary

PREFACE

Language is only the instrument of science, and words are but the signs of ideas.   Samuel Johnson (1709–1794)

This book introduces, analyzes, and evaluates the important concepts found in current programming languages. The book is based on two premises: that programming languages exist for the purpose of software production, and that they comprise one of many tools required for this task. The merits of a programming language, or a programming language concept, must thus be judged on how it affects software production and how well it can be integrated with other software production tools.

This book is *not* an introduction to any one programming language. It is *not* a feature-by-feature examination of programming languages. Rather, it presents and evaluates concepts common to programming languages and those likely to dictate the evolution of programming languages in the future. We have taken a comparative approach: the concepts are illustrated by contrasting their appearance in different languages. The languages emphasized most are Pascal, ALGOL 68, and SIMULA 67 because (1) these languages have provided the starting point for many ideas of the recent languages, and (2) they illustrate well the important characteristics of the earlier languages. Many other languages, ranging from old ones such as FORTRAN and ALGOL 60 to infants such as CLU, Euclid, Mesa, and Ada, are used in examples, with particular emphasis on Ada. A chapter is also devoted to functional languages, with special attention given to LISP and APL. The reader, however, will not become a proficient programmer in *any* of these languages. Rather, we hope that this book will improve your ability to appreciate and evaluate programming languages (or proposals). In addition, we hope you will be able to identify the important concepts in programming languages and recognize their limits and capabilities.

This ability is essential if one is to choose a language, design a language, or even use a language to maximum advantage. Thus, the book will prove useful to software managers, professional programmers, and language designers, both as a study guide and as a reference text.

vii

These professionals' tasks have become increasingly difficult with the rapid information explosion in the field of programming languages, coupled with the recognition that our current languages are inadequate. This trend is vividly demonstrated by the rise in the number of professional conferences on programming languages; by the rise in the number of microprocessor languages, spurred on by advances in hardware technology; and by the decision of the U.S. Department of Defense to undertake the development of yet another programming language. It is our intention to enable the reader to take advantage of these developments, rather than be overwhelmed by them.

We have designed this book to be used as a textbook in a course on programming languages. In such use, it should be supplemented with manuals on specific languages. We have made a deliberate decision not to include in the text any detailed "summaries" of languages. A language summary can provide only a superficial view and therefore cannot be used as a reference document; only the language manual or its official definition can serve that purpose. Furthermore, one of the basic skills that a student should acquire in a programming languages course is the ability to learn and evaluate a language solely on the basis of its official definition. The glossary of programming languages at the end of the book directs the user to the required documents. Nevertheless, the book is a self-contained analysis of programming language concepts.

Prerequisites for the book are fluency in one programming language and working knowledge of another; preferably, one of the two should be block-structured. Reading knowledge of Pascal is helpful but not essential. The reader should also have some software development experience. The emphasis on systematic program design requires that the reader have some familiarity with the difficulties and problems of software production. In particular, the reader should be aware of the need for a disciplined approach to programming and should know how to use a language in a disciplined way—although this is not a prerequisite if the reader is willing to take some of our assertions on faith.

The emphasis on modern languages such as Pascal, rather than on traditional ones such as FORTRAN or PL/I, makes the book particularly suitable for university curricula that share this emphasis. Most curricula are moving in that direction. We also cover the basics of the traditional languages, however.

Parts of the book have been used over the last five years in a beginning graduate-level course on programming languages. The material is suitable either for this level or for advanced undergraduates.

PURPOSE AND CONTENTS OF THE BOOK

If any one notion distinguishes this work from other books on programming languages, it is the theme that programming languages should support software development. Indeed, one purpose is to evaluate programming language concepts in terms of their contribution to the software development process and to develop the criteria needed for such evaluation. These criteria are based principally on the relationship between programming languages and design methodologies and—to a lesser extent—on the relationship between programming languages and other software production tools. This point of view is developed in Chapter 1. In Chapter 2, we present four concepts—data types, control structures, program correctness, and programming in the large—that can be used to examine and evaluate programming languages. These concepts also are used to explain the evolution of the field over the past 25 years. Each of Chapters 4 through 7 is devoted to detailing and illustrating one of these concepts. An important point in these chapters is how language features in support of these concepts can be implemented. Chapter 3 provides the background on language processing that is necessary for following the discussions of Chapters 4 through 7.

Although we are concerned primarily with those languages classified as imperative, or statement-oriented, we devote Chapter 8 to a discussion of functional, or applicative, languages. The contrast between these two styles—imperative versus applicative—serves to illustrate their strengths and weaknesses.

Finally, in Chapter 9 we discuss the subject of language design. The field of language design has been and promises to remain one of the most active areas of computer science. The recent Department of Defense language Ada and the many microcomputer languages being developed today, indicate this high level of activity.

ACKNOWLEDGEMENTS

The comments of a number of people have been extremely helpful in reducing errors and improving the presentation. We especially would like to thank J. P. Banatre, Dan Berry, Laurence Chan, Jon Cohen, Richard LeBlanc, Gyula Magó, Dino Mandrioli, David Moffat, and Kuo-Chung Tai.

Carlo Ghezzi acknowledges the support of CNR (the Italian Research Council). Mehdi Jazayeri acknowledges the support of TRW Vidar.

We were extremely fortunate to have had the help of Edith Coon, who provided pleasant, accurate, and fast typing service. For the many versions she has typed and retyped, we thank her. Vicki Baker typed early versions of several chapters. We also would like to thank our families, who put up with the many hours with "the book."

A NOTE TO THE INSTRUCTOR

Chapters 2 through 9 contain exercises. A few of the exercises require the student to consult official language definitions. There are two kinds of exercises that we did not list explicitly but that are particularly valuable. One is the reading of a language manual and evaluating that language based on the concepts of this book. The language glossary at the end of the book can serve as a starting point. The other exercise we recommend is the writing of programs in different languages. Some of the languages discussed here, however, might not be available at a particular installation. What we recommend in that case is to use these languages as program design languages when appropriate (e.g., CLU for designing an abstract-data type) and then manually to translate the solution to a locally available language. This kind of exercise helps the student appreciate the usefulness of languages that directly support a design methodology.

Chapter 7 contains a discussion of software development tools with emphasis on UNIX™*. If UNIX is available at a particular installation, we recommend programming assignments that require the student to use these different tools. It can cause a real change of attitude towards programming, especially if one is used to writing programs in less friendly environments (e.g., using cards, cryptic JCL commands). Also, to help students to appreciate the problems of programming in the large, some team projects should be assigned in relation to Chapter 7.

Carlo Ghezzi

Mehdi Jazayeri

---

*UNIX is a trademark of Bell Laboratories.

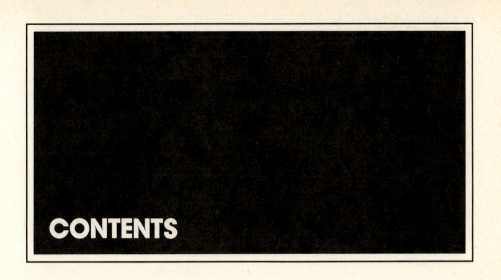

CONTENTS

PROGRAMMING LANGUAGE CONCEPTS

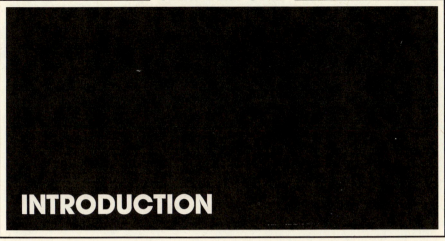

CHAPTER ONE

INTRODUCTION

This book is concerned with programming languages. Programming languages, however, do not exist in a vacuum: they are tools for writing software. A comprehensive study of programming languages must take this role into account. We begin, therefore, with a discussion of the software development process and the role of programming languages in this process. The purpose of this chapter is to provide a perspective from which to view programming languages and their intended uses. From this perspective, we will weigh the merits of many of the language concepts discussed in the rest of the book.

1.1 SOFTWARE DEVELOPMENT PROCESS

The software development process can be divided into five phases. These phases usually are followed as five sequential steps in software development. Each step, however, may identify deficiencies in the previous one, which then must be repeated. Each phase involves a distinct activity and results in a set of clearly identifiable products. These phases can be listed as follows.

i. *Requirements analysis and specification*
A software system is developed in order to meet a need perceived by a user community. User needs are stated in the form of a set of *requirements* that the system is expected to satisfy. These requirements are developed jointly by users and software developers. The success of a system is measured eventually by how well the software mirrors these stated requirements; how well the requirements mirror the users' perceived needs; and how well the users' perceived needs reflect the real needs.

The result of this phase is a requirements document stating *what* the system is to do, along with users' manuals, feasibility and cost studies, performance requirements, and so on. The requirements document does not specify *how* the system is going to meet its requirements.

ii. *Software design and specification*

Starting with the requirements document, software designers design the software system. The result of this phase is a system design specification document identifying all of the modules comprising the system, and their interfaces. Of the various approaches to software design and specification, none is universally accepted. The design methodology followed in this step can have a great impact on the choice of the programming language to be used in system implementation. We will come back to this point later in the chapter.

iii. *Implementation (coding)*

The system is implemented to meet the design specified in phase 2. This is the only step in which a programming language is used directly. The result is a fully implemented and documented system.

iv. *Certification*

The purpose of this step is to ensure that the system meets the stated requirements. This usually is done by testing the system against the design specifications. It is often assumed that the design specifications capture the requirements accurately, although this should be demonstrated before the system can be considered certified.

The result of step 4 is a certified system delivered to the user. Some testing is, of course, performed by each programmer during the implementation phase. There are three kinds of testing: module testing, integration testing, and system testing. *Module testing* is done by each programmer on the module he or she is working on, to ensure that it meets its interface specifications. *Integration testing* is done on a partial aggregation of modules; it is basically aimed at uncovering intermodule inconsistencies. *System testing* is performed during the final certification phase, to ensure that the entire system works properly according to the requirements document.

Besides testing, included in the certification phase are all the activities concerned with assessing the correctness of the program. Any program verification efforts, for example, are covered by this step.

v. *Maintenance*

Following delivery of the system, changes to the system may become necessary either because of detected malfunction (error) or because of a desire to add new capabilities or to improve old ones. These changes are referred to as maintenance. The importance of this phase can be seen in the fact that maintenance costs are typically at least as large as those of all the other steps combined.

We next will examine the role of the programming language in the software development process, by illustrating the relationship between the programming language and other software development tools in Section 1.2 and the relationship between the programming language and design methodologies in Section 1.3.

1.2   THE PROGRAMMING LANGUAGE AS A COMPONENT OF A SOFTWARE DEVELOPMENT FACILITY

The work in any of the five phases of software development may be supported by computer-aided tools. The phase currently supported best is the coding phase, with such tools as text editors, compilers, linkers, and libraries. These tools have evolved gradually, as the need for automation has been recognized. In the early days of computing—and not even the earliest—one had to punch a program on cards, pick the necessary routines from a library of card decks, combine all the routines, and submit them to the compiler. The possibilities for clerical errors—let alone the possibility of wearing out the library decks—were great. Advances in many areas of computer science have led to the automation of many of these tasks. One can now use an interactive editor to create a program and a file manager to store it in a library for future use. When needed, several previously created and (possibly) compiled programs may be linked to produce an executable program. These computer-aided program development tools have increased programming productivity by reducing the chances of errors.

Yet, as we have seen, software development involves much more than programming. If we want to increase the productivity of software development, we must devise computer support for all of its phases.

By a *software development facility* we mean an integrated set of tools and techniques that aid in the development of software. The facility is used in all phases of software development: that is, requirements, design, implementation, certification, and maintenance.

An idealized scenario for the use of such a facility would be the following. A team of application and computer specialists, interacting with the facility, develops the system requirements. The facility keeps track of the requirements as they are being developed and updated, and guards against incompleteness or inconsistency. It also ensures the currency of the documentation as changes are being made to the requirements.

Following the completion of the requirements, system designers, interacting with the facility, gradually design the system: that is, they specify the needed modules and the module interfaces. Test data may also be produced at this stage. The implementers then undertake to implement the system based on the design. The tools provided by the software development facility at this phase are the most familiar. They include programming languages, editors, compilers, simulators, interpreters, linkers, and others that one normally uses in programming.

As far as the usefulness of the facility is concerned, it is important that these tools not only work well together but that they be compatible with tools used in the other phases. For example, the programming language must be compatible with the design methodology supported by the facility at the design stage. If the methodology is top-down design, the language must support this approach in the sense of allowing the hierarchical levels of the design to be apparent in the program. The next section is devoted to the effect of the design methodology on programming languages. The point we would like to impress upon the reader is that the facility must be viewed as consisting of tools and methodologies, and that these ought to be compatible, for maximum benefits.

In the certification phase, the help provided by the facility can be quite varied. The facility could be used to collect test data during the requirements, specification, and implementation phases. It could ensure that these tests are kept current (as changes are made to the specifications, for example). It could also support the use of formal specification and verification of modules. The results of tests could be collected and classified. Suitable measures could be used to determine the adequacy of the testing strategy.

The result of all this interaction with the facility is a fully documented and certified system that corresponds to the requirements set down initially. If at any future time there is need to modify the system—that is, the requirements—the facility must be capable of tracing the change to the design specification, code, test data, and documentation and to identify all affected areas.

The foregoing scenario provides a particularly simple and ideal illustration of the use of a software development facility. Although no such facility exists at present, current technology is not too far from making such a system possible. (In fact, all of the components of the facility exist; what is needed is the engineering job of integrating these components into a unified system.) In any case, the point of this discussion is to focus attention on the overall activity in which software developers are involved and the role that a programming language plays in this work. Whether or not these activities are supported by a computer system, they must be undertaken, and the programming language is only one tool that software developers use. Since the usefulness of this tool can only be measured by its contribution to the software development process, it is necessary to examine the relationship of the programming language to other components of a software development facility.

We must mention that this view has not always been accepted. Certainly, the first programming languages were designed for "programming" rather than for "software development." Nevertheless, even if a language was not designed with the goal of software production in mind, it must be evaluated based on that criterion, since that is the desired end. Such is the criterion used in this book.

1.3 SOFTWARE DESIGN METHODOLOGY AND PROGRAMMING LANGUAGES

As mentioned earlier, the relationship between software design methodologies and programming languages is a most important one. This is so whether or not one views the programming language as a component of a software development facility. In trying to follow a certain design methodology, we will find that some languages are better suited than others.

Older languages, such as FORTRAN, were not designed to support specific design methodologies. For example, the absence of suitable high-level control structures in FORTRAN makes it difficult to systematically design algorithms in a top-down fashion. Conversely, Pascal was designed with the explicit goal of supporting top-down design and structured programming. The developing trends in languages show that the idea that languages should support a design methodology is increasingly becoming accepted.

The fields of software design methodology and programming language design can converge, and in some cases they already have. The most striking example of this trend is information hiding (as a design methodology) and data abstraction (as a language design principle).

Information hiding is a design technique for decomposing systems into modules. Each module hides a *secret,* often the format of a particular data structure (record, file, etc.). The module provides *access functions* that can be used to inquire or update the information contained in the data structure. Thus, users of the module (i.e., other modules) may access, through function calls, the information that the module is willing to provide. They cannot access the information by directly manipulating the module's data structure, or by using global variables.

Languages with data abstraction facilities, such as SIMULA 67, Mesa, CLU, and Ada, are quite capable of implementing this methodology. In fact, as we will see, a SIMULA class, a Mesa module, a CLU cluster, or an Ada package can directly represent an information-hiding module.

It is not clear if the concept of information hiding spawned the idea of the SIMULA class as a mechanism for describing abstractions. It is likely that the concepts of information hiding and the SIMULA class progressed independently and met in their maturation. The lesson is that the choice of design methodology can influence language design and should also influence the choice of the language to be used.

1.4 COMPUTER ARCHITECTURE AND PROGRAMMING LANGUAGES

Design methodologies influence programming languages in the sense of establishing requirements for the language to meet. Computer architecture has exerted influence from the opposite direction in the sense of restraining language designs to what can be implemented efficiently on current-day machines. Accordingly, languages have been constrained by the ideas of Von Neumann, since most current computers are very similar to the original Von Neumann architecture. To go one step further with this argument: what is most discouraging is that most so-called high-level language-directed architectures are not in fact being driven by real language needs, since the language motivating the architecture was itself motivated by computer architecture in the first place.

Backus (Backus 1978) has strongly argued this point of view and has called for the use of a functional style of programming, both because of its simpler (and sounder) mathematical foundations and because of its higher expressive power. LISP is the best-known example of a language promoting such style, but many of LISP's original functional characteristics have been modified to make the language efficiently implementable on traditional machine architectures. Backus argues that we will abandon our traditional languages and adopt a radically different language only if the computers exist to execute these languages efficiently; he predicts that hardware technology will soon make this possible.

Backus attacks the concepts of assignment statements and variables as the roots of much evil and a curse passed on by the Von Neumann architecture. However, although examples of functional programming languages, such as LISP, have been around for a number of years, they have succeeded in replacing the conventional programming languages only in certain application areas. Besides implementation problems, there are probably questions of the psychology and sociology of programming languages that favor the traditional approaches. These issues are highly controversial, and the debate on traditional versus functional programming languages is currently in the research stage.

This book considers the prevalent languages of the last 25 years and the issues that have influenced their design. We are thus confined to the examination of what are called statement-oriented languages. We do, however, cover the important issues in functional programming languages in Chapter 8.

1.5 LANGUAGE DESIGN GOALS IMPOSED BY THE SOFTWARE DEVELOPMENT PROCESS

Returning to the theme of viewing a programming language as a tool for the development of software, this section identifies the requirements that this viewpoint places on the programming language.

i. *Software must be reliable*

In other words, users should be able to rely on the software. They should feel comfortable in using it even in the presence of infrequent or undesirable events such as hardware or software failures. This informal and hard-to-quantify property is strongly related to the more formal property of correctness. Software is correct if it behaves according to its specifications: the more rigorously and unambiguously the specifications are set down, the more convincingly program correctness can be proved. The reliability requirement has gained importance as software has been called upon to accomplish increasingly complicated tasks.

ii. *Software must be maintainable*

Again, as software costs have risen and increasingly complex software systems have been developed, economic considerations have reduced the possibility of throwing away existing software and developing similar applications from scratch. Existing software must be modified to meet new requirements. Also, since for such complex systems it is almost impossible to get the real requirements right in the first place, one can only hope to gradually evolve a system into the desired one.

iii. *Software must execute efficiently*
Efficiency has always been a goal of any software system. This goal affects both the programming language (features that can be efficiently implemented on present-day architectures) and the choice of algorithms to be used.

These three requirements—reliability, maintainability, and efficiency—can be achieved by appropriate tools in the software development facility, and by certain characteristics of the programming language. We now will discuss language issues directly in support of these goals.

1.5.1 Language and Reliability

The goal of software reliability is promoted by the following programming language qualities.

Writability This is a hard-to-quantify property. Basically, it refers to the possibility of expressing a program in a way that is natural for the problem. The programmer should not be distracted by details and tricks of the language from the more important activity of problem solving. Even though it is a subjective criterion, we can agree that higher-level languages are more writable than lower-level languages (e.g. assembly or machine languages). For example, an assembly language programmer is often distracted by the addressing mechanisms needed to access certain data, for example by positioning index registers, and so on. The easier it is to concentrate on the problem solving activity, the less error-prone is program writing.

Readability It should be possible to follow the logic of the program, and to discover the presence of errors, by examining the program. Readability is also a subjective criterion that depends a great deal on matters of taste and style. However, the simpler the language is and the more naturally it allows algorithms to be expressed, the easier it is to understand what a program does by examining the code. For example, the **goto** statement has the potential of making programs hard to read, because it can make it impossible to read a program in one top-to-bottom pass and to understand it. Rather, one must jump around in the program in search of the targets of the **goto** statements. Although many programmers did not agree when it first was suggested that the **goto** statement is harmful, there is now a general consensus that in most cases the **goto** statement should not be used.

As we will see, many of the qualities that make programs readable by humans also make them more easily checkable by a computer. Automatic checks performed by the computer contribute to program correctness very effectively.

Ability to deal with exceptions   The language should make it possible to trap undesired events (arithmetic overflows, invalid input, etc.) and to specify suitable responses to such events. In this way, the behavior of the system becomes totally predictable even in anomalous situations.

1.5.2   Language and Maintainability

The need for maintainable programs imposes two requirements on the programming language: programs written in the language must be readable, and they must be modifiable. Like readability (discussed above), modifiability is somewhat subjective. It is possible, however, to identify features that make a program more modifiable. For example, several programming languages allow constants to be given symbolic names. Choosing an appropriate name for a constant promotes the readability of the program (e.g., we may use *pi* instead of 3.14). Moreover, a future need to change the value would necessitate a change only in the definition of the constant, rather than in every use of the constant.

Example (Pascal)

```
const no_of_words = 65536;
var memory: array [1. .no_of_words] of integer;
    . . .
    . . .
    . . .
    if m > no_of_words then . . . memory exhausted . . .
    . . .
    . . .
    . . .
```

The symbolic constant *no_of_words* represents the size of memory. Each memory element is an integer and can be accessed by a subscript in the range 1 through *no_of_words*. If at any time the memory is expanded, all that needs to be changed is the first line of the program, even if the information that is changed is used in several places in the program.

1.5.3 Language and Efficiency

The need for efficiency has guided language design from the beginning. Many languages have had efficiency as a main design goal, either implicitly or explicitly. For example, FORTRAN originally was designed for a specific machine (the IBM 704). Many of FORTRAN's restrictions, such as the number of array dimensions or the form of expressions used as array indices, are based directly on what could be implemented efficiently on the IBM 704.

The issue of efficiency has changed considerably, however. Efficiency is no longer measured only by the execution speed and space. The effort required to produce a program or system initially and the effort required in maintenance can also be viewed as components of the efficiency measure. And, once again, the programming language can have a great impact.

A language supports efficiency if it has the qualities of writability, maintainability, and optimizability. Writability and maintainability are discussed above. "Optimizability" refers to the quality of allowing automatic program optimization.

Optimizability is important because much of the time traditionally spent in programming is devoted to trying to find efficient ways of doing things. However, the preoccupation with optimization should be removed from the early stages of programming. The ideal approach would be first, to produce a program that is demonstrably correct, and then, through a series of efficiency-improving transformations, modify this program to obtain a correct and efficient one. A language is optimizable if it makes possible the automatic application of these transformations. For example, the existence of **goto** statements complicates automatic optimization. More generally, it has been shown that many features that reduce optimizability also hamper readability.

1.6 A BRIEF HISTORICAL PERSPECTIVE

This section examines briefly the developments in language design by following the evolution of ideas and concepts from a historical perspective.

The software development process originally consisted only of the coding phase. In the early days of computing, the computer was used mainly in scientific applications. An application was programmed by one person. The problem to be solved (e.g., a differential equation) was well-understood. As a result of all this, there was not much need for requirements analysis or design specification, or even maintenance. A programming language, therefore, only needed to support one programmer, who was programming what would be by today's standards an extremely simple application.

The desire to apply the computer in more and more applications led to its being applied in increasingly less-understood and more-sophisticated environments. This, in turn, led to the need for "teams" of programmers and for more formal approaches. The requirements and design phases, which up to then essentially were performed in one programmer's head, now required a team, with the results being communicated to other people. And since so much effort and money was being spent on the development of systems, old systems could not simply be thrown away when a new system was needed. Economic considerations persuaded people to enhance an existing system to meet the newly recognized needs. Also, program maintenance now became an important issue.

System reliability is another issue that has gained importance gradually, because of two major factors. One factor is that systems are being developed for users with little or no computer background; hence, they are not as tolerant of system failures as the system developers themselves. The second factor is that systems are now being applied in areas such as nuclear power plants and patient monitoring, where system failures can have disastrous outcomes.

The shortcomings of programming languages in these areas has led to a great number of language design efforts. The purpose of this book is to examine these influences on language design and assess the extent to which the resultant languages meet their goals. Table 1 gives a genealogy of the major programming languages discussed in this book.

TABLE 1 Genealogy of Programming Languages

Language	Year	Originator	Predecessor Languages	Intended Purpose
FORTRAN	1954–57[b]	J. Backus (IBM)	—	Numeric computation
ALGOL 60	1958–60[c]	Committee	FORTRAN	Numeric computation
COBOL	1959–60[c]	Committee	—	Business data processing
APL	1956–60[b]	K. Iverson (Harvard)	—	Array processing
LISP	1956–62[b]	J. McCarthy (MIT)	—	Symbolic computation
SNOBOL	1962–66[b]	R. Griswold (Bell Labs)	—	String processing
PL/I	1963–64[c]	IBM Committee	FORTRAN ALGOL 60 COBOL	General purpose
SIMULA 67	1967[a]	O.-J. Dahl et al. (Norwegian Computing Center)	ALGOL 60	General-purpose simulation
ALGOL 68	1963–68[c]	Committee	ALGOL 60	General purpose
Bliss	1971[a]	Wulf et al. (Carnegie Mellon U.)	ALGOL 68	Systems programming
Pascal	1971[a]	N. Wirth (ETH Zurich)	ALGOL 60	General and educational purpose. Supporting structured programming

Table 1 Continued

Language	Year	Originator	Predecessor Languages	Intended Purpose
C	1974[a]	D. Ritchie (Bell Labs)	ALGOL 68 BCPL	Systems programming
Mesa	1974[c]	Xerox PARC	Pascal SIMULA 67	Systems programming
Concurrent Pascal	1975[a]	P. Brinch Hansen (Cal. Tech)	Pascal	Concurrent programming
CLU	1974–77[b]	B. Liskov et al. (MIT)	SIMULA 67	Supporting a methodology based on abstraction
Euclid	1977[a]	Committee	Pascal	Verifiable systems programs
Gypsy	1977[a]	Good et al. (U. of Texas–Austin)	Pascal	Verifiable systems programs
PLZ	1977[a]	Zilog Inc.	Pascal	Systems programming
Modula	1977[a]	N. Wirth (ETH Zurich)	Pascal	Systems programming real-time
Ada	1979[a]	J. Ichbiah et al. (CII Honeywell Bull)	Pascal SIMULA 67	General purpose, embedded applications, real-time

[a]First official language description.

[b]Language design and initial implementation.

[c]Language design.

SUGGESTIONS FOR FURTHER READING AND BIBLIOGRAPHIC NOTES

Numerous texts that discuss the entire life cycle of software have been published in recent years. (Tausworthe 1977) gives a comprehensive view of all aspects of software production and a proposal for standardized development. Other texts on software production are (Aron 1974), (Yourdon 1975), (Jackson 1975), (Myers 1976), (Zelkowitz et al. 1979).

The programming phase is discussed in depth in the collection of papers in a special issue of the **ACM Computing Surveys** (ACM-CS 1974). The emphasis is on programming style and systematic derivation of programs. In particular, the paper by

Knuth discusses the uses and misuses of **goto**s and the paper by Wirth discusses the writing of well-structured programs in Pascal. This language is suitable for supporting a top-down program design methodology—programming by stepwise refinement (Wirth 1971*b*). The origin of many ideas on systematic programming can be traced back to (Dijkstra 1968*a*), which is the starting point of the vast amount of research on "structured programming" of the early 1970s. (Dahl et al. 1972) is an excellent reference on the topic. A more elementary view of structured programming is provided in the introductory programming textbook by N. Wirth (Wirth 1973).

The principle of "information hiding" has been proposed by (Parnas 1972*b*) as a basis for a design methodology supporting modularity, reliability, and modifiability of software. Further references on this point are (Myers 1975), (Myers 1976), and (Myers 1978).

Friendly programming environments that support program development with a large variety of tools are becoming increasingly popular. (Kernighan and Mashey 1979) presents an overview of UNIX. Another program development system is described in (Cheatham et al. 1979). (Sandewall 1978) discusses a LISP environment. Requirements for a programming environment based on Ada are specified in (DOD 1980a).

(Wegner 1976) and (ACM-SIGPLAN 1978) provide a historical perspective of programming language developments. (Backus 1978*a*) argues that such developments display no real evolution and advocates a purely functional style of programming.

CHAPTER TWO

PREVIEW: EVOLUTION OF CONCEPTS IN PROGRAMMING LANGUAGES

At the present time I think we are on the verge of discovering at last what programming languages should really be like. I look forward to seeing many responsible experiments with language design during the next few years; and my dream is that by 1984 we will see a consensus developing for a really good programming language (or, more likely, a coherent family of languages). Furthermore, I'm guessing that people will become so disenchanted with the languages they are now using—even COBOL and FORTRAN—that this new language, UTOPIA 84, will have a chance to take over. At present we are far from the goal, yet there are indications that such a language is very slowly taking shape. . . . A great deal of research must be done if we're going to have the desired language by 1984. (Knuth 1974)

We must recognize the strong and undeniable influence that our language exerts on our way of thinking, and in fact defines and delimits the abstract space in which we can formulate—give form to—our thoughts. (Wirth 1974)

*Language is the vehicle by which we express our thoughts, and the relation between those thoughts and our language is a subtle and involuted one. The nature of language actually shapes and models the way we think. . . . If, by providing appropriate language constructs we can improve the programs written using these structures, the entire field will benefit. . . . A language design should **at least** provide facilities which allow comprehensible expression of algorithms; **at best** a language suggests better forms of expression. But language is **not** a panacea. A language cannot, for example, prevent the creation of obscure programs; the ingenious programmer can always find an infinite number of paths to obfuscation. (Wulf 1977)*

Chapter 1 discussed the many facets of the relation between programming languages and the entire production cycle of software. On the one hand, the language can favor the adoption of systematic program design methodologies; on the other, the language has a strong influence on the reliability, readability, and modifiability of programs. Rules and methodologies that have been found to be helpful in the development of reliable and high-quality software can be, and increasingly are, incorporated into programming languages in order to encourage users to apply these methodologies, or at least to make their application easier.

The above quotation from Knuth expresses a perhaps-optimistic view of the current state of the art in the field of programming languages. The purpose of this book is to present the important ideas that have influenced the evolution of language designs, in order to outline how UTOPIA 84 is slowly taking shape. This chapter develops the criteria that will be used in the book to classify programming language concepts and explain their evolution.

The chapter is organized as follows. Section 2.1 introduces the concept of abstraction and shows its fundamental role in programming. Two particular instances of this concept in programming languages—data and control abstractions—are analyzed in Sections 2.2 and 2.3. Program correctness, another concept that has influenced the evolution of programming languages, is illustrated in Section 2.4. Finally, Section 2.5 shows the influence exerted on programming languages by the need for producing large programs.

The purpose of this chapter is mainly introductory. Rather than examining language features in any detail, we will only motivate the concepts and criteria that will be used throughout the book in the presentation and evaluation of programming languages.

2.1 THE ROLE OF ABSTRACTION

Computers are increasingly replacing humans in many applications, from business administration to process control. To replace a manual procedure, software designers must reproduce its behavior in a computer program. Computer programs can be thought of as models of these manual procedures.

Like any model, a computer program is an *abstraction* from reality. Abstraction is the process of identifying the important qualities or properties of the phenomenon being modeled. Using the abstract model, one is able to concentrate only on the relevant qualities or properties of the phenomenon and to ignore irrelevant ones. What is relevant depends on the purpose for which the abstraction is being designed. For example, someone learning to drive can represent a car simply by four properties: the gas, brake, and clutch pedals, and the steering wheel. The engineer designing the car would use a model that also shows the relationship between the pedals and the engine. For the driver's abstraction, the engine is an irrelevant property; for the engineer, it is a crucial one.

Abstraction permeates the whole of programming. In particular, it has a twofold relationship with programming languages. On the one hand, programming languages are the tools by which software designers can implement the abstract models. On the other, programming languages are themselves abstractions from the underlying processor where the model is implemented.

The early programming languages, however, did not recognize the crucial role that abstraction plays in programming. For example, in the early 1950s the only abstraction mechanism provided by assembly languages over machine languages was symbolic naming. The programmer could use relatively self-explanatory terms to name operation codes and could symbolically name memory locations. Thus the programmer could abstract away from the machine representation of programs, and in particular from the identity of memory locations and the particular bit-representation of operation codes.

The contributions of this facility to the readability and modifiability of programs are well known. The vast amount of bookkeeping required in machine language programming is automatically performed by the translator, and this makes programming easier and less error-prone. For example, in a program for geometric modeling, the user can freely use self-explanatory names, such as VOLUME, AREA, SIZE, to denote the values of geometric entities, without keeping track of the memory locations where such values are actually stored. Moreover, some very simple correctness checks can be performed on the program at translation time. For example, undefined and multiply defined symbols can be caught by the assembler, and this can help the programmer in the production of correct programs. Additional help can be provided by simple tools such as cross-reference tables. In our example, the source of an error in the evaluation of the volume of an object can be discovered by examining the list of statements that assign values to variable VOLUME. Such a list may be provided by the cross-reference table.

Subprograms (and macros) also were introduced by assembly languages as a means for the programmer to name an activity described by a group of actions and to consider it as a single action. In our example, scale reductions, perspective views, planar projections, and so on might be drawn by suitable subprograms.

Subprograms are useful tools for methodical programming, because they are mechanisms for building abstractions. A subprogram is the implementation of an abstraction, whereas a subprogram call represents the use of the abstraction. When designing a subprogram, the programmer is concerned with *how* it works. Afterward, when the subprogram is called, the programmer can ignore the ''how,'' and concentrate on *what* it does. This is another example of the use of abstraction in programming. The subprogram can be viewed as an extension of the programming language by a new operation. When using the operation, the programmer abstracts away from its actual implementation. The machine is viewed as an abstract, special-purpose processor whose instruction repertoire contains the new operation.

The late 1950s and early 1960s saw the design of the first higher-level languages, which provided a richer set of mechanisms for defining abstractions. These mechanisms can be used to define data abstractions and control abstractions. Data abstractions model the data manipulated by programs. Control abstractions model computations by combining elementary actions into patterns of arbitrary complexity. Sections 2.2 and 2.3 outline the evolution of data and control abstractions in programming languages.

2.2 DATA ABSTRACTION

2.2.1 Data Abstraction in Early Languages

Machine-level languages view stored data as strings of bits that can be manipulated by the machine's instructions. The instruction repertoire includes shifts, logical operations, fixed-point arithmetic, and several other operations.

A first step toward introducing abstractions on data was taken by FORTRAN, COBOL, and ALGOL 60. In these languages, the information stored in certain memory locations is viewed not as a sequence of anonymous bits, but rather as an integer value, a real, a boolean, or something else. The decision about the particular data abstractions to be included in a programming language was mainly dictated by the machines for which the languages were intended (e.g., the machine provided fixed- and floating-point arithmetic) and by the spectrum of applications the languages were supposed to cover (e.g., the language was intended to cover scientific applications).

As a result, no language turns out to be appropriate for all applications, since the programmer is limited by the expressive power of the fixed set of abstractions provided by the language. For example, FORTRAN is not the appropriate language for string manipulation problems, nor is COBOL for solving a system of differential equations; and neither one is particularly suitable for matrix manipulation or for applications requiring highly dynamic data structures with a variety of access paths.

PL/I tried to overcome these problems by collecting many of the abstractions provided by the previous programming languages—namely, FORTRAN, ALGOL 60, and COBOL. However, many data-related features of the language turned out to be difficult to master, and often unsafe. Examples will be given in Chapter 4. Moreover, the proliferation of built-in abstractions, as opposed to mechanisms for defining new abstractions, has the principal effect of making the language large without exhausting all the needs that may arise in different applications.

2.2.2 Data Abstraction in ALGOL 68, Pascal, and SIMULA 67

The approach followed by the languages of the next generation—SIMULA 67, ALGOL 68, Pascal—is in some sense less ambitious, but has proved to be more effective. Such languages try to achieve generality not by providing an exhaustive set of built-in abstractions, but rather by providing flexible and easy-to-use mechanisms by which the programmer can define new abstractions. Such an approach quite naturally fits in with a design methodology based on the recognition of abstractions. Moreover, the abstractions identified for the design of the software become mirrored, at least to some extent, by the resulting structure of the program. As a consequence, programs are more easily understandable and modifiable, and have a higher likelihood of being correct.

ALGOL 68 and Pascal allow the programmer to use the built-in data types and constructors (arrays, records, etc.) to define new types. For example, using the Pascal notation, the following definitions and declarations define two new types (*student* and *course*) and three variables (*comp_sci_15, comp_sci_140, comp_sci_240*) of type *course*.

type *student* = **record** *first_name:* **array** *[1..10]* **of** *char;*
 mid_init: char;
 last_name: **array** *[1..15]* **of** *char*
 end;
course = **record** *no_of_students: 0..20;*
 attendants: **array** *[1..20]* **of** *student*
 end;
var *comp_sci_15, comp_sci_140, comp_sci_240: course;*

The newly defined type *student* is a data structure, with three components, used to store a student's identification. Type *course* is defined as a table of students (*attendants*), together with the number of students (*no_of_students:* an integer between 0 and 20) who are registered for the course. Thus, any of the above variables (*comp_sci_240*, say) can be viewed as shown in Figure 2.1.

A natural question is, Why did we choose to represent students and courses as described above? More basically, Why do we need a data structure for students and courses? The answers to these questions lay in the motivations of the program and in the abstractions that are identified during design, and it is impossible to find them by looking at the program. However, it would be helpful to have a language that allows the clarification of such issues as part of the program.

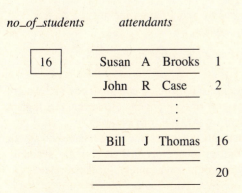

Figure 2.1 Data structure for variable *comp_sci_240*.

For example, we may imagine that the program solves an application for a computer science professor who teaches *comp_sci_15, comp_sci_140,* and *comp_sci_240*. This professor receives from the registration office a deck of cards containing data on the students who signed up for these courses and wants to produce a sorted listing of the students, grouped together by course taken.

We may also imagine that type *course* has been introduced because it is necessary to operate on data objects, such as *comp_sci_15,* by inserting a new student (in the appropriate order) and printing the names of the enrolled students. The initial abstract version of the program could be

for *each card of the card deck* **do**
      let S be the student's identification and let C be the course name;
      insert S into the table for course C in appropriate order
end-of-do;
print table for comp_sci_15;
print table for comp_sci_140;
print table for comp_sci_240;

The (imaginary) approach followed by the designer consists of characterizing a set of *logical* operations on course tables before deciding on how to implement such tables in the computer. Any specific way of implementing course tables must provide a *representation* for the tables as well as *concrete operations:* that is, algorithms expressed in the programming language, corresponding to the logical operations on course tables. However, the decision as to how to represent course tables and how to implement the operations is at a lower level of abstraction than the decision that course tables are needed to store the students' identification.

In Pascal (and similarly, in ALGOL 68) these decisions lead to the declaration of the new types described above, and to the implementation of the following procedures, one for each logical operation.

- *Insert:* takes a parameter of type *course* and a parameter of type *student* and inserts the value of *student* in *course*.

- *Print:* takes a parameter of type *course* and prints its contents.

Procedures *insert* and *print* are related very closely to type *course*. They are exactly the concrete operations that manipulate objects of type *course*. However, this logical relationship is not apparent from the Pascal (or ALGOL 68) program.

On the other hand, SIMULA 67 provides a construct (the **class**) that allows both the representation and the concrete operations to be specified in a single syntactic unit. This construct considerably improves program readability, because related entities implementing a certain abstraction are grouped together.

2.2.3   Toward Abstract Data Types

There are similarities between the user-defined types of Pascal, ALGOL 68, and SIMULA 67 and the built-in types of these languages. As an example, consider the built-in type *integer* and the user-defined type *course* of Section 2.2.2. Both types are abstractions built upon an underlying representation—a bit string for *integer,* a record for *course.* Both types have an associated set of operations—arithmetic operations and comparisons for *integer, insert* and *print* for *course.*

In one important point, however, built-in types and user-defined types differ from one another. Built-in types hide from the programmer the underlying representation; it cannot be directly manipulated. For example, the programmer cannot access a particular bit of the bit string representing an *integer.* Procedures *insert* and *print,* on the other hand, are not the only means to manipulate a *course.* The programmer can operate directly on the components of objects of type *course* and is not forced to call the operations defined for the new type. For example,

comp_sci_240.no_of_students: = 17

would be a legal—but quite possibly undesirable—operation that modifies the number of students enrolled in comp_sci_240. In other words, there is no language-enforced distinction between two abstraction levels: the level at which one can use courses as new objects, and the level at which one implements courses in terms of lower-level abstractions. At the same time, the programmer can view courses as abstract objects manipulable via *insert* and *print* operations and as particular data aggregates whose components can be accessed and modified individually.

This confusion between levels of abstraction can lead to the production of programs that are hard to read. Even more important, it reduces program modifiability. For example, suppose that we decide to change the representation of tables to a sequential list structure or to a binary tree. The change is not localized within the declarations of data and the concrete operations. It is also necessary to check out all direct accesses to the representation of data, which may be spread throughout the program.

In conclusion, in order to define new data types in a program, one would like to have language features that allow (*a*) the association of a representation to the concrete operations in a suitable language unit that implements the new types; and (*b*) the hiding of the representation of the new type from the units that use the new type.

User-defined types that satisfy properties (*a*) and (*b*) are called *abstract data types.* Property (*a*) makes the final version of the program reflect the abstractions discovered during program design. The resulting structure of the program becomes self-explanatory. Property (*b*) enforces the distinction between levels of abstraction and favors program modifiability. ALGOL 68 and Pascal do not provide features that satisfy points (*a*) and (*b*). The SIMULA 67 **class** satisfies point (*a*), not point (*b*). Recent languages, such as CLU and Ada, provide facilities for defining abstract data types that satisfy both properties (*a*) and (*b*).

The concept of an abstract data type derives from the more general principle of information hiding; a program part implementing an abstract data type is an example of an information hiding module (Section 1.3). Abstract data types hide representation details and route accesses to abstract objects via procedures. The representation is *protected* from any attempt to manipulate it directly. A change in the implementation of an abstract data type is confined within the program part that describes the implementation and does not affect the rest of the program.

2.3   CONTROL ABSTRACTION

Control structures describe the order in which statements or groups of statements (*program units*) are to be executed. Just as with data abstraction facilities, control abstraction mechanisms can determine the suitability of a language for particular application areas. Control structures can be classified as either *statement-level* control structures—that is, those that are used to order the activation of individual statements—and *unit-level* control structures—that is, those that are used to order the activation of program units. The evolution of control abstractions according to this classification is outlined below.

2.3.1   Evolution of Statement-Level Control Structures

Conventional hardware provides two very simple mechanisms to govern the flow of control over individual instructions: sequencing and branching. Sequencing is implemented by automatically incrementing the program counter after executing each instruction. This mechanism allows instructions stored in consecutive memory locations to be fetched and executed one after the other. The program counter can also be explicitly altered by branch instructions in order to accomplish control transfer to a specified location other than the next one in the sequence.

In assembly languages, instructions to be executed consecutively are written one after the other. Branching is represented by a **jump** instruction. For example, looping N times over a certain set of instructions requires initializing, modifying, and testing a counter value (often stored in a register), as in the following scheme (many machines include an instruction to modify, test and branch in one instruction).

```
        set register to N;
loop :  if the value in register is zero jump to after;
        < loop body >;
        restore the counter value in register (if necessary) and decrease it by one;
        jump to loop;
after : . . . . . .
```

Machine-level control structures are difficult to use and error-prone. The resulting programs are difficult to read and maintain, because these structures are not natural for humans. Humans organize their computational processes according to some standard patterns, such as repetition or selection among different choices. For example, a more natural way to describe the above program would be

do the following N times
< loop body >

User-oriented control structures have been incorporated in higher-level languages in order to facilitate programming and to promote a better programming style. However, most higher-level languages retain branching, in the form of **goto** statements, and therefore also support a low-level programming style. **Goto** statements are a source of obscurity in programming (see Section 1.5.1). The **goto** controversy of the early 1970s, however, did not provide a definitive solution to the problem of which control structures should be included in a programming language. Nevertheless, there is general agreement that **goto** statements should be used only as a technique to synthesize ''legitimate'' control structures if the language does not include those control structures.

2.3.2 Evolution of Unit-Level Control Structures

2.3.2.1 Subprograms and Blocks

Programming languages provide facilities for grouping statements implementing an abstract action into a suitable program unit. The most common and useful example is the subprogram, which has been present since the first assembly languages were formulated. A subprogram definition gives a name to a certain program unit. A subprogram call *invokes* a program unit—that is, forces control to transfer to the called unit, which upon completion of its task *returns* control to the calling point. *Parameter passing* conventions allow units explicitly to exchange information.

A simpler example of a program unit is the ALGOL 60 block, which provides for the grouping of actions, but not for the naming of the group. A block, therefore, cannot be invoked explicitly and is executed when it is encountered during the normal progression of execution.

Subprograms and, to a lesser extent, blocks are useful tools for program structuring. In particular, subprograms support the distinction between the definition of an abstract action (the subprogram body) and its use (the subprogram call). However, there are cases in which the control regime of subprogram call and return unduly constrains the programmer. Several programming languages of the recent generation recognize this constraint and provide additional unit-level control structures.

2.3.2.2 Exception Handling

The events or conditions that a program unit encounters during its execution can be classified as either usual or exceptional. Examples of exceptional conditions include the following: a subprogram discovers that some values of parameters can cause the execution of an illegal division by zero; a storage allocator runs out of storage to allocate; a protocol error is caught during reception of a message on a transmission line.

To increase the readability of the program and to indicate the programmer's assumptions about the expected and unexpected events, it is desirable to be able to divide the program into several units. Some units handle the usual events and can detect the occurrence of anomalous or exceptional conditions (called *exceptions*). The occurrence of an exception implicitly transfers control to an appropriate unit, called an *exception handler*, that deals with the exception.

Conventional programming languages provide little help in dealing with exceptions. A subprogram that may raise the exception could be coded by introducing an additional return parameter (e.g., an integer) denoting an exception code (e.g., 0 = no exception, 1 = exception number one, etc.). The calling unit would explicitly test the exception code after each call and then transfer control to the appropriate exception handler, if necessary. This limitation of the expressive power of the language forces programmers to state their intentions and assumptions in an awkward way that obscures the logic of the program.

PL/I was the first higher-level language to provide (*ad hoc*) features for exception handling. Other exception handling facilities have been adopted by later language designs (e.g., Bliss, Mesa, CLU, and Ada).

2.3.2.3 Coroutines

Conventional subprograms cannot describe program units that proceed concurrently, as happens in discrete simulation. For example, the simulation of a four-player card game could be done by designing four program units, one for each player. After each move, a unit should activate the unit that corresponds to the next player. When activated, a unit should resume execution wherever it left off when it last transferred control to another unit. Several programming languages provide a facility—the *coroutine*—to implement this form of interleaved execution. Each coroutine representing a player of the card game would have the following general structure.

coroutine for player *i*
declarations of local data (e.g., the cards of player i);
while *game_not_finished* **do**
     select card;
     play card;
     resume execution of the coroutine corresponding to the next player
end-of-do

Conventional subprograms are subordinate to their caller and upon termination, return to the caller. In most programming languages the return operation causes the deletion of the subprogram's local data. In our example, this means that the information about the cards of the player would be lost. Unlike subprograms, coroutines are symmetric units that explicitly activate each other; they do not return, but rather *resume* each other. When coroutine **A** resumes coroutine **B**, **A**'s local data are retained.

A later resumption of **A** allows **A** to continue its execution from wherever it had left off. In the example, the information about the cards held by a player is retained when another player is resumed.

2.3.2.4 Concurrent Units

Coroutines are quite adequate to model activities that are executed in an interleaved fashion. In many applications, however, it is useful to model a system as a set of units, called *concurrent units,* whose execution proceeds in parallel (whether or not they are actually executed in parallel). This facility is particularly important in areas such as operating systems. In describing concurrent units, it is necessary to abstract from the physical architecture of the underlying machine, where the units are executed. The machine might be a multiprocessor, with each processor dedicated to a single unit, or it might be a multiprogrammed uniprocessor. Allowing for the possibility of different machines means that the correctness of a concurrent system cannot be based on an assumption of the speed of execution of the units. Indeed, the speed can differ greatly if every unit is executed by a dedicated processor, or if a single processor is shared by several units. Moreover, even if the architecture is known, it is difficult to design a system in such a way that its correctness depends upon the speed of execution of the units.

Coroutines are a low-level language construct for describing concurrent units. They can be used to simulate parallelism on a uniprocessor by explicitly interleaving the execution of a set of concurrent units. Therefore they describe, not a set of concurrent units, but rather a particular way of sharing the CPU of a processor in order to simulate concurrency. Many recent programming languages provide specialized features to deal with concurrency.

Even though concurrency is becoming an important aspect of programming languages, its main motivations and principles have traditionally arisen from the area of operating systems. The following example should help clarify the basic problems and concepts of concurrent programming.

Suppose that a certain system contains two concurrent activities: a producer and a consumer. The producer produces a stream of values and places them into a buffer of a certain size, **N**; the consumer reads these values from the buffer in the same order as they are produced. This model represents many operating system functions, such as file input and output. In the sample solution to this example shown below, the units implementing the two activities are described by cyclic and, ideally, nonterminating program units.

unit producer

repeat   *produce an element;*
            append the element to the
            buffer
forever

unit consumer

repeat   *remove one item from the*
            buffer;
            perform some computation on
            the item
forever

The two units represent activities that cooperate to achieve a common goal. The common goal is to transfer data from the producer (which could be reading it from an input device, for example) to the consumer (which could be storing it in a file, for example). It is desirable to make the units insensitive to the variations in speed of the two activities (e.g., the speed of the input device). The buffering mechanism does precisely that, by smoothing such variations. However, to guarantee the correctness of the cooperation, the programmer must assure that no matter how fast or slowly the producer and the consumer progress, there will be no attempts to write into a full buffer or to read from an empty buffer. Concurrent programming languages provide *synchronization statements* that allow the programmer to delay a unit whenever necessary for the purpose of correct cooperation with other concurrent units. In the example, the producer must be delayed if it tries to append an element when the buffer is full, until the consumer removes at least one element. Similarly, the consumer must be delayed if it tries to remove an item when the buffer is empty, until the producer appends at least one new element.

Another, more subtle, need for synchronization may arise when both activities can legally have access to the buffer. For example, suppose that operations *append* and *remove* update the value of t, the total number of buffered items, by performing (1) $t: = t + 1$ and (2) $t: = t - 1$, respectively. Also, suppose that (1) and (2) are implemented as

read **t** *into a private register;*
update the value stored in such register;
write the value stored in the private register into **t**

where *update* is "increment by one" and "decrement by one," respectively, for (1) and (2). The actions that form (1) and (2) are indivisible machine instructions, in the sense that if one such action starts to execute, it is guaranteed to finish before any other machine operation is started. This is in contrast with the operations (1) and (2) themselves: since they are not indivisible, the execution of their constituent actions may be interleaved. One of many possible sequences of interleaved actions could be as follows: the first action of (1); the first action of (2); the second action of (1); the second action of (2); the third action of (1); and finally, the third action of (2).

Given that (1) and (2) are not indivisible actions, it is easy to verify that if m is the value of t before the concurrent execution of a pair (append, remove), the value of t after the execution can be m, $m + 1$, or $m - 1$—the first value being the only correct result. To guarantee correctness, the programmer must assure that (2) does not start while (1) is in progress, and vice versa. We say that (1) and (2) must be executed in *mutual exclusion,* as if they were "indivisible" operations.

We are now in a position to state some requirements for the abstractions we need to deal with concurrency, as well as for the language constructs that can be used to define such abstractions.

A concurrent system should be viewed as a set of *processes,* each process being represented by a program unit. Processes are *concurrent* if their executions can be (conceptually) overlapped in time: that is, if the start of a process can occur when the previously executing process is not terminated. Processes $P_1, P_2, \ldots P_N$ are *disjoint* if they describe activities that never interact with one another: that is, do not access any shared objects. The result of the execution of one process is independent of the other processes; in particular, processes can have arbitrary speeds. Very often, however, processes are *interacting*. Interaction results from one of the following two reasons.

Competition Processes compete for access to a certain shared resource, which is to be used in mutual exclusion (e.g., a line printer).

Cooperation Processes cooperate to achieve a common goal.

Processes interact correctly only if a certain precedence relation holds among their elementary actions: that is, certain actions must precede certain other actions. Such a relation defines a *partial ordering* among actions. For example, in the producer/ consumer example, if $P_j(C_j)$ denotes the production (consumption) of the jth element, correct cooperation requires ("$\rightarrow$" should be read as "precedes")

$$C_j \rightarrow P_{j+N} \text{ and } P_j \rightarrow C_j \text{ for all } j$$

Correct competition requires that no two updates of shared variable t be executed at the same time. If IT_j (DT_j) denotes the jth increment (decrement) of variable t performed by the producer (consumer), correct competition requires

$$IT_j \rightarrow DT_k \text{ or } DT_j \rightarrow IT_k \text{ for all } j \text{ and } k$$

Concurrent programming languages provide language facilities for the definition of processes and suitable synchronization statements to enforce the required partial ordering of actions. Coroutines, as mentioned above, can be used to implement concurrency on a uniprocessor, but they provide an inadequate level of abstraction for this task. They overspecify the system by explicitly showing when a process resumes another. In other words, they impose a total ordering on actions even when a partial ordering is a completely adequate description of the system.

2.4 PROGRAM CORRECTNESS

Correctness is one of the basic requirements for any software. There are two different approaches to the production of correct programs. The first, *error correction,* consists of treating an already-written program every time the symptom of an error is discovered. The second, *error prevention,* consists of trying to develop programs that are correct in the first place.

Obviously, no programs are developed with complete disregard for correctness, and no programs are developed so carefully as to be free of possible errors. It is true, however, that much of the cost of software production results from error correction, and that the adoption of suitable systematic approaches to software design can help prevent the introduction of errors.

One way to favor the production of correct programs is to make the design and coding effort easily manageable, so that we can be confident of the desired behavior of the system. Abstractions on data and control, as discussed in Sections 2.2 and 2.3, are powerful ways of mastering the complexity of program design. Language constructs that allow the mapping of design abstractions into program structures promote the production of well-structured, correct programs. Such program structures make it possible to break down the complex task of reasoning about a large object—the entire program—to reasoning about smaller, manageable, largely autonomous, abstract objects. Also, individual program units must be easy to write and to understand, so that possible errors can be located and fixed easily. A number of harmful features—that is, features that make it difficult to reason about programs—have been identified in programming languages, starting with the well-known case of the **goto** statement. (A review of such features and of a number of alternative solutions proposed by language designers is presented in Chapter 6.)

Even systematically designed programs can contain errors, however, and so it still is necessary to devise strategies for isolating and removing such errors. A solid basis for a systematic certification of programs—at different levels—is provided by the programming language itself. At the lower level are *consistency checks,* which verify that programs adhere to the language definition. For example, programs must be syntactically well-formed (that is, consistent with the syntactic rules of the language); program variables must be used in a way that is consistent with their type; subprograms must be called with actual parameters that are consistent, in number and type, with the formal parameters that appear in the subprogram's heading.

Consistency checks performed before executing the program are called *static checks;* those performed during execution are called *run-time* (or *dynamic*) *checks.* *Syntax checks* performed by the translator are an example of static checks. *Type checks* are another example of consistency checks that most languages require, and that often can be done statically. The following Pascal program fragment illustrates these points.

```
var x, y : integer;
    z: char;
    .

    .

    .

    x: = (((x+y) * 5 + x * y);
    if x<0 then y:=z;
    .

    .

    .
```

The assignment statement contains a syntax error, because of a missing closing parenthesis. The **if** statement contains a type error because a character-valued variable (*z*) is assigned to an *integer*. Both errors can be caught statically.

Although any statically detectable error could also be detected at run-time, it would be unwise to delay such error checking to run-time, for two reasons. One reason is that potential sources of error would only be detected at run-time by providing input data that cause the error to be raised: for example, the above-cited incorrect program fragment would signal the type error only if the value of x is negative. Secondly, dynamic checking slows down the program execution.

Not all languages, however, allow programs to be type-checked completely before run-time. For example, in APL the type of a variable is determined by the variable's current value and thus can change during program execution, as the following fragment shows.

.

.

.

.

A ← 'STRING'

.

.

.

.

A ← 3.77

.

.

.

.

As a consequence, adding a numeric value to A is correct only if the current value of A is a number, and not a character string. But in general, this can only be ascertained at run-time.

We can conclude that correctness can be enhanced by a language whose definition requires extensive checks on programs: and all the more so if the checks can be done statically. Early programming languages did not recognize the need for language features supporting program correctness. Most recent languages, however, have been designed with the goal of supporting extensive program checking.

Even in the presence of extensive static checking, the programmer can still produce a program that does not meet its specifications. The program is therefore gradually modified until it can be certified. The traditional approach to program certification consists of *testing* the program by submitting a sample of inputs, taken from the program specification documents, and observing whether the output produced by the program adheres to the specified behavior of the program. Incorrect results are symptoms of errors that must be removed from the program. Correct results, however, do not imply the correctness of the program, since all that can be said is that the program behaved correctly for those particular input data. Thus, following a remark by Dijkstra, we can say that testing can be used to prove the presence of bugs, not their absence!

This intrinsic deficiency of program testing has stimulated a large amount of research in *program verification*. As opposed to testing, verification aims at verifying correctness of a program independently of its execution. Program verification in the strict sense means proving that a program *implementation* is consistent with its *specification*. Specification, in turn, is intended here as a formal and precise description of what the program is to do.

Program verification can be done manually, but in such a case the confidence in the correctness of the program depends on the confidence in the correctness of the proof itself. Automatic systems for program verification have also been implemented, but there is no real experience with their use in the verification of large, practical systems. One example is reported in (Walker et al., 1979). The authors of this experiment come to the conclusion that "there appears to be no technical reasons, other than the necessity for engineering a suitable (computer assisted) verification system . . . that program proving methods could not be employed for the development of software where correct operation is critical. . . . Current techniques, however, are still not suitable for general use."

Neither testing nor verification are likely to provide the exclusive, final answers to the need of proving programs correct. Program verification is theoretically sounder than testing. However, in the early stages of program development, when many errors are likely to be present in the program, testing can be more economical than proving. In other words, the techniques complement one another and together provide greater assurance of correctness than can either one alone. Unfortunately, a practically usable and theoretically well-founded methodology that embodies a blend of the two approaches is still to be found.

2.5 PROGRAMMING IN THE LARGE

The production of large software systems often requires coordination of the activities of a large number of people. Programs are assembled as collections of individual modules, possibly written by different persons and coded in different languages. Very large programs ("nearly impossible programs," according to [Yourdon 1975]) may be up to 10^6 source-statements long, may be written by hundreds of programmers over a period of several years, and may consist of several hundred modules with complex interactions among themselves and with other, separately developed systems. Systems software for large computers, government and military applications, large banking projects, management information systems, and several other applications fall into this category. Successful management of the design, production, certification, and maintenance of such software systems is a formidable task, involving problems ranging from the sociology of human relations to software production methodologies.

At a lower level of size and complexity, projects that require production of large programs (several thousands of source statements long, written by 5 to 20 programmers over a period of two to three years) are becoming increasingly common. Managing the design and production of such large systems requires suitable methodologies and tools in order to keep the complexity under control.

The entire life-cycle of software production in the case of large software systems can be rather different from that of small-sized programs. In (DeRemer and Kron 1976) it is argued that "*programming in the large* is an essentially distinct and different intellectual activity from that of constructing the individual modules"—that is, from *programming in the small*. Consequently, they conclude that "essentially distinct and different languages should be used for the two activities."

We have implicitly assumed that large systems are made up of individual components, called *modules*. Modularity, in fact, is generally recognized as the only guideline available for mastering the complexity of design and implementation of large and complex systems. However, "modularity" is a buzz-word that often is used to denote several properties of software. In many cases, modularity is defined in terms of size of the program units that comprise a system. Thus, for example, there are organizations that adopt production standards such as "Each FORTRAN subroutine must be contained in a page of printout." Restrictions that apply only to the size of modules, however, do not improve the quality of programs in any real sense: chopping the long text of a program into a sequence of smaller pieces does not make the program any better.

A more helpful notion of modularity is in terms of independence. This means that each module should be understood and, possibly, implemented independently of the other modules of the system. Each module should realize a single and simple conceptual function of the system; consequently, restrictions on module size result automatically as a by-product of the design process. Information hiding as a design principle favors the production of highly independent modules. In fact, design decisions internal to a module are hidden and do not affect the correctness of the cooperation among the modules. Once the module interfaces have been (carefully) designed, modules can be developed independently of each other, stored in a library, and later assembled to construct a unique program.

The goal of modular software design exerts a strong influence on programming languages. Languages should provide facilities for the definition of modules and for information hiding. They should also provide facilities for structuring a collection of modules in a unique system. Finally, it should be possible to develop and certify modules separately. Some recent language designs (e.g., Ada) have been strongly influenced by these concepts.

The need for producing large and complex, reliable software systems has also influenced the development of a number of tools that can assist the programmer in designing, coding, certifying, and maintaining individual programs. As we argued in Chapter 1, programming languages and program development methodologies in isolation are not enough to significantly increase programmer productivity. Rather, the combination of a suitable programming language with a number of powerful, integrated, easy-to-use, language-sensitive tools—that is, a software development facility—can become the key factor in improving the quality of programs. The first step in this direction has been taken with systems such as UNIX, which was developed by Bell Laboratories for the DEC family of computers. The development of a consistent and complete program-development system, however, is still an open research problem.

SUGGESTIONS FOR FURTHER READING
AND BIBLIOGRAPHIC NOTES

(Sammet 1969) is a compendium of a large number of programming languages and provides a comprehensive view of the evolution in the field. (Wegner 1976) surveys the evolution of programming languages until 1975. The proceedings of the ACM SIGPLAN Conference on the History of Programming Languages (ACM-SIGPLAN 1978) put earlier successful language-design efforts into a historical perspective. Several papers of (ACM-SIGPLAN 1978) explicitly point out the strong influence exerted by hardware upon the abstractions provided by languages (see, for example, Backus's paper on FORTRAN).

The evolution of the concept of abstraction in programming languages is discussed in (Guarino 1978).

Wegner's paper in (Wegner 1979) presents a comprehensive overview of research directions in programming languages.

A solution to Exercise 2.6 can be found in (Conway 1963), which is the origin of coroutines.

This chapter has emphasized programming language concepts and their evolution. A detailed analysis and a critical evaluation of the solutions adopted by several programming languages will be presented in Chapters 3 through 8. Suggestions for further reading and bibliographic notes on the topics outlined in Sections 2.2 through 2.5 are given in the Further Reading sections of Chapters 4 through 7.

Exercises

2.1   Programming language abstractions can be classified according to how naturally they support program writing. Often, the more natural they are, the more difficult it is to implement them on a computer.

Based on this characterization, compare the IF statement of FORTRAN to the IF-THEN-ELSE statement of ALGOL-like languages.

2.2   Because only a finite number of values can be represented in a computer, the hardware-supported integer data type does not fully correspond to the mathematical notion of integer. What happens on your computer when the result of an integer expression is out of the acceptable range of values?

2.3   As part of a large programming project, you are asked to design and implement a queue data structure, called STORE, for storing and retrieving integer values. Values are extracted from the queue in first-in/first-out order. The queue must be able to detect attempts at insertion into a full queue or retrievals from an empty one. Since the requirements for the project are not quite firm yet, you must design your program to be easily modifiable. For example, the maximum size or the storage organization of the queue might need to be changed later.

    a. Specify the requirements for STORE as abstractly as you can, and then produce a concrete implementation.

    b. Code your concrete implementation in your favorite programming language.

    c. Discuss the modifiability of your solution and the ways in which the language helped or hindered in achieving it.

2.4 The ALGOL-like program fragment

while $a>b$ **do**

    .

    .

    .

end-of-do

can be rewritten by using (conditional and unconditional) jumps. Briefly compare the two approaches in terms of readability and writability.

2.5 A program must read an integer value and print "yes" if the value is zero and "no" otherwise. Write a solution using the FORTRAN IF statement but no **goto**'s. How natural is your solution? Can you write a better solution using the ALGOL-like IF statement?

2.6 This exercise illustrates the use of coroutines. Design a program to read characters from cards and print them out. Every occurrence of a pair of asterisks ("**") in the input must be replaced with the single character " ↑ " in the output. All other characters simply are copied. Your solution should consist of two coroutines: an input coroutine to provide the next character and an output coroutine to print characters.

2.7 The values of two variables, **v**1 and **v**2, are interchanged by each one of two concurrent processes, P1 and P2. The interchange is accomplished by the following sequence of indivisible machine-level operations.

        Load **v**1 into register R1.

        Load **v**2 into register R2.

        Store value from register R1 into **v**2.

        Store value from register R2 into **v**1.

What is the effect of concurrent execution if P1 and P2 do not execute the interchange in mutual exclusion?

2.8 Give examples of static and dynamic checks supported by your favorite programming language.

2.9 *Exhaustive testing* is the testing of a program for all possible values of its input variables. Give arguments (and examples) to show that exhaustive testing is impractical.

2.10   What are the criteria you follow to select data for testing your programs? How confident are you of the correctness of your program after testing?

2.11   Which of the languages familiar to you is more supportive of programming in the large, and why?

2.12   Have you ever been a member of a team working on a program of substantial size? If so, what difficulties did you face that you would not face when writing a simpler program by yourself?

CHAPTER THREE

AN INTRODUCTORY SEMANTIC VIEW OF PROGRAMMING LANGUAGES

A programming language is a formal notation for describing algorithms to be executed by a computer. Like all formal notations, a programming language has two components: *syntax* and *semantics*.

The syntax is a set of formal rules that specify the composition of programs from letters, digits, and other characters. For example, the syntax rules may specify that each open parenthesis must match a closed parenthesis in arithmetic expressions and that any two statements must be separated by a semicolon. The semantic rules specify ''the meaning'' of any syntactically valid program written in the language. Such meaning can be expressed by mapping each language construct into a domain whose semantics is known. For example, one way of describing the semantics of a language is by giving a description of each language construct in English. Such a description, of course, suffers from the informality, ambiguity, and wordiness of natural language, but it can give a reasonably intuitive view of the language.

In this chapter, we will take the *operational* approach to semantics, in which the semantics of a programming language is described by specifying the behavior of an abstract processor that executes programs written in the language. This semantic characterization of a language could be presented using a rigorous and formal notation. Instead, we will follow a more traditional and informal approach, because it is more easily and intuitively understood by computer programmers and, additionally, provides a high-level view of the problems found in implementing the language.

This chapter describes the basic concepts of programming languages and introduces the basic semantic features that are needed to understand them. We will use FORTRAN, the family of ALGOL-like languages, and APL as examples to illustrate the fundamental issues (without assuming prior familiarity with these languages). The principles and techniques described here are general and extend to the newer languages, which will be discussed in the rest of the book.

We will not discuss the syntax of programming languages in any detail. We are concerned with the capabilities of a language, which are not affected by syntax. We must emphasize, however, that the syntax of a programming language has a great impact on the ease of use of the language for most programmers, and on the readability of programs written in that language.

The chapter is organized as follows. Section 3.1 presents two strategies for processing a programming language: interpretation and translation. Section 3.2 defines the general concept of binding, which will be used to describe several semantic properties of programming languages. Section 3.3 illustrates program variables and their basic attributes. Section 3.4 is about program units and their run-time representation. Sections 3.5 through 3.7 further detail these concepts in the case of FORTRAN, ALGOL-like languages, and APL.

3.1 LANGUAGE PROCESSING

Although in theory it is possible to build special-purpose computers to execute directly programs written in any particular language, present-day computers directly execute only a very low-level language, the *machine language*. Machine languages are designed on the bases of speed of execution, cost of realization, and flexibility in building new software layers upon them. On the other hand, programming languages often are designed on the basis of the ease and reliability of programming. A basic problem, then, is how a higher-level language eventually can be executed on a computer whose machine language is very different and at a much lower level.

There are basically two alternatives for an implementation: interpretation and translation.

3.1.1 Interpretation

In this solution, the actions implied by the statements of the language are executed directly. Usually, for each possible action there exists a subprogram—written in the machine language of the host machine—to execute the action. Thus, interpretation of a program is accomplished by calling subprograms in the appropriate sequence.

More precisely, an interpreter is a program that repeatedly executes the following sequence.

1. Get the next statement.

2. Determine the actions to be executed.

3. Perform the actions.

This sequence is very similar to the pattern of actions carried out by a traditional computer: that is,

1. Fetch the next instruction (i.e., the instruction whose address is specified in the program counter).

2. Advance the program counter (i.e., set the address of the instruction to be fetched next).

3. Decode the instruction.

4. Execute the instruction.

This similarity shows that interpretation can be viewed as a simulation, on a host computer, of a special-purpose machine whose machine language is the higher-level language.

3.1.2 Translation

In this solution, programs written in a high-level language are translated into an equivalent machine-language version before being executed. This translation is performed in several steps. Subprograms might first be translated into assembly code; then, assembly code is translated into relocatable machine code; then, units of relocatable code are linked together into a single relocatable unit; and finally, the entire program is loaded into main memory as executable machine code. The translators used in each of these steps have specialized names: compiler, assembler, linker (or linkage editor), and loader, respectively.

In some cases, the machine on which the translation is performed (the *host machine*) is different from the machine that is to run the translated code (the *target machine*). This kind of translation is called *cross-translation*. Cross translators offer the only viable solution when the target machine is too small to support the translator.

Pure interpretation and pure translation are two extremes. In practice, many languages are implemented by a combination of the two techniques. A program may be translated into an intermediate code that is then interpreted. The intermediate code might be simply a formatted representation of the original program, with irrelevant information (e.g., comments and spaces) removed and the components of each statement stored in a fixed format, in order to simplify the subsequent decoding of instructions. In this case, the solution is basically interpretive. Alternatively, the intermediate code might be the (low-level) machine code for a virtual machine that is to be later interpreted by software. This solution, which relies more heavily on translation, can be adopted for generating portable code: that is, code that is more easily transferable to different machines than is machine language code.

In a purely interpretive solution, executing a statement may require a fairly complicated decoding process to determine the operations to be executed and their operands. In most cases, this process is identical each time the statement is encountered. Consequently, if the statement appears in a frequently executed part of a program (e.g., an inner loop), the speed of execution is strongly affected by the identical decoding process. On the other hand, pure translation generates machine code for each high-level statement. In doing so, the translator decodes each high-level statement once only. Frequently used parts are then decoded many times in their machine language representation; since this is done efficiently by hardware, pure translation can save processing time over pure interpretation. On the other hand, pure interpretation may save storage. In pure translation, each high-level language statement may expand into tens or hundreds of machine instructions. In a purely interpretive solution, high-level statements are left in the original form and the instructions necessary to execute them are stored in a subprogram of the interpreter. The storage saving is evident if the program is large and uses most of the language's statements. On the other hand, if all of the interpreter's subprograms are kept in main memory during execution, the interpreter may waste space for small programs that use only a few of the language's statements.

3.2 THE CONCEPT OF BINDING

Programs deal with *entities,* such as variables, subprograms, statements, and so on. Program entities have certain properties, called *attributes*. For example, a variable has a name, a type, a storage area where its value is kept; a subprogram has a name, formal parameters of a certain type, certain parameter-passing conventions; a statement has associated actions. Attributes must be specified before an entity is processed. Specifying the exact nature of an attribute is known as *binding*. For each entity, binding information is contained in a repository called a *descriptor*.

Binding is a central concept in the definition of programming-language semantics. Programming languages differ in the number of entities they can deal with, in the number of attributes to be bound to entities, and in the time when such bindings occur (*binding time*). In particular, a binding is *static* if it is established before run-time and cannot be changed later; it is *dynamic* if it is established at run-time and can be changed according to some language-specified rules.

The concepts of binding and binding time help clarify many semantic aspects of programming languages. In the next section we will use these concepts to illustrate the notion of a variable.

3.3 VARIABLES

Conventional computers are based on the notion of a main memory consisting of elementary *cells,* each of which is identified by an address. The contents of a cell comprise its *value*. The value of a cell can be read and/or modified. Modification implies replacing a value with a new value. Furthermore, hardware allows for access to cells on a one-at-a-time basis. With a few exceptions, programming languages can be viewed as abstractions, at different levels, of the behavior of such conventional computers. In particular, they introduce the notion of variables as an abstraction of the notion of memory cells and the notion of assignment statements as an abstraction of the destructive modification of a cell.

In most of this and the following chapters we basically will restrict our considerations to these conventional, ''assignment-based'' programming languages. Alternative languages that support a functional style of programming will be discussed in Chapter 8.

A variable is characterized by a *name* and four basic attributes: scope, lifetime, value, and type. The name is used to identify and refer to the variable. Some languages allow variables that do not have names; examples of these so-called *anonymous* variables are given later in the chapter. Discussed below are each of these four attributes and the different policies adopted by programming languages for binding attributes to variables.

3.3.1 The Scope of a Variable

The *scope* of a variable is the range of program instructions over which the variable is known, and thus manipulable. A variable is *visible* within its scope and invisible outside it. Variables can be bound to a scope either statically or dynamically. *Static scope binding* defines the scope of a variable in terms of the lexical structure of a program: that is, each reference to a variable is statically bound to a particular (implicit or explicit) variable declaration. Static scope rules are adopted by most of the languages we will be discussing in this text.

Dynamic scope binding defines the scope of a variable in terms of program execution. Typically, each variable declaration extends its effect over all the instructions executed thereafter, until a new declaration for a variable with the same name is encountered. APL, LISP, and SNOBOL4 are examples of languages with dynamic scope rules.

Dynamic scope rules are rather easy to implement but have disadvantages in terms of programming discipline and efficiency of implementation. Programs are hard to read because the identity of the particular declaration to which a given variable is bound depends on the particular point of execution, and so cannot be determined statically.

3.3.2 The Lifetime of a Variable

The lifetime of a variable is the interval of time in which a storage area is bound to the variable. This area is used to hold the value of the variable. We will use the term *data object* (or simply, *object*) to denote the storage and the value together.

The action that acquires a storage area for a variable is called *allocation*. In some languages, allocation is performed before run-time (*static allocation*). In other languages, it is performed at run-time (*dynamic allocation*), either upon explicit request from the programmer via a *creation statement* or automatically upon the entering of the variable's scope. Sections 3.4 through 3.7 present an extensive analysis of these issues.

3.3.3   The Value of a Variable

The value of a variable is represented in coded form in the storage area bound to the variable. The coded representation is then interpreted according to the variable's type.

In some programming languages, the value of a variable can be a *reference* (*pointer*) to an object. In such languages, an object can be made accessible via a chain of references (or *access path*) of arbitrary length. Two variables *share* an object if each has an access path to the object. A shared object modified via a certain access path makes the modification known to all possible access paths. Sharing of objects is used to conserve storage, but it can lead to programs that are hard to read, because the value of variables can be modified even when they are not referenced. References are the primary means for accessing anonymous variables.

The binding between a variable and the value held in its storage area is usually dynamic, since the value can be modified by an assignment operation. An assignment such as $b:=a$ causes a copy of a's value to be made into the storage area bound to b.

Some languages, however, allow for freezing of the binding between a variable and its value once it is established. The resulting entity is, in every respect, a user-defined *symbolic constant*. For example, in Pascal one can write

const *pi = 3.1416*

and in ALGOL 68

real *pi = 3.1416*

and then use *pi* in expressions such as

circumference:= *2 * pi * radius*

Variable *pi* is bound to value 3.1416 and its value cannot be changed—that is, the translator reports an error if there is an assignment to *pi*.

Pascal and ALGOL 68 differ in the time of binding between the variable and its unchangeable value. In Pascal the value is either a number or a string of characters, and thus it is possible to establish binding at translation time. The translator can legally substitute the value of the constant for its symbolic name in the program. In ALGOL 68 the value can be yielded by an expression involving other variables and constants; consequently, binding can only be established at run-time, when the variable is created. A *manifest constant* is a symbolic constant whose value can be bound at translation time.

A subtle question concerning the binding between a variable and its value is, What is the value immediately after the variable is created? There are a number of possible approaches. Unfortunately, the adopted solution often is left unspecified in the language definition and is solved differently by different implementations. This fact makes it difficult to prove the program correct, because correctness may depend on the implementation. Furthermore, moving an apparently correct program to a different installation may produce unforeseen errors or unexpected results.

One obvious and frequently adopted solution to the above problem is to ignore it. In this case, the bit string found in the area of storage associated with the variable is considered as its initial value. Another solution is to provide a system-defined initialization strategy: for example, integers are initialized to zero, characters to blank, and so on. Yet another solution consists of viewing an uninitialized variable as initialized with a special *uninitialized-value* and forbidding any read accesses to such variables until a meaningful value is assigned to the variable. This solution, by far the cleanest, can be enforced in different ways. Its only drawback could be the costs associated with the run-time checks necessary to ensure that an uninitialized value is never used in the program.

3.3.4 The Type of a Variable

The type of a variable can be viewed as a specification of the class of values that can be associated with the variable, together with the operations that can be legally used to create, access, and modify such values.

When the language is defined, a type name is usually bound to a certain class of values and to a set of operations. For example, type *boolean* is bound to the values *true* and *false* and to the operations **and, or**, and **not**. Values and operations are bound to a certain machine representation when the language is implemented. For example, *true* might be bound to the bit string 00 . . . 001, *false* might be bound to 00 . . . 000. Operations **and, or**, and **not** might be implemented via suitable machine instructions that operate on the bit strings representing booleans.

There are languages in which the programmer can define new types, by means of a type declaration. For example, in Pascal one can write

type *t* = **array** [1..10] **of** *boolean*

This declaration estalishes a binding—at translation time—between the type name *t* and its implementation (i.e., an array of 10 booleans, each accessible via an index in the subrange 1 to 10). As a consequence of this binding, type *t* inherits all the operations of the representation data structure (the array); thus, it is possible to read and modify each component of an object of type *t* by indexing within the array.

In languages that support the definition of abstract data types there is no default binding between a new type and the set of operations; the operations must be specified as a set of subprograms in the declaration of the new type. The declaration of the new type has the following general form.

type *t* =   data structure representing objects of type *t;*
           procedures to be used for manipulating data objects of type *t*
end

Types can be bound to variables either statically or dynamically. The static solution is adopted by most of the languages we will be discussing in the following, that is Pascal, ALGOL 68, SIMULA 67, CLU, Ada, etc., but also by older languages like FORTRAN, COBOL, ALGOL 60, and PL/I.

In such languages, the binding between a variable and its type is usually specified by a *variable declaration*. For example, in Pascal one can write

var *x,y: integer;*
    z: boolean;

However, there are languages (such as FORTRAN) in which the first occurrence of a new variable name is taken as an implicit declaration. The advantage of explicit declarations lies in the clarity of the programs and in improved reliability, since such things as spelling errors in variable names can be caught at translation time. For example, in FORTRAN the declaration of variable ALPHA followed by a statement such as ALPA = 7.3 intended to assign a value to it, would not be detected as an error. ''ALPA'' would not be considered as an incorrect occurrence of an undeclared variable (i.e., as a misspelled ALPHA), but rather as the implicit declaration of a new variable, ALPA.

APL and SNOBOL4 are two languages that use a dynamic binding between variables and types. For example, in APL a variable name may denote at different points during execution a simple variable, a one-dimensional array, a multidimensional array, or even a label. Actually, APL variables are not explicitly declared; rather, their type is implicitly determined by the value they currently hold. For example, after executing the assignment statement

$$A \leftarrow 5$$

A is an integer variable holding ''5'' as its value. A later statement

$$\rightarrow A$$

would treat *A* as a label variable and jump to the statement whose number is the value of *A*. Still later, *A* may be modified by the following assignment:

$$A \leftarrow 1\ 2\ 51\ 0$$

Now *A* denotes a one-dimensional array of length 4. The lower bound of the index is implicitly set to 1.

Dynamic binding provides great flexibility in creating and manipulating data structures. However, it has disadvantages in terms of programming discipline, program correctness, and efficiency of implementation. Programs are hard to read because the type of a variable that occurs in a statement is not immediately known, but depends on the paths of execution followed by the program. As a consequence, an APL statement such as

$$A[2;3] \leftarrow 0$$

intended to assign zero to the component in row 2, column 3, of a two-dimensional array, is correct only if, at that particular point of execution, A is a two-dimensional array. For example, it would be incorrect if $A \leftarrow 0$ were the latest assignment to A. In other words, APL requires *dynamic type checking* to verify that the use of each variable is consistent with its type. In contrast, static binding is the basis of static type checking, whose benefits to program correctness were discussed in Section 2.4.

As another example, consider the APL statement

$$A \leftarrow B + C$$

This statement is correct if either one or both of the variables B and C are simple variables, but also if B and C are arrays with the same number and size of dimensions. Moreover, the actions necessary to execute the statement depend on the types of B and C. If B and C are simple variables, the implied actions are a simple addition and an assignment. If B and C are one-dimension arrays, the implied actions comprise a loop of additions and assignments.

This example shows that information about types of APL variables must be used at run-time not only to perform dynamic type checking, but also to choose the appropriate actions for executing statements. In order to use type information, descriptors must exist at run-time and must be modified every time a new binding is established. Conversely, other languages (such as Pascal) are designed so that type information is known at translation time. Consequently, descriptors need to exist only at translation time.

Programming languages that adopt dynamic binding between variables and types are processed more naturally by interpretation. As the above example shows, there generally is not enough information before run-time to generate code for the evaluation of expressions involving variables of unknown type. The choice between translation and interpretation in the implementation of a language is therefore heavily influenced by the binding rules between variables and types. Languages with dynamic binding are interpretation-oriented, whereas languages with static binding are translation-oriented.

3.4 PROGRAM UNITS

Programming languages allow a program to be composed of a number of *units*. Program units can be developed in a more or less independent fashion and can sometimes be translated separately and combined after translation. Variables declared within a unit are *local* to the unit. A unit can be *activated* at execution time. Assembly language subprograms, FORTRAN subroutines, and ALGOL 60 procedures and blocks are well-known examples of program units. This section reviews some elementary mechanisms that control the flow of execution among program units and the bindings established when a unit is activated. The important issue of subprogram parameter passing and additional mechanisms that control the flow of execution are discussed in Chapter 5.

The representation of a program unit during execution is called *unit activation*. A unit activation is composed of a *code segment* and an *activation record*. The code segment, whose contents are fixed, contains the instructions of the unit. The contents of the activation record are changeable. The activation record contains all the information necessary to execute the unit, including, among other things, the data objects associated with the local variables of a particular unit activation. The relative position of a data object in the activation record is called *offset*. To reference a data object, the processor can use the starting address of the activation record that contains the data object and the offset for the object.

A unit is not a self-contained, completely independent piece of program. If it is a subprogram, it can be activated by a subprogram call issued by another unit, to which control is to be returned after execution. Therefore, the return point is a piece of (changeable) information that must be saved in the activation record at subprogram call. Moreover, units can reference variables other than those declared locally, if the scope rules of the language allow this. Nonlocal variables that can be referenced by a unit are called *global* for that unit.*

The *referencing environment* of a unit activation **U** consists of **U**'s local variables, which are bound to objects stored in **U**'s activation record (*local environment*); and of **U**'s global variables, which are bound to objects stored in the activation records of other units (*global environment*). Two variables of a unit's referencing environment that denote the same data object are called *aliases*. The modification of a data object bound to a global variable is called a *side-effect*.

Units can often be activated recursively: that is, a unit can call itself either directly or indirectly through some other unit. In other words, a new activation of a unit can occur before termination of a previous activation. All the activations of the same unit are composed of the same code segment but different activation records. Thus, in the presence of recursion, the binding between an activation record and its code segment is necessarily dynamic. Every time a unit is activated, a binding must be established between an activation record and its code segment to form a new unit activation.

Some languages, such as FORTRAN, do not support recursive activations. Thus the binding between the code segment and the activation record can be static, and the creation (and initialization) of the data objects for the local variables of a unit can be done before program execution. The following sections discuss these issues in more

---

*Some authors (e.g., Pratt 1975) distinguish between the terms "nonlocal" and "global." The latter is used to denote a nonlocal variable belonging to an activation record that is active throughout program execution. We will use the two terms interchangeably.

detail. The case of FORTRAN is presented in Section 3.5. ALGOL-like languages are studied in Section 3.6. The basic issues of interpretive languages, exemplified by APL, are discussed in Section 3.7.

3.5 THE STRUCTURE OF FORTRAN

A FORTRAN program is composed of a set of units: a main program and a (possibly empty) set of subprograms (subroutines and functions). The amount of storage required to hold each local variable is fixed; it is known at translation time and cannot be changed during the execution of the unit.

Each unit is compiled separately and is associated with an activation record that can be allocated before execution: that is, variables can be created before run-time and their lifetimes extend over the entire program execution (*static variables*). The scope of a variable, however, is limited to the unit in which it is declared.

Units can access global variables declared via COMMON statements. These variables can be viewed as belonging to a system-provided activation record, global to all program units. A view of a FORTRAN program is illustrated in Figure 3.1.

When a unit is translated, consecutive locations of the unit's activation record are reserved for local variables as variable declarations are processed: that is, offsets are statically bound to variables. However, the binding between a variable and its storage area cannot be completed, because the area where the activation record will be stored is not known. The area becomes known when the units are linked and loaded prior to execution.

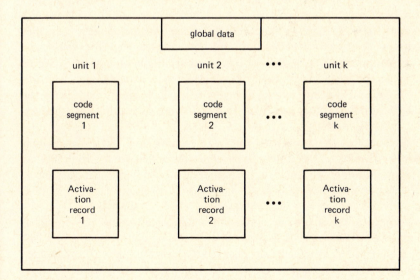

Figure 3.1 A view of a FORTRAN program during execution.

In short, FORTRAN permits a *static memory allocation scheme*. Storage required by each unit is fixed and known before run-time; it can be associated with the unit before run-time; it remains bound to the unit during the entire course of program execution, even if the unit is not active. A consequence of static memory allocation is that most FORTRAN processors allow units to display a "history-sensitive" behavior, even though this feature is explicitly ruled out by the standard definition of the language. A history-sensitive subprogram may produce different results when activated twice with the same values of parameters and global variables, because the values kept in the local environment may be different in each activation. For example, some local values can be initialized before run-time (via a DATA statement), and updated at each activation of the unit. History-sensitive units often are difficult to understand and analyze. A subprogram cannot be described simply by relating inputs and outputs; its behavior may depend on the *state* of computation (i.e., the values stored in the activation record).

Static memory allocation is simple and easily implementable, but the resulting language lacks flexibility. It is not possible to write recursive subprograms. Every variable (in particular, arrays) must have a fixed, statically known size. And finally, storage is occupied by activation records even when the corresponding units are not active.

3.6 THE STRUCTURE OF ALGOL-LIKE LANGUAGES

Most of the languages discussed in the following chapters are descendants of ALGOL 60 and often are called ALGOL-like languages. ALGOL-like languages provide a feature—the *block structure*—to control the scope of variables and to divide the program into units. Any two units in the program text can be either *disjoint* (i.e., they have no portion in common) or *nested* (i.e., one unit completely encloses the other). The structure of the program can thus be viewed as a *static nesting of units* (Figure 3.2*a*). Such a static nesting can also be represented by a tree structure. The tree structure in Figure 3.2*b* for the program of Figure 3.2*a* clearly shows that units B and E are statically enclosed within unit A; units F and G are statically enclosed within E; C within B; and D within C.

If a variable is locally declared in a unit U, it is visible in U, but not in the units that enclose U. However, it is visible (with an exception) to all the units that are statically nested within U. In Figure 3.2, a variable declared in unit B is not visible to A, E, F, and G; it is visible to B, C, and D. It is local to B and global to C and D.

The exception to the above rule occurs when a variable local to a given unit is given the same name as a variable declared in an enclosing unit. In such a case, the same name might denote either the locally declared object or the global object declared in the outer unit. The convention in ALGOL-like languages is that local declarations mask global declarations. This implies that in Figure 3.2, if variable v is declared both in A and C, any references to v within A, B, E, F, and G refer to the variable v local to A, whereas any references to v within C and D refer to the variable v local to C.

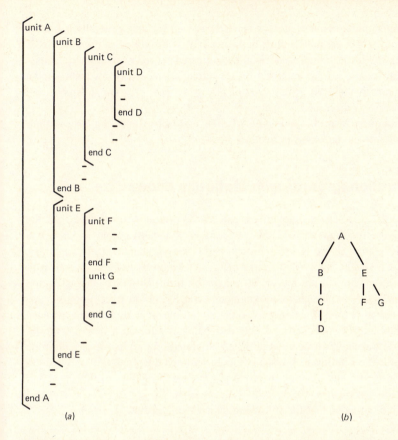

Figure 3.2   Static nesting of ALGOL-like units. (*a*) Unit layout. (*b*) Static nesting tree.

In general, in determining the variables visible to a unit, it is necessary to proceed from that unit outward, through all the enclosing levels of static nesting. Every declaration of a variable that was not previously encountered defines a name visible to the unit.

In ALGOL-like languages, units fall into one of two categories: blocks and subprograms. Blocks are activated when they are encountered during the normal progression of execution and only serve to define a new environment by means of local declarations. Subprograms, on the other hand, are named units activated only when they are called explicitly. The scope rules of subprogram names are the same as those described above for variables.

In order to model the run-time behavior of ALGOL-like languages, it is necessary to specify the rules that govern the life-time of variables and the creation of referencing environments for unit activations. Usually, all the local variables of a unit are automatically created when the unit is activated: that is, there is no explicit "create" operation. Furthermore, some languages require that the amount of storage needed for each variable be fixed and statically known; this case is discussed in Section 3.6.1.

In other languages, the amount of storage needed for each variable generally is known only at run-time, when the unit is activated; this case is discussed in Section 3.6.2. In still other cases, local variables are explicitly created by the programmer. Consequently, the amount of storage required by an activation record is not even known when the unit is activated, but grows dynamically when new creation statements are executed. This case is discussed in Section 3.6.3.

A final important aspect—how ALGOL-like unit activations can access their global environment—is discussed in Section 3.6.4.

3.6.1 Activation Records with Statically Known Size

In this case, local variables are implicitly created when the unit is activated, and the amount of storage required to hold the value of each local variable is known at translation time. Pascal (if we ignore pointers) and C are two languages in this class.

As in the case of FORTRAN, the size of the activation record and the offset of each local variable within it are known at translation time. However, the activation record cannot be bound to the unit's code segment statically, before execution, because there may be several recursive activations of the unit at the same time. The activation record must therefore be allocated and bound dynamically for each new activation. Consequently, at translation time a variable can be bound only to its offset within the activation record; the binding to physical storage requires knowledge of the address of the activation record and can only be done at run-time. Variables of this class will be called *semistatic variables*.

For example, suppose that the following declaration appears in a unit:

a : **array** [*0.. 10*] **of** *integer*

(i.e., *a* is an array of integers with subscripts in the range 0 to 10). Also suppose that each integer occupies one location in the activation record, and that consecutive storage cells are allocated to the array. At translation time, *a*'s address is known relative to the address of the first location of the activation record, which will become known at execution time. If x is a variable holding this address, a reference to $a[i]$ is translated as a reference to location $x + \mathit{offset\_a} + i$.

Dynamic allocation of activation records has two major effects: it allows the implementation of recursive unit activations and, as we will see, it allows more-efficient utilization of main storage. To make return from an activation possible, activation records must contain enough information to identify the instruction to be executed and the activation record to become active upon return. The first (*return point*) is encoded by a pair: a pointer to the caller's code segment and an offset within that segment. The second is represented by a pointer to the activation record of the calling unit; this pointer is called the *dynamic link*. The chain of dynamic links originating in the currently active activation record is called the *dynamic chain*. The dynamic chain represents the dynamic nesting of unit activations.

For example, if units **F** and **G** of the program shown in Figure 3.2 are mutually recursive subprograms, Figure 3.3 represents a partial description of the state of our abstract processor after the following chain of calls.

Call E issued by instruction 3 within **A**'s code segment.

Call F issued by instruction 5 within **E**'s code segment.

Call G issued by instruction 7 within **F**'s code segment.

Call F issued by instruction 3 within **G**'s code segment.

Call G issued by instruction 7 within **F**'s code segment.

Call F issued by instruction 3 within **G**'s code segment.

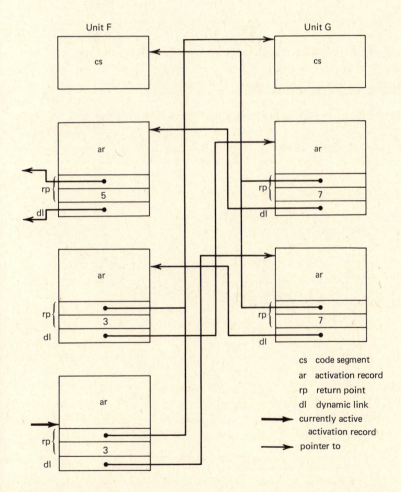

Figure 3.3   Partial representation of the state of the abstract processor during execution of the program in figure 3.2.

When a unit **U** completes its current activation, the activation record is no longer needed. The lifetime rules specify that each activation of **U** must have a new activation record. The local variables of **U** can be global only to units that are nested within **U** and that are activated after the current activation of **U**. Hence, such activations are completed before **U**'s current activation. Therefore, after a unit completes its current activation, it is possible to free the space occupied by the activation record and make it available to store new activation records. Since the activation record that is freed is the most recently allocated, activation records can be allocated with a last-in/first-out policy, on a stack-organized storage.

Stack management can be implemented as follows. Let FREE and CURRENT be two variables pointing to the first free location above the stack and to the first cell of the topmost activation record (the one that is currently active) respectively (Figure 3.4).

The actions performed when a unit is activated are

1. STACK [FREE]: = CURRENT {set the dynamic link for the new activation record}

2. CURRENT: = FREE {set the new value of CURRENT}

3. FREE: = FREE + S {S is the size of the new activation record}

When the unit completes execution, the dynamic link can be followed to arrive at the activation record of the caller. The needed actions are

1. FREE: = CURRENT

2. CURRENT: = STACK [CURRENT]

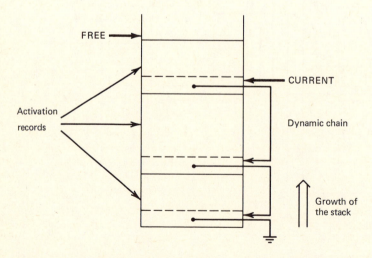

Figure 3.4 Dynamic links and chain in the execution stack.

A stack-based storage management for ALGOL-like languages is an implementation choice and is not strictly implied by the semantics of the language. The semantics of the language only requires that local variables be bound to a new activation record for each new activation, and, conceptually, the local objects of previous activations can continue to exist forever. However, thanks to the scope rules of the language, an activation record becomes inaccessible as soon as the activation terminates. This is why we can choose to allocate activation records on a stack. Ability to reuse the storage released by activation records is the reason why dynamic storage allocation is in principle more efficient than static allocation in the use of storage.

3.6.2 Activation Records Whose Size Is Known at Unit Activation

In ALGOL 60 and other languages of the family, such as ALGOL 68 and, more recently, Ada, neither the size of the activation record nor the position of each local variable within the activation record is always known statically. Variables are automatically created when the unit is activated, but their size can depend on values that are known only at run-time when the unit is activated. Such is the case for *dynamic arrays,* that is, arrays whose bounds become known at run-time. Variables of this class will be called *semidynamic variables*.

The complication that the introduction of semidynamic variables adds to the case discussed in Section 3.6.1 is that local variables cannot be bound to a constant offset within the activation record at translation time, and more address binding must be delayed to run-time. For example, suppose that the following (ALGOL 68) declarations appear within unit U.

$[1{:}n]$ **int** $a;$
$[1{:}m]$ **real** $b;$

(That is, a is an array of integers with subscripts in the range 1 to $n,$ and b is an array of reals with subscripts in the range 1 to m). Let m and n be two global variables. Since the values of n and m are not known at translation time, the amount of storage needed for a and $b,$ and therefore for **U**'s activation record, cannot be determined statically. However, the language semantics require that the values of m and n (and therefore the size of the activation record) be known at unit activation time. This provides the basis for a rather efficient implementation as described below.

At translation-time, we can reserve, within the activation record, storage for the descriptors of the dynamic arrays a and b. The descriptor includes at least one cell in which a pointer to the storage area for the dynamic array will be stored and one cell each for the lower and upper bounds of each array dimension. Since the number of dimensions of the array is known at translation time, the size of the descriptor is known statically. All accesses to semidynamic variables are translated as indirect references through the pointer in the descriptor, whose offset is determined statically.

At run-time, the activation record is allocated in several stages. First, the storage required for semistatic variables and for descriptors of semidynamic variables are allocated. When the declaration of a semidynamic variable is encountered, the dimension entries in the descriptors are entered, the actual size of the semidynamic variable is evaluated, and the activation record is expanded to include the variable. (This expansion is possible because, being the active unit, the activation record is on top of the stack.) The pointer in the descriptor, finally, is set to point to the area just allocated.

3.6.3   Activation Records with Dynamically Variable Size

The languages described in the previous sections are characterized by having all local variables implicitly created at unit activation time. Moreover, the size of the activation records either is known statically or, at worst, known when units are activated. Languages of the ALGOL family—except for ALGOL 60—from PL/I and Pascal to ALGOL 68 and Ada, also allow programmers to deal with data objects whose size can vary during execution. Consequently, the amount of storage required by an activation record is not known when the unit is activated. Such variables will be called *dynamic variables*.

One notable example of dynamic variables is the *flexible array* provided by ALGOL 68 and a few other languages. A flexible array is an array whose bounds can vary during program execution to accommodate the size of the object assigned to it. Consider the following ALGOL-like program structure.

begin Unit A;
      begin Unit B;
      end B;
end A;

Let x be a flexible array declared locally in unit A, and let x be assigned within unit B. Storage for holding the value of x cannot be reserved on the stack within A's activation record, because the amount of space necessary to hold the value assigned by unit B is known only when B is executed (i.e., when B's activation record is on top of the execution stack). At that point of execution, A's activation record is farther down in the execution stack, and changing its size to accommodate the object newly assigned to x would require reshaping the execution stack—an obviously infeasible solution.

Another example of dynamic variables is provided by variables that are allocated under program control. These exist in PL/I, Pascal, and other languages and allow the creation of data structures that can be expanded and contracted. Such a data structure can be modeled as consisting of a set of nodes; nodes may be added to and deleted from the structure dynamically. Examples of these data structures are linked lists and trees. The nodes are often connected via pointers. Since the nodes are allocated while the program is executing and their numbers are not known at the time of writing the program or at translation time, it is impossible to name them explicitly.

They are accessed indirectly through pointers. For example, in Pascal, every pointer is qualified such that it is able to point to objects of only one type. Assuming that p has been declared to be a pointer of type t, then the statement

new (p)

creates an object of type t and assigns its address to p. The lifetime of the object created in this way, unlike that of semistatic and semidynamic variables, does not end when the block containing the allocation statement is exited. Instead, some languages (e.g., PL/I) provide statements for deallocating such objects explicitly. Other languages (e.g., Pascal) state that the object lives as long as a reference (i.e., a pointer) to it exists. Furthermore, it is possible to create several such objects without deallocating any of them. It is easy to see, therefore, that such objects cannot possibly be allocated on the stack.

Consider again, for example, the above mentioned program structure. Let p be a pointer declared in unit A, and let B contain the allocation statement "new (p)." When the allocation statement is executed, the activation record on top of the stack is that of unit B. The object cannot be allocated on top of the stack, because when B is exited the object would be deallocated (while p still points to it). Allocation in A's activation record is also infeasible, because, as we saw in the case of flexible arrays, it would require reshaping the execution stack.

In summary, dynamic variables denote data objects whose size and/or number can vary dynamically during their lifetimes. This fact prohibits the allocation of these variables on a stack; instead, they are allocated in a memory area called a *heap*. The term "heap" is meant to indicate freedom from the last-in/first-out connotation of the stack. For this reason, dynamic variables are called *heap variables*, as opposed to semistatic and semidynamic variables, which are called *stack variables*. Further discussion of heap variables and hints on the run-time management of the heap are given in Sections 4.7.2.6 and 4.7.4.

3.6.4 Accessing the Global Environment

So far we have only examined how a unit activation can reference its own local environment. We will now discuss how unit activations can refer to their global environment; the problem of parameter passing will be delayed until Chapter 5.

In a language such as FORTRAN, as we saw, global variables can be considered to belong to a system-provided activation record that is global to all units, and all bindings between global variables of a unit and storage allocated to such global variables can be established statically.

In ALGOL-like languages, the activation records that are on the stack at any given time represent the dynamic chain of unit activations. Figure 3.5 shows the stack of our abstract processor after the sequence of calls described in Section 3.6.1 for the program shown in Figure 3.2. Suppose that the integer variable x is declared within both E and G, and that the integer variable y is declared within G, B, and A. Moreover, let z be an integer variable locally declared within F. Suppose that the abstract processor reaches the assignment $z := x+y$ when the execution stack is that shown in Figure 3.5. As we have seen, the appropriate binding to a stack location for z is partially established at translation time by translating each occurrence of z into a reference to CURRENT + offset_z (offset_z is a statically known value), and is completed at run-time when the value of CURRENT (the starting address of F's activation record) becomes known. But what about x and y? Note that the binding between x (or y) and the stack location allocated to it is *not* the most recently established binding. In fact, the most recent binding to a stack location for variable x has been established by the latest activation of unit G, but the scope rules of the language require variable x referenced within F to be the one declared within E. Similarly, variable y referenced within F is the one declared within A, and not the one most recently allocated by the latest activation of G. In other words, the sequence of activation records stored in the stack represents the sequence of unit activations dynamically generated at run-time. But what determines the nonlocal environment are the scope rules of the language, based on the static nesting of unit declarations.

3.6.4.1   Static Chain

One way to make possible access to global variables is for each activation record to contain a pointer (*static link*) down the stack to the activation record of the statically

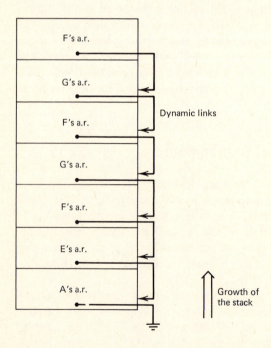

Figure 3.5   The abstract processor's stack for the case of Figure 3.3.

enclosing unit in the program text. Figure 3.6 shows the static links for the example of Figure 3.5. The sequence of static links that can be followed from the topmost activation record is called the *static chain*. Referencing global variables can be intuitively explained as a search that traverses the static chain. To find the correct binding between a variable and a stack location, we search down the static chain until a binding is found. In our example, a reference to x is bound to a stack location within E's activation record, whereas a reference to y is bound to a stack location within A's activation record—as indeed it should be.

In practice, searching, which would entail considerable run-time overhead, is never necessary. A more efficient solution is based on the fact that the activation record containing a variable named in a unit U is always at a fixed distance from U's activation record along the static chain. If it is a local variable, the distance is obviously zero; if it is a variable declared in the immediately enclosing unit, the distance is one; and so on. This distance attribute can be evaluated and bound to the variable at translation time. Consequently, variables may be statically bound to a pair (distance, offset within the activation record). If the variable is semistatic, the offset is the relative position of the object within the activation record. If the variable is semidynamic, the offset is the relative position of a pointer to a stack location where the object is stored. If the variable is dynamic, the offset is the relative position of a pointer to a heap area where the object is stored.

The pair (distance, offset) is used at run-time as follows. If d is the value of the

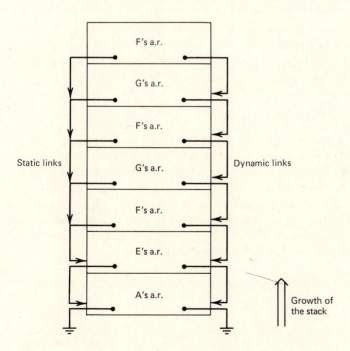

Figure 3.6   Example of Figure 3.5 with static links.

distance, starting from location CURRENT, we traverse d steps along the static chain. The value of the offset is then added to the address so found, and the result is the actual run-time address of the global data object. In the case of semidynamic and dynamic variables, this process leads to a location through which an extra level of indirection is required to reach the actual data object.

So far we have seen how to use the static chain to access global variables. We will now show how the static link can be installed at run-time when a unit is activated. If unit U is a block, the static link for an activation of U is installed very easily, since it is obviously the same as the dynamic link. If U is a subprogram, the operation is more complex. First, for each local subprogram declared in a unit, an entry in the unit's activation record is used to store a pointer to the subprogram's code segment. A subprogram call can then be represented in our abstract processor as "jump (d,o),"* where (as for variables) d is the number of steps down the static chain and o is the offset within the activation record of the location that contains a pointer to the appropriate code segment.

Suppose now that unit V is being processed and that instruction "jump $(2,4)$" is executed to call a subprogram U locally declared within unit W. The static link for U's activation record is set to point to the base of the activation record that lies two steps down the static chain (see Figure 3.7).

When the execution of the currently active unit terminates, the return to the previously active environment does not require any additional machinery. The topmost activation record simply is deleted, and the static chain needed for accessing the new global environment is found already installed.

The main drawback to the use of static links is the need for following the static chain for each reference to a nonlocal variable. The time required to locate a global data object is not constant and depends on the number of steps descended down the static chain.

3.6.4.2   Display

An alternative implementation technique, which speeds up the referencing of global data objects at the cost of making unit activation and return more complex, is based on the use of a display. This new solution is attractive if nonlocal referencing occurs more frequently than subprogram entry and exit.

Instead of static links, a vector of variable length (the *display*) is used to record the pointers to the activation records on the static chain at any given point during execution. Figure 3.8 illustrates the display for the example of Figure 3.6. An identifier represented by the pair (d,o) is now accessed in two steps:

1.   Find the base address b of the activation record. If m is the current number of entries in the array DISPLAY (that is, $0 \ . \ . \ m-1$ is the

---

*Remember that we are considering parameterless subprograms.

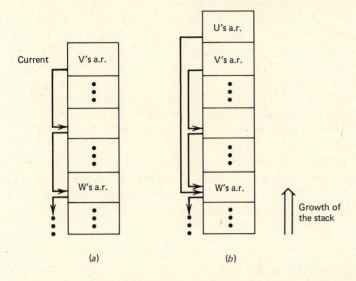

Figure 3.7 (*a*) Static links before calling *U*. (*b*) Static links after calling *U*.

range of subscripts), then DISPLAY $[m-d-1]$ contains the required value of b.

2. Evaluate $b+o$ to obtain the address of the variable.

Referencing a global variable via a display is therefore very simple and takes a constant time for all global variables. However, it is necessary to implement actions

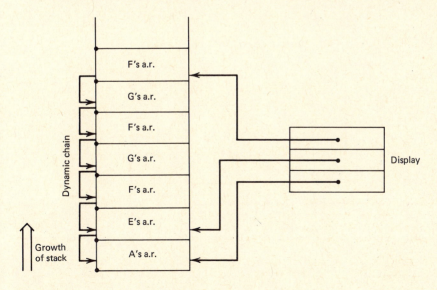

Figure 3.8 Display solution for the example of Figure 3.6.

that modify the display at unit entry and exit to reflect the currently active static chain. Once again, if the unit is a block, the actions are very simple, and they are left to the reader as an exercise. In the case of a subprogram call, let $P_0, P_1, \ldots P_m$ be the values stored in DISPLAY at subscripts $0, 1, \ldots m$ before the call, and let "jump (d,o)" be the call to be processed. If $j = m - d - 1$, then P_j ($0 \leqslant j < m$) is the reference to the activation record of the unit where the subprogram is locally declared. Consequently, the new display will contain $j + 2$ entries—the first $j + 1$ remaining the same as before the call, and the topmost being a reference to the new value of CURRENT. This case for the example of Figure 3.7 is shown in Figure 3.9.

Return from a subprogram, on the other hand, requires restoring the contents of the display to what they were before the call was executed. In the abovementioned case, this means that the values $P_{j+1}, P_{j+2}, \ldots P_m$ must have been saved in the activation record of the called subprogram. Upon exit, these values are copied back into the display.

3.7   THE STRUCTURE OF AN INTERPRETIVE LANGUAGE: APL

Section 3.3.1 stated that some languages are translation-oriented and others are interpretation oriented. From the discussion of Section 3.6, we can conclude that ALGOL-like languages are translation-oriented. The adoption of static binding rules for scopes requires the binding of a variable reference to a variable declaration based on the examination of the program structure. This examination is done more appropriately by a translator than by an interpreter. The adoption of dynamic scope rules, on the other hand, favors the use of an interpreter. Although this text gives major emphasis

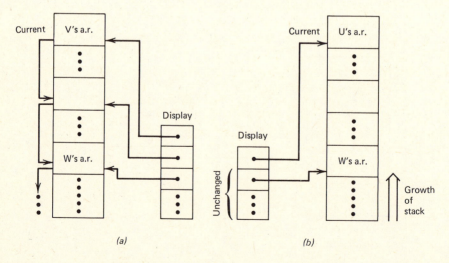

Figure 3.9   Implementation of the example of Figure 3.7 with a display. (*a*) Executions stack and display before calling *U*. (*b*) Execution stack and display after calling *U*.

to translation-oriented languages, the discussion of an interpretive language such as APL should help clarify the basic issues and contrast the difference between the two approaches.

APL has many interesting and unusual features, from being interactive—and providing a number of special features for use in an interactive environment—to providing facilities for array manipulation. However, we will ignore most such features here and will simply outline the run-time behavior of an abstract APL processor. In Chapter 8 we will study the functional aspects of APL.

An APL program usually consists of a number of subprograms and of a sequence of statements, which can be viewed as the main program (Figure 3.10). The first line of a subprogram definition declares the formal parameters (I in the case of SUB, N in the case of FUN). Function subprograms also indicate the result parameter (R in the case of FUN). Local variables (X in the case of FUN, Y in the case of SUB) are also declared.

Global variables are implicitly declared by an assignment to an identifier that has not been declared as local. A variable declaration does not specify the variable's type. Subprogram names are considered as global identifiers.

APL scope rules are dynamic: that is, the scope of a name is totally dependent on the run-time call chain (i.e., on the dynamic chain), rather than on the static structure of the program. In the example shown in Figure 3.10, consider the point when the call SUB 2 is issued. The nonlocal references to X and Z within the activation of SUB are bound to the global X and Z defined by the main program. When function FUN is activated from SUB, the nonlocal reference to Y is bound to the most recent definition of Y: that is, to the data object associated to Y in SUB's activation record. The next instruction of the main program calls function FUN again. In this case, the nonlocal reference to Y from FUN is bound to the global Y defined in the main program.

The implementation of the APL global-referencing mechanism can be very simple. Activation records are allocated on the execution stack and joined together by dynamic links. Each entry of the activation record explicitly records the name of the variable and contains a pointer to a heap area, where the value can be stored. Allocation on a heap is necessary because the amount of storage required by each variable can vary dynamically (see Section 3.3.1). For each variable—say, T—the stack is searched by following the dynamic links. The first association found for T in an activation record is the proper one. Figure 3.11 illustrates the execution stack for the program of Figure 3.10 when FUN is called by SUB, which is, in turn, called by main.

Although very simple, this accessing mechanism is very inefficient. Following the same philosophy that leads to the idea of the display for ALGOL-like languages, it is possible here to maintain a table of currently active nonlocal references. Instead of searching down the dynamic chain, a single search in this table is sufficient. We will not discuss this solution in any detail. However, the reader will notice that as in the case of the display, this solution speeds up referencing nonlocal variables, at the expense of more-elaborate actions, to be executed at subprogram entry and exit, that update the table of active nonlocal references.

APL's dynamic scope rules represent a sharp departure from the static rules of

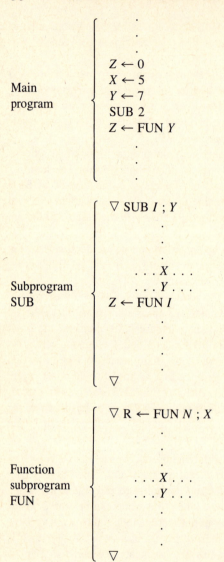

Main program
$$Z \leftarrow 0$$
$$X \leftarrow 5$$
$$Y \leftarrow 7$$
SUB 2
$$Z \leftarrow \text{FUN } Y$$

Subprogram SUB
$$\nabla \text{ SUB } I\, ;\, Y$$
$$\ldots X \ldots$$
$$\ldots Y \ldots$$
$$Z \leftarrow \text{FUN } I$$
$$\nabla$$

Function subprogram FUN
$$\nabla \text{ R} \leftarrow \text{FUN } N\, ;\, X$$
$$\ldots X \ldots$$
$$\ldots Y \ldots$$
$$\nabla$$

Figure 3.10   Structure of an APL program.

ALGOL-like languages. Before ending this section, let us turn briefly to an evaluation of the programming style that these scope rules support and the reliability of the resulting programs. Dynamic scope rules help reasoning about the program *as it is executed*: the most recently established binding is the one that is valid at any instant. Thus, dynamic scope rules make programs amenable to interactive execution performed by an interpreter. In contrast, static scope rules help reasoning about the

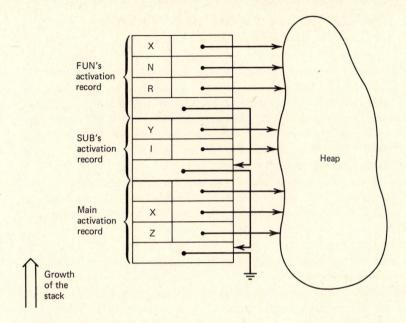

Figure 3.11   Execution stack at a particular point of execution of the program of Figure 3.10.

program *as it is written*: the referencing environment at any point during the execution of a program depends not on the history of the computation, but on the textual structure of the program. Thus, with static scope rules it is more natural to develop a program by first writing the program, then going through the written text to assess its correctness, translating it, and finally, executing it.

Interactive program interpretation is in fact typical of dynamic languages such as APL, and the solution is appealing for programs of moderate size. As we will see in Chapter 8, the availability of extremely powerful built-in operations on arrays makes the language particularly suitable for interactive execution, because even a single statement can express a considerable amount of computation. There are two main reasons, however, why dynamic languages are less suitable for the construction of large programs to be used repeatedly in a production environment. First, the compilation choice is more attractive in this situation, because the compiler can generate efficient object code, which can be saved for later reuse. Second, the language itself favors the production of more reliable programs. The programmer can more easily reason about the program, and the translator can help in assessing correctness by extensively checking the program.

This is a striking example of how a language feature—scope rules—can have effects that extend far beyond the strict boundaries of the programming language. Not only can it affect the programming style and the reliability of the produced programs, but it can also demand an entirely different implementation and a different set of programming tools.

SUGGESTIONS FOR FURTHER READING
AND BIBLIOGRAPHIC NOTES

Programming language semantics has been informally studied here by describing the behavior of a processor for the language. This operational description intentionally has been left rather informal. The reader interested in formal approaches to operational semantics can refer to (Wegner 1972). Other approaches to the formal specification of semantics are presented in (Tennent 1976), (Gordon 1979), (Bjørner and Jones 1978), and (Hoare 1969). (Hoare and Wirth 1973) and (Alagić and Arbib 1978) give a formal definition of Pascal based on the theory of (Hoare 1969).

Our view of semantics is more oriented to language implementation. We have emphasized the important concepts of binding and binding time. This viewpoint is also taken by other textbooks on programming languages, such as (Elson 1973) and (Pratt 1975).

The results of the experiments reported in (Gannon and Horning 1975) and (Gannon 1977) support the assertion that languages that statically bind a type to variables lead to more-reliable programs.

We have emphasized the run-time representation of programs. Additional details on this topic can be found in compiler textbooks such as (Gries 1971), (Bauer and Eikel 1976), (Aho and Ullman 1977), and (Barrett and Couch 1979).

A different approach to the description of the operational semantics of programming languages is taken by (Organick et al. 1978).

Exercises

3.1 Design a program unit that prints a randomly generated number each time it is activated. The unit must not access any global variables and does not receive parameters. Can this problem be solved with a history-insensitive unit?

3.2 Design and run an experiment to check whether your FORTRAN compiler allows the implementation of history-sensitive subprograms.

3.3 Consider the following ALGOL-like program:

```
program A;
    procedure B;
        procedure C;
                .
                .
            call B;
                .
                .
        end C;
                .
                .
```

```
        call C;
    end B;
    procedure D;
            .

            .

        call B;
    end D;
        .

        .

        call D;
    end A;
```

Describe each stage in the life of the stack until *B* is called within procedure *C*. In particular, show the dynamic and static links before and after every call.

3.4 Explain why the static and dynamic links have the same value for ALGOL-like blocks.

3.5 Nonlocal referencing for a language with dynamic scope rules can be implemented via a table that keeps track of the referenceable nonlocal variables (Section 3.7). Detail the actions that must be executed at subprogram entry and exit in order to keep this table up-to-date.

3.6 "Early binding supports efficient implementation and favors reliable programming; late binding provides flexibility." Give examples that support this statement. Give counter-examples.

3.7 Explain why APL requires more run-time support than ALGOL-like languages and why ALGOL-like languages require more run-time support than FORTRAN. Is this phenomenon a function of the compiler/interpreter, or is it inherent in the language? Draw some conclusions about the comparative run-time efficiency of these languages. How about space efficiency? Programming efficiency?

3.8 In ALGOL 60, a variable may be declared to be **own**. An own variable is allocated storage the first time that its enclosing unit is activated, and its storage remains allocated until program termination. Normal scope rules apply, so that the variable is known only within the unit in which it is declared. In essence, the effect of the own declaration is to extend the lifetime of the variable to cover the entire program execution.

    a. Own variables are *not* automatically initialized to certain default values. This, in practice, turns out to limit their usefulness greatly. To appreciate this weakness, write a function that keeps track of the number of times it has been called. This value is kept in an own variable and returned each time the function is called.

    b. Outline an implementation model for **own** variables. For simplicity, assume that **own** variables can only have simple (unstructured) type.

3.9 Design an interpreter for a mini-language (a language consisting of five types of statements or less).

3.10 Design a translator for a mini-language.

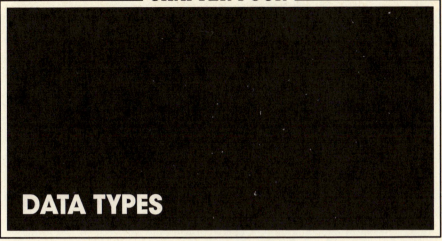

CHAPTER FOUR

DATA TYPES

Computer programs can be viewed as functions that are to be applied to certain input data in order to produce certain desired results. In conventional programming languages, this function is evaluated through a sequence of steps that produce intermediate data that are stored in program variables. There are basic differences among languages in the kinds of data they use, the available kinds of operations on data, and the way data can be structured and used.

Programming languages usually provide a fixed, built-in set of elementary data types, as well as mechanisms for structuring more complex data types starting from the elementary ones. These issues are discussed in general throughout this chapter. We will concentrate on languages that establish a static binding between a variable and its type. In particular, we will review and discuss the data-type features provided by ALGOL 68, Pascal, SIMULA 67, CLU, and Ada.

The chapter is organized as follows. Section 4.1 discusses built-in types. Section 4.2 classifies the basic mechanisms provided by programming languages to aggregate elementary data into complex data structures. Section 4.3 discusses how such mechanisms can be used to define new data types in ALGOL 68 and Pascal. Section 4.4 discusses type conversions. Section 4.5 presents several controversial issues regarding types in ALGOL 68 and Pascal and shows the solutions adopted by Ada. Section 4.6 presents language features for defining abstract data types, with emphasis on SIMULA 67 and CLU. Section 4.7 discusses implementation models.

4.1 BUILT-IN TYPES

Programming languages provide a fixed set of built-in types, which, as mentioned in Sections 2.1 and 2.2, in most cases reflect the behavior of the underlying hardware. At the programming-language level, the concept of built-in type appears as a way of identifying the abstract behavior of a set of data objects with a common set of operations. Therefore, integers can be viewed as the set of values $\ldots -2, -1, 0, 1, 2, \ldots$

that can be manipulated by the well-known operators $+$, $-$, $*$ and $/$. The translator for the programming language maps this abstract view into a concrete implementation. For example, the implementation maps the abstract object "25" into a certain bit string—for example, 00011001 in two's-complement representation. Similarly, the adding of two integers is mapped into the machine's fixed-point addition operation.

Based on some of the points already raised in Sections 2.2 and 2.4, we can say that built-in types introduce four useful properties. The first of these properties holds for both static and dynamically-typed languages, whereas the other three hold only for statically typed languages.

1. *Invisibility of the underlying representation*
   The programmer does not have access to the underlying bit string that represents a value of a certain type. Such a bit string is changed as a result of the application of operations, but the change is visible to the programmer as a new value of the built-in type, not as a new bit string. Invisibility of the underlying representation has the following two beneficial effects.

   - **Programming style**   The abstraction provided by the language increases program readability by protecting the representation of objects from undisciplined manipulation. This is in contrast to the underlying conventional hardware, which does not enforce protection. Any object is viewed as an uninterpreted string of bits that can be manipulated by the instruction repertoire of the machine. For example, a location containing an instruction can be added to a location containing a string of characters, or even to another instruction.

   - **Modifiability**   The implementation of abstractions can be changed without affecting the programs that make use of the abstractions. As a consequence, *portability* of programs is also improved: that is, programs can be moved to machines that use different internal representations for data.

   Programming languages provide instructions to read and write values of built-in types. Most languages also provide features for formatting the output. Machines perform input/output by interacting with peripheral devices in a complicated and machine-dependent way (which will be ignored in this text). High-level languages hide these complications and the physical resources involved in machine input/output (registers, channels, etc.).

2. *Correct use of variables can be checked at translation time*
   If the declaration of variables is required, illegal operations on a variable can be caught by the translator: that is, protection of variables can be enforced at translation time.
   We have already mentioned, however, that static type-checking does not exhaust all the checks that can be done on a program. For

example, the expression *i/j* might be statically checked as correct (e.g., *i* and *j* are both *real*) and yet might require a run-time check if a division by zero is to be trapped. Another example is given in point **4** below.

3. *Disambiguation of operators can be done at translation time*
   There are languages in which a few operator symbols can be used to represent a large number of operators. For example, the symbol '' + '' can represent both addition of reals and addition of integers. In a statically typed language (Section 3.3.1), the machine operation to be invoked for executing *A + B* can be chosen by the translator, since the types of the operands are known. This makes the implementation more efficient than in a dynamically typed language such as APL, in which it is necessary to keep track of types in run-time descriptors. An operator whose meaning depends on the type of its operands is called *overloaded*, or *generic*. The '' + '' operator is overloaded because it is defined for both integers and reals (and implemented by different machine instructions on the underlying representation). A judicious use of overloading can contribute to the simplicity and usability of a programming language. For example, having two different symbols for integer and real addition would make programming more complicated. However, excessive use of overloading can generate programs that are hard to understand, because a unique name denotes completely different entities.

4. *Accuracy control*
   In some cases, the programmer can explicitly associate with the type a specification of the relative accuracy of the representation. For example, FORTRAN allows the user to choose between single- and double-precision floating-point numbers. ALGOL 68 allows one to specify the required (relative) precision by declarations such as **long real**, **long long real** (for floating-point values), and **long int**, **long long int**, (for fixed-point values). The number of **long** (or **short**) prefixes supported is determined by the implementation and available in constants *int lengths, int shorts, real lengths,* and *real shorts*. Accuracy of numeric data types can also be controlled in Ada.

   Accuracy specification can be viewed both as a space optimization directive to the translator and as a request to the translator to insert run-time checks to monitor the values of variables. The latter provides an effective aid for the programmer in assessing the correctness of programs. Finally, programs with accuracy specifications are more easily adaptable to different installations with different memory word lengths, because source program changes are localized to declarations.

4.2 DATA AGGREGATES

Programming languages allow the programmer to specify aggregations of elementary data objects and, in turn, aggregation of aggregates. A well-known example is the

array constructor, which constructs aggregates of homogeneous-type elements. An aggregate object has a unique name. Manipulation can be done on a single elementary component at a time, each component being accessed by a suitable *selection* operation. In many languages it is also possible to assign and compare entire aggregates.

Sections 4.2.1 through 4.2.4 classify the basic structuring mechanisms provided by programming languages.

4.2.1 Cartesian Product

The Cartesian product of n sets $A_1, A_2, \ldots A_n$, denoted by $A_1 \times A_2 \times \ldots A_n$, is a set whose elements are ordered n-tuples $(a_1, a_2, \ldots, a_n)$, where $a_i \in A_i$. For example, regular polygons might be characterized by an integer—the number of edges—and a real—the length of an edge. Any polygon would thus be an element in the Cartesian product

integer $\times$ *real*

Cartesian products are called *records* in COBOL and Pascal, *structures* in PL/I and ALGOL 68.

Programming languages view Cartesian product data objects as composed of a number of symbolically named fields. In the above example, variables of type *polygon* could be declared as composed of an integer field (*no_of_edges*) holding the number of edges, and a real field (*edge_size*) holding the length of each edge. The fields of Cartesian products are selected by specifying, in an appropriate syntactic notation, the *selectors* (or *field names*) *no_of_edges* and *edge_size*. For example, following the Pascal syntax, to make the polygon *t1* an equilateral triangle of edge 7.53, one should write

t1.no_of_edges:= 3;
t1.edge_size:= 7.53

In ALGOL 68, this could be done in one statement.

t1:= (3,7.53)

4.2.2 Finite Mapping

A finite mapping is a function from a finite set of values of a domain type *DT* onto values of a codomain type *CT*. Programming languages possess an **array** constructor that allows one to define finite mappings. The Pascal declaration

var *a:* **array** *[1..5]* **of** *real*

can be viewed as a mapping from integers in the subrange 1 to 5 to the set of reals.

An object of the codomain can be selected by *indexing:* that is, by providing as index an appropriate value in the domain. Thus, the Pascal notation *a*[*k*] can be viewed as an application of the above mapping to the argument *k*. Indexing with a value out of the domain results in an error that usually can only be caught at run-time.

In some languages, such as APL, ALGOL 68, and Ada, indexing can be used to select more than one element of the codomain. For example, in ALGOL 68, *a*[3:5,5:12] specifies a two-dimensional subarray of *a* containing 24 elements.

The strategy for binding the domain of the function to a specific subset of values of type *DT* varies according to the language. Basically, there are three possible choices.

1. *Compile-time binding*
   The subset is fixed when the program is written and frozen at translation time. This restriction was adopted by FORTRAN, C, and Pascal. It supports static and semistatic variables.

2. *Object creation-time binding*
   The subset is fixed at run-time, when an instance of the variable is created. This choice (*dynamic arrays*) initially was used by ALGOL 60 and has been adopted by SIMULA 67 and Ada. Following the terminology introduced in Chapter 3, such array variables are called semi-dynamic.

3. *Object manipulation-time binding*
   This is the most flexible but also the most costly choice in terms of run-time execution. The size of the subset can be changed at any time during the object's lifetime (*flexible arrays*). This is typical of interpretive languages such as SNOBOL4 and APL. Of compiled languages, AL-GOL 68 was the first to allow it (in the form of **flex** arrays); then, subsequently, CLU. According to the terminology introduced in Chapter 3, such array variables are called dynamic.

4.2.3 Sequencing

A sequence consists of any number of occurrences of data items of a certain component type *CT*. This structuring mechanism has the important property of leaving unspecified the number of occurrences of the component, and therefore it requires the underlying implementation to be able to store objects of arbitrary size (at least in principle).

Strings provide a well-known example of sequences in which the component type is character. The concept of sequence also captures the familiar data-processing idea of sequential *file*.

It is difficult to abstract a common behavior from the examples of sequences provided by existing programming languages. For example, SNOBOL4 views strings as data objects with a rich set of operations. Conversely, Pascal and C view strings simply as arrays of characters, with no special primitives for string manipulation. Taking somewhat of a middle ground, PL/I and Ada provide string manipulation primitives but, to reduce the problem of dynamic storage allocation, require that maximum size of a string be specified with the declaration of the string. Files present more serious problems in that they often have peculiar, system-dependent aspects as a result of the necessary interface with the operating system.

Conventional operators on strings include the following.

1. Concatenation. The concatenation of *THIS_IS_* and *AN_EXAMPLE* gives *THIS_IS_AN_EXAMPLE*.

2. Selection of the first (last) component. Selection of the last component of the above string yields *E*.

3. Slicing. A substring can be extracted from a given string by specifying the positions of the first and last desired characters.

Simple primitives are usually provided for files. For example, a Pascal file can be only modified by appending a new value to the end of an existing file, and reading is possible only by sequential scanning.

4.2.4 Recursion

A recursive data type T can contain components that belong to the same type T. To define a recursive type, one can use the type name inside the type's definition. For example, type *binary_tree* can be defined either as empty or as a triple composed of an atomic element, a (left) *binary_tree*, and a (right) *binary_tree*.

Recursion is a structuring mechanism that can be used to define aggregates whose size can grow arbitrarily and whose structure can have arbitrary complexity. As opposed to sequencing, it allows the programmer to create arbitrary access paths for the selection of components.

Data objects of recursive type are implemented by using pointers. Each component specified as belonging to the recursive type is represented by a location containing a pointer to the data object, rather than the data object itself. It is necessary to do so because data objects may be of arbitrary size. For example, each node of a binary tree has two associated locations: one containing a pointer to the left subtree (if any); the other containing a pointer to the right subtree (if any). (We ignore other information being kept at each node.) The tree itself is identified by another location containing a pointer to the root node of the tree. Starting from this location, it is possible to access each node by following a suitable chain of pointers. A null pointer corresponds to an empty (sub)tree. Sections 4.3.1.2.3 and 4.3.2.2.4 illustrate how binary trees can be defined in ALGOL 68 and Pascal, respectively.

4.2.5 Discriminated union

The discriminated union is a structuring mechanism that specifies that a choice is to be made between different, alternative structures. Each alternative structure is called a *variant*.

COBOL supports discriminated unions with its REDEFINES clause. This construct supports the common data-processing situation in which the structures of some stored records are identical for the most part, differing only for some fields. In a payroll program, a field may refer either to the employee's monthly salary or to his hourly pay, depending on how he is paid. In the following example, *SALARY* and *HOUR_RATE* refer to the same record-field, but each has a different picture (which, in COBOL, is analogous to the concept of type).

```
01  EMPLOYEE_RECORD.
    05  NAME                        PIC X(20).
    05  SALARY                      PIC 9999.
    05  HOUR_RATE REDEFINES SALARY  PIC 99V99.
```

Most modern programming languages allow the programmer to define—to a more-or-less general degree—the type of a variable as a discriminated union. Two examples are the *union* of ALGOL 68 and the *variant record* of Pascal, which will be discussed later.

4.2.6 Powerset

It is often useful to define variables whose value can be any subset of a set of elements of a certain type T. The type of such variables is *powerset* (T)—the set of all subsets of elements of type T. Type T is called the *base type*. For example, suppose a language processor accepts the following set O of options.

LSTS: produce listing of source program.

LSTO: produce listing of object program.

OPTM: optimize object code.

SSRC: save source program on backup storage.

SOBJ: save object code on backup storage.

EXEC: execute object code.

A command to the processor can be any subset of O, such as

{LSTS,LSTO}

{LSTS,EXEC}

{OPTM,SOBJ,EXEC}

The type of command is powerset (O).

Variables of type powerset (T) represent sets. The operations permitted on such variables are set operations such as union and intersection. It is also possible to test whether a given object of type T is in the set. Pascal's use of this concept is shown in Section 4.3.2.2.3.

4.3 USER-DEFINED TYPES

The constructors reviewed in the previous sections allow the programmer to define complex data objects as aggregates of elementary items. An example of a structured variable declaration in Pascal is

var *a : record* *x : integer;*
              y : **array** *[1..10]* **of** *char*
      end

The type of variable *a* has no explicit name, but is described in terms of its representation (a Cartesian product, one of whose fields is a finite mapping).

Several modern programming languages, such as ALGOL 68, Pascal, and Ada, also provide a facility for defining a new type name. The programmer can define data types by renaming existing types or by aggregating a number of elementary and/or user-defined types via some of the constructors discussed in Section 4.2. The notion of type is used in these languages in a limited framework, just to capture a uniform mechanism to access the components of structured objects. A type declaration defines a prototype data structure (a *template*) that can be instantiated by declaring as many variables of that type as are necessary.

For example, in Pascal one can declare the following Cartesian product type.

type *complex* = **record** *radius: real;*
                   angle: real
        end

All variables of type *complex* are composed of two fields—*radius* and *angle*—for holding the absolute value and argument of a complex number. The declaration

var *c1,c2,c3: complex*

instantiates three complex variables named *c1*, *c2*, and *c3*.

The basic advantages of providing facilities to give explicit names to types are

1. *Readability*
    Appropriate choice of the new type names can improve the readability of programs. The stepwise refinement process that leads to the definition of a class of data is mirrored by the hierarchical structure of type definitions.
        For example, after the previous declaration of *complex,* one could declare the following types.

voltage = complex;
voltage_table = **array** *[1..10]* **of** *voltage*

These declarations show quite explicitly that variables of type *voltage_table* can represent the values of voltage in a space of 10 points, a *voltage* being represented by a complex number.

2. *Modifiability*
   A change to the data structures that represent the variables of a given type requires a change only in the type declaration, not in the declarations of all the variables (i.e., it is localized to small portions of the program). However, it still may require a change to the instructions of the program that manipulate variables whose type is changed.

3. *Factorization*
   The definition of a complicated data structure prototype is written only once and then used as many times as necessary to declare variables. This reduces the amount of coding necessary to copy the same definition for each variable and reduces the possibility of clerical errors.

4. *Consistency checking*
   The possibility of defining new types allows the programmer to extend the application of a simple but effective validation tool such as type checking, from the limited class of built-in types to any class of user-defined types. The amount of type checking that can be done depends on the notion of type *compatibility* (or *equivalence*) specified by the language. The type-checking mechanism treats two compatible types as being the same type. This topic will be discussed in Section 4.5.2.

Sections 4.3.1 and 4.3.2 will review user-defined types as provided by ALGOL 68 and Pascal. More powerful mechanisms that allow the programmer to define abstract data types are discussed in Section 4.6.

4.3.1 The Type Structure of ALGOL 68

The type structure of ALGOL 68 is rich and elaborate. One of the design goals of the language, carried through and clearly visible in its type structure, is *orthogonality*. To achieve simplicity, the language provides a small number of independent primitive concepts; to achieve expressive power, these concepts can be applied orthogonally (i.e., independently or in any combination).

ALGOL 68 uses a precise but rather unusual terminology. For the sake of uniformity, we will describe the language using the terms and concepts developed in Chapter 3. The reader should be aware that some of our terms (e.g., "name") may have a different meaning in the official ALGOL 68 terminology.

ALGOL 68 uses the term "mode" for "type." A variable declaration has the form

type *variable_name*

where **type** may be a language-defined or a user-defined type. There are five primitive types (*plain modes*) and five ways of constructing new types. The language-defined types also include some nonprimitive types that have been defined by the language in terms of primitive types and the type construction facilities.

4.3.1.1 Primitive Types (Plain Modes)

There are five primitive types, of which four are quite usual: **int**, **real**, **bool**, and **char**. Whole numbers are represented by **int**, rational numbers by **real**. Two implementation-defined constants, *max int* and *max real* give the largest (respectively) integer and real number representable. Booleans are represented by **bool**, which consists of the two values, **true** and **false**. Single characters are represented by **char**.

The fifth mode is **void**, whose only value is **empty**. The purpose of the mode **void** is to add consistency to the language. Every statement has a mode, including assignment statements and procedure call statements. The mode of an assignment statement is the mode of the left-hand side value; the mode of a call statement is the mode of the returned value; if the procedure does not return a value, the call has the mode **void**.

4.3.1.2 Nonprimitive Types (Nonplain Modes)

The language provides five ways to construct new modes from the plain modes. The new mode may be given a name or simply used in variable declarations without a name.

For example, if **X** stands for the definition of a new mode, we could give it the name *newmode* with the following definition:

mode newmode = X

and then use **newmode** to declare variables:

newmode *x,y,z*

Or we could say

X *x,y,z*

without giving the mode a name. Notice that when a new mode is defined, it becomes part of the language (for this program), and therefore its name appears in boldface.

Presented below are the type construction mechanisms of ALGOL 68.

4.3.1.2.1 References Two attributes of a variable are the value and the reference to the area of storage where the value is kept (Section 3.3). Most languages do not emphasize the distinction between these two concepts. For example, in the Pascal statement

$$x: = x + 2$$

assuming x has been declared as integer, the right-hand side x stands for the value of the variable, whereas the left-hand side x stands for the reference to the storage area where the value is kept. And in the declaration

var x: *integer*

integer qualifies the values that may be assigned to variable x. It is not quite right to say "the type of x is integer"; it is more correct to say "the type of values assigned to x is integer." In most languages, however, the two quoted phrases can be used interchangeably.

ALGOL 68 makes this distinction between value and reference to a data object quite explicit. A variable always stands for a reference to a data object. The effect of the following ALGOL 68 declaration

int x

is to declare x as a reference to data objects of type **int**: that is, the type of x is **ref int**.

Now, for a statement

$$x: = x + 2,$$

ALGOL 68 states that the x on the right-hand side is "dereferenced" in order to yield the value needed for " + "; on the left-hand side, what is needed is a reference to a data object and no dereferencing takes place. Whether dereferencing is needed is determined from context (as in the above).

Notice that the *effect* of the declaration or the assignment statement is the same as in Pascal. The difference is in ALGOL 68's clear definition of the difference between references and values and the dereferencing operation.

The concept of a reference is used as a mechanism for defining new modes. Preceding a previously defined mode with the symbol **ref** results in a new mode. For example, the declaration

ref int *ri*

creates *ri* of mode **ref ref int**: that is, the value stored in the area referenced by *ri* is of mode **ref int**—a reference to an integer. In other words, *ri* is what other languages call a pointer. We can assign to *ri* names of mode **ref int**, such as x above:

$$ri: = x$$

Here, *ri* requires a value of mode **ref int**, which *x* is. Therefore, no dereferencing on *x* is necessary—*ri* will simply hold the reference to the data object bound to *x*.

The general rule for an assignment statement is that the mode of the left-hand side is used to determine whether dereferencing (or any other conversion) is necessary on the right-hand side. In fact, the left-hand side variable is to be a **ref** to some mode **x**. If the right-hand side is not of the mode that the left-hand side can refer to (i.e., **x**), dereferencing is applied automatically until the assignment can be done.

Using a pointer such as *ri,* we can access both a **ref int** value and an **int** value (the value held by the object referenced by the **ref int** value).

For example,

int *x,y;*
ref int *ri;*
x: = 2;
ri: = x;
y: = ri

will assign 2, the value of *x,* to *y.* In the last assignment, *y* requires a value of mode **int**; *ri* is dereferenced twice to get such a value; in this case, this value is the one assigned most recently to *x.*

The assignment

ri: = 1

is not valid because *ri* requires a value of mode **ref int** and 1 is of mode **int**. In general, the right-hand side must be of a mode with one less **ref** than the left-hand side, or be dereferenceable to such a mode (which 1 is not).

We can assign a value to the object currently pointed to by *ri* by explicitly dereferencing *ri*. Explicit conversion is called *casting* in ALGOL 68.

The statement

(**ref int**) *ri: =* 1

causes the retrieving of a **ref int** object from *ri* and then assigning 1 to that object. In this case, casting *ri* to **ref int** will yield a reference to the same data object referenced by *x*, since *ri: = x* is the most recent assignment to *ri*. The value of this object is changed to 1.

Casts can be used on the right-hand side as well. For example,

(**ref int**) *ri: =* (**int**) *ri +* 1

adds 1 to the value of the object pointed to by *ri*. The cast on the right-hand side, however, is not required in this case, since the dereferencing would have been determined from context and applied automatically.

Since any mode may be preceded by **ref**, all the following modes (as well as others) are valid in ALGOL 68.

ref int
ref ref int
ref ref ref real

We can create as many levels of indirection as we like. This is an example of the orthogonality of design. There are no exceptions such as "only one **ref** may precede a mode."

A problem associated with the use of pointers in most languages is the *dangling reference* problem. A dangling reference is a pointer (i.e., reference) that points to a storage area that has been deallocated. Such problems can occur if we allow pointers to refer to program variables. Program variables are deallocated upon exit from the unit where they are locally declared; consequently, a pointer to them may remain dangling.

ALGOL 68 has a simple-looking rule that prevents the occurrence of dangling references: in an assignment to a reference variable, the scope of the value being assigned must be the same as, or enclose, the scope of the reference variable.
The following program fragment shows some legal and illegal assignments.

begin **ref int** *ri*; **int** *i;*

> . . . . .
> **begin ref int** *rx;* **int** *x;*
>
> > . . . . .
> > *rx:= x;*   ¢ *legal*   ¢
> > *rx:= i;*   ¢ *legal*   ¢
> > *ri:= i;*   ¢ *legal*   ¢
> > *ri:= x*   ¢ *illegal*   ¢
> **end**
> > ¢ *at this point, rx and x have disappeared, no pointers to them should exist; ri and i, however, still exist* ¢
> . . . .

end

As discussed in Chapter 3, pointers in programming languages can be used to point to anonymous objects. In ALGOL 68, such objects may be created via *generators*. A generator creates a data object of a given mode and yields a reference to the data object. There are two kinds of generators: one creates stack variables (**loc**); the other, heap variables (**heap**).

The statement

ri: = **heap int**

creates an integer data object on the heap and assigns its address to *ri* (which should be a **ref int**).

The statement

ri: = **loc int:** *= 2*

creates a local variable (on the stack), assigns the value 2 to it, and makes *ri* (a **ref int**) point to it. As usual, this object will cease to exist upon exit from the scope in which it is declared. It differs from program variables only in that it does not have an explicit name.

4.3.1.2.2 Multiples *Multiple,* the ALGOL 68 term for "array," can be used to create finite mappings. The domain of the finite mapping is a subrange of integers. The new modes are called rows. For example, "[ ] **int**" is the mode "row of integers" (a one-dimensional array), "[,] **int**" is a "row row of integers" (two-dimensional array), and so on. We can also have the mode "[ ] [ ] **int**," which is the mode "row of row of integers." The difference between values of mode "row row of integers" and "row of row of integers" is that the former is a two-dimensional array, whereas the latter is a one-dimensional array, each of whose elements is itself a one-dimensional array.

We may have multiples of values of any mode. For example,

[ ] **ref** [,] **int**

is a valid mode: row of references to row row of integers, or an array of pointers to two-dimensional arrays of integers.

Note that although the number of dimensions of an array is part of its type, the size of an array—that is, the number of elements in each dimension—is not. Any variable declared to be a multiple, however, must indicate this size—at least in terms of variables.

[*m:n*] **int** *ri*

declares the data object referenced by *ri* to be a semidynamic array with indexes in the range *m..n*. When this declaration is encountered at execution time, the array is allocated according to the current values of *m* and *n; ri* preserves this size until it disappears at exit from its scope.

On the other hand, arrays may be declared to be flexible, in which case their size may be changed when an assignment is made to them. These are an example of what we have called dynamic variables.

flex [*1:0*] **int** *a*

declares the data object referenced by *a* to be a row containing (initially) no integers.

a: = (*2,3,49*)

changes the bounds to [1:3] and assigns values to all its elements. The bounds may be changed only by assignment to the whole array.

The mode **string** is predefined by the language as a flexible array of characters.

mode string = **flex** [*1:0*] **char**

The actions allowed on strings, which are the same as for arrays, are subscripting, with which one element is retrieved; and trimming, with which a cross section (or "slice," in ALGOL 68 jargon) of the array is retrieved.

4.3.1.2.3 Structures   Rows allow the creation of a finite mapping: that is, a mode consisting of homogeneous elements. A new mode may also be constructed from inhomogeneous elements by a Cartesian product. This can be done by the ALGOL 68 *structure*. A structure (or *structured value*) consists of a set of values, called *fields*, which may have different modes.

mode person = **struct** (**string** *name*, **int** *age*)

creates a new mode consisting of the two fields *name* and *age*. Having created variables of this mode, for example, we may assign values to them.

person *mom, dad;*
mom: = *("helen",35);*
dad: = *("tom",36)*

Individual fields can also be accessed for retrieval or assignment by using the selector **of**, as illustrated in the following example:

age **of** *dad:* = *age* **of** *dad* + *1*

Again, structures may be made of any modes.

struct (**ref ref** [,] **int** *one*, **flex** [*1:0*] **real** *two*, **int** *three*, **person** *four)*

is an allowable (although not obviously useful!) mode.

Recursive data structures can be created by combining references and structures. For example, the mode of nodes of a binary tree can be declared as

mode binary_tree_node = **struct** (**string** *info*, **ref binary_tree_node** *left, right)*

The predefined modes **compl, bits** and **bytes,** and **sema** have been defined using the structures

mode compl = **struct** (**real** *re, im);*
mode bits = **struct** (*[1:bits width]* **bool** *x);*
mode bytes = **struct** (*[1:bytes width]* **char** *x);*
mode sema = **struct** (**ref int** *x)*

The implementation-defined constants *bits width* and *bytes width*, respectively, indicate the number of bits and bytes in a machine word. The mode **sema** is the semaphore (see Section 5.2.4.1) and can be used for parallel programming. The operations **up** and **down** are defined for **sema.** The names of the fields of the **bits, bytes,** and **sema** structures are not available to the programmer, so, for example, one cannot use indexing with a **bits** value.

Mode **bits** may be used to implement power sets, which are not directly supported by the language (see Exercise 4.17).

4.3.1.2.4 Unions   In a sharp departure from previous ALGOL-like languages, AL-GOL 68 allows discriminated unions—in the form of **united** modes.

mode ib = **union (int, bool)**

defines the new mode **ib,** whose values may be integers or booleans. Notice that variable *x* declared as

ib *x*

at any moment holds a value of type either **int** or **bool,** but the type of *x* is always **ref ib.**

Assignments to a variable *x* of type **ib** are like other assignments:

ib *x,y;*
y: = *5;*
x: = *y;*
x: = **true**

Accessing the value of *x,* however, cannot be done so easily, because the type of the value must be established before the value can be used. The determination of the type is done with the use of a *conformity clause*. The conformity clause ensures that no type mismatch may occur at run-time: that is, the programmer is forced to anticipate all such events.

case *x* **in**
    (int *x1):* . . . . . *x1.* . . .
    (bool *x2):* . . . . *x2.* . . .
esac

is an example of such a clause. Within each alternative of the **case** clause, the type of *x* is established and a new name is used to refer to *x*. More precisely, *x*1 and *x*2 are constants "initialized" with the value of *x* at entry to the conformity clause; their types are (respectively) integer and boolean, and therefore type checking on the use of *x*1 and *x*2 can be done statically.

United modes may be derived from any other mode, including **void,** as in

union (integer, ref [ ] int, void)

United modes are often used in procedures that may take parameters of different types. They represent the introduction into a programming language of an important, but possibly dangerous, concept—discriminated union—in an elegant, systematic, and safe way.

4.3.1.2.5 Procedures The final method of constructing new types in ALGOL 68 is through the use of procedures. The concept of mode in ALGOL 68 is more general than type in other languages. For example, a procedure is an object of mode **procedure** with specified modes for its parameters and its result.

mode pl = proc(bool, real)int

defines a new mode **pl,** which is a procedure accepting a boolean and a real parameter and returning an integer result. Just as with other modes, variables of mode **pl** may also be declared and assigned (in contrast to most other languages).

pl x, y;
x: = **proc(bool** b, **real** r) **int**: . . . . body of procedure . . . ;
.
.
.
y: = x;

   With procedures, the full generality of ALGOL 68 modes and the systematic application of orthogonal design can be seen clearly. Procedure modes may be made up of any other modes: for example, uniteds, references, or other procedures. Thus, the following is a valid definition.

mode funnyproc = proc(int, ref [ ] bool)proc([ ] ref int, proc(real) int)void

It defines a mode that is a procedure that happens to return another procedure as its result; the returned procedure takes a procedure as its second parameter and returns a value of type **void.**
   Orthogonality of design makes the rules of the language simple and uniform. It does not, and is not intended to, prevent the coding of complicated constructs. The type structure of ALGOL 68 is summarized in Figure 4.1.

4.3.2 The Type Structure of Pascal

4.3.2.1 Unstructured Types

As in ALGOL 68, data types in Pascal must be ultimately built from unstructured components belonging to primitive, unstructured types. Some of these unstructured types are built-in, others are user-defined. The built-in unstructured types are *integer, real, boolean,* and *char*. A value of type *integer* is an element of an implementation-defined ordered subset of whole numbers. The implementation-defined standard identifier *maxint* denotes the largest integer value that can be handled by the given Pascal implementation. A value of type *real* is an element of an implementation-defined

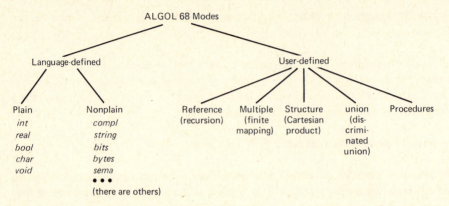

Figure 4.1　ALGOL 68 type structure.

subset of rational numbers. Both the maximum magnitude and the precision of real values are implementation-dependent, the limits being imposed by the underlying floating-point arithmetic of the machine. A value of type *char* is an element of a finite, ordered set of characters. Both the set of characters and their ordering relation are implementation-defined. Booleans can have one of the two values *true* and *false;* they can be compared (*false* is considered to be less than *true*) and manipulated by the boolean operators **and**, **or**, and **not.**

Integers, booleans, and characters can be collectively called *ordinal types,* because each element of the type has a unique *predecessor* and a unique *successor.* For booleans, *true* is defined to be the successor of *false.* The successor and the predecessor of an ordinal value are evaluated by the built-in functions *succ* and *pred.* Such functions are examples of overloaded operators, because they can accept a parameter of any ordinal type.

Pascal programmers can define new ordinal types in two ways. The first is by *enumeration* of the possible values. For example,

type *day = (sunday, monday, tuesday, wednesday, thursday, friday, saturday)*

This declaration has the following effects.

1.　It introduces a new data type *day;*

2.　It defines *sunday, monday, . . . saturday* as the constants of this new type.

3.　It defines an ordering relation among constants: *sunday < monday < . . . < saturday.*

The only implicitly defined operations on variables of this new type are assignments and comparisons. Thus, after declaration of the variables

var *today, tomorrow, yesterday, my_birthday: day*

the following statements represent correct manipulations of the variables.

today: = *thursday;*
tomorrow: = *succ(today);*
yesterday: = *pred(today);*
my_birthday: = *tomorrow*

Unfortunately, values of enumerated types cannot be read or written by a program. Although we can say that type *day* includes all weekday names, we must read the value of a day in some coded form— say,*integer*—and then explicitly convert it into a value of type *day*.

The second way of defining new ordinal types is by specifying the *subrange* of an ordinal type (the *associated ordinal type* or *base type*). For example, having defined the type *day,* we may define *work_day* as the subrange *monday* through *friday*. The following fragment illustrates this feature.

type *work_day* = *monday . . friday;*
      age = *0 . . 120 {subrange 0 through 120 of integers}*
var *my_age: age;*
      class_day: work_day;

New types may be used without being given an explicit name, as in

var *course_taught: (comp_sci_15, comp_sci_140);*

which specifies the (anonymous) type of *course_taught* as the enumeration of the values *comp_sci_15* and *comp_sci_240*.

The above declarations legally can be followed by the statements

course_taught: = *comp_sci_240;*
my_age: = *33;*
if *course_taught* = *comp_sci_15*
   then *class_day:* = *tuesday*
   else *class_day:* = *wednesday*

Variables of a subrange type have the same behavior as the variables of the base type—except for the set of values they may assume, which is a subset of the set of values of the associated ordinal type. A verification of this property intrinsically requires a run-time check. For example, execution of *class_day:* = *succ(class_day)* would raise a run-time error if *class_day* is equal to *friday,* because *succ(friday)* is *saturday,* and *saturday* does not belong to type *work_day*.

4.3.2.2 Aggregate Constructors

4.3.2.2.1 The Array Constructor   The **array** constructor allows the programmer to define finite mappings. The general form of an array structure is

array [*t*1] **of** *t*2

where *t1*, the *index* (or domain) *type*, is an ordinal type; and *t2*, the *component* (or codomain) type, is the type of each component of the array.

For example,

type *flavor* = *(chocolate, mint, peach, strawberry, vanilla, bluecheese, catsup,*
                 garlic, onion);
    icecream_flavor = *chocolate . . vanilla;*
    icecream_order = **array** *[icecream_flavor]* **of** *boolean;*
var *my_order, your_order: icecream_order;*
    choice: icecream_flavor;

can be followed by

for *choice:* = *chocolate* **to** *vanilla* **do**
    my_order [choice]: = *false;*
my_order [mint]: = *true;*
your_order: = *my_order*
{both my_order and your_order are mint}

Note that the legality of an array access such as

my_order [suçc(choice)]

requires a run-time check in order to verify that the index has a value within the bounds. In fact, if *choice* = *vanilla, succ(choice)* would generate *bluecheese*: that is, a value that does not belong to type *icecream_flavor*. Pascal regards as being of different types arrays with different index types, such as in

type *a1* = **array** *[1 . . 50]* **of** *integer;*
    a2 = **array** *[1 . . 70]* **of** *integer*

Since procedures require formal parameters to have a specific type, it is not possible, for example, to write a procedure that sorts both arrays of type *a1* and arrays of type *a2*.

Multidimensional arrays can be defined in Pascal as arrays whose elements are themselves arrays. For example,

type *row* = **array** *[−5 . . 10]* **of** *integer;*
var *my_matrix:* **array** *[3 . . 30]* **of** *row*

However, the abbreviation

var *my_matrix:* **array** *[3 . . 30, −5 . . 10]* **of** *integer*

is also allowed.

4.3.2.2.2 The Record Constructor The **record** constructor can be used to define Cartesian products. The general form of a **record** structure is

record *field_1: type_1;*
     field_2: type_2;
         .

         .

         .

     field_N: type_N
end

where *field_i*, $1 \leq i \leq N$, is a *field identifier*, and *type_i*, $1 \leq i \leq N$, is a *field type*. The record can be accessed as a whole or individual fields can be accessed by using the symbol "." as a selector (dot notation). For example, the declarations

type *reg_polygon* = **record** *no_of_edges: integer;*
                       edge_size: real
             end;
var *t,q,p: reg_polygon;*

can be legally followed by

t.no_of_edges:= 3; t.edge_size:= 7.53;
    {t is an equilateral triangle. The length of the edge is 7.53}
q.no_of_edges:= t.no_of_edges + 1;
*q.edge_size:= 2*t.edge_size;*
p:= q

A record type can also have a *variant part*, in which case it is possible to define discriminated unions. For example,

type *dept* = *(houseware, sports, drugs, food, liquor);*
    month = *1. .12;*
    item = **record** *price: real;*
               case *available: boolean* **of**
                   true: (amount: integer;
                     where: dept);
                 false: (month_expected: month)
      end

The field identifier *available* is the discriminating component (the *tag field*) of the above **record** structure. If the value of *available* is *true*, then an *item* is characterized by the available amount and the name of the department in which it is kept. If it is *false*, then an item is characterized by the month its delivery is expected. In both cases, the item has an associated price.

Pascal allows the programmer to access all fields of a record structure, including the tag field. Therefore, if *i*1 and *i*2 are declared and manipulated as follows

var *i1, i2: item;*

      .

      .

      .

    i1.price:= 5.24;
    i1.available:= true;
    i1.amount:= 29;
    i1.where:= liquor;
    i2.price:= 324.99;
    i2.available:= false;
    i2.month_expected:= 8

the resulting structures can be illustrated as in Figure 4.2.

Type checking for variant records generally can be done only at run-time. For example, if *i* is of type *item,*

i.amount

is a correct field selection only if the current variant has a *true* value in its tag field. Dynamic type checking requires keeping track of the current variant in a run-time descriptor for each variant record. Unfortunately, the possibility of resetting the tag field and the variants independently of each other, and inconsistently, makes run-time checking hard to implement. For example, if the tag field is passed to a procedure as a modifiable parameter, the procedure should update the descriptor for each assignment to the tag field. However, the procedure does not know if it is changing a tag field of a variant record, unless such information is also passed as an additional flag associated with each actual parameter. Each access to a formal parameter within the procedure—whether or not it is a tag field—would then require checking the flag and, possibly, updating the descriptor. This solution would make the implementation of procedures quite inefficient.

We will show later that the conventional implementation of variant records consists of overlapping all variants over the same storage area. Therefore, variant records allow the programmer to interpret the string of bits stored in this area under the

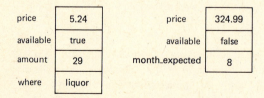

Figure 4.2   An example of Pascal variant record.

different views provided by the types of each variant. In our example, after setting under one variant fields *amount* and *where* of variable *i*1, it is possible to change the variant by setting *available* to *false* and then interpret the value previously stored into field *amount* as the value of *month_expected*.

This is an insecure—though legal—use of variant records. Viewing the same storage area under different names and types can be useful in modeling some practical situations. For example, a program unit that simulates an input device might view a variable as a sequence of *k* characters, whereas a program unit that simulates a special-purpose processor might view the same variable as an integer to be read. In general, however, giving different names (and types) to the same data object is a dangerous programming practice. The fact that an object can be modified under one name and the effect of the modification become visible under a different name makes programs particularly hard to read and write. Moreover, in order to view a certain bit string under different types, one should know how the different types are represented by the translator. In the above example, one should know that a sequence of *k* characters and an integer occupy the same amount of storage—say, a word. Consequently, the program's correctness becomes implementation-dependent; for example, moving the program to an installation in which both integers and single characters occupy an entire word would make the program incorrect.

Still worse is the fact that the tag field of a variant record is optional. The above type *item* could be declared as

```
record price: real;
        case boolean of
            true: (amount: integer;
                   where: dept);
            false: (month_expected: month)
end
```

In this case, the variant record construct is intrinsically insecure. Either *amount* and *where* or *month_expected* can be used when they are not present, and there is no way to catch the error, even at run-time, because there is no field of the record to denote the currently applicable variant. The solution of making the compiler insert an appropriate tag field, though feasible, has no real justification, because the absence of the tag field is a deliberate choice provided to the programmer in order to save storage. Therefore, the absence of the tag field makes run-time type checking impossible.

It is interesting to contrast the insecurities of the Pascal discriminated union with the conceptual soundness of the ALGOL 68 counterpart (union modes). This shows how the apparent simplicity of Pascal, which is responsible for much of its popularity, sometimes hides unsuspected problems.

4.3.2.2.3 The Set Constructor The **set** constructor is a restricted version of the powerset constructor, in that the base type can only be an ordinal type. As a consequence, it is not possible to define sets of reals, sets of tables, sets of sets, and so on.

The following declarations define an enumerated type and two variables of type set.

type *vegetable = (bean, cabbage, carrot, celery, lettuce, onion, mushroom,*
    zucchini);
var *my_salad, leftover:* **set of** *vegetable {variables may contain any set of*
    vegetables; their type is powerset of vegetable};

The following statements represent legal manipulations.

leftover: = . . . ;
my_salad: = *[carrot..onion] {assigns a set value with four members to my_salad};*
if not *bean* **in** *leftover {membership test}*
    then *my_salad: = my_salad + leftover {"+" stands for "union of sets"}*

4.3.2.2.4 Pointers The lifetime of Pascal variables is related to the static structure of procedure nesting: storage is automatically allocated for variables on the stack when the procedure to which they are local is activated; it is deallocated when the activation terminates. Pascal also provides pointers to reference anonymous data objects allocated on the heap. Heap data objects are allocated by the explicit creation statement *new* (see Section 3.6.3).

    The following example illustrates the use of Pascal pointers in the building of recursive types such as binary trees.

type *tree_ref= ↑ binary_tree_node;*
    binary_tree_node = **record** *info: char;*
                              left, right: tree_ref
               end;
var *my_tree: tree_ref*

my_tree is defined as a pointer (↑) to the root node of a binary tree of characters.
    An empty binary tree can be constructed by the following assignment.

my_tree: = **nil**

    The value **nil** can be held by any pointer (independently of the type of the object to which it points) and points to no element at all. If *p* is a pointer and *p* is not equal to **nil**, the object pointed to by *p* is denoted by *p* ↑ . Unlike ALGOL 68, dereferencing must always be written explicitly.
    A binary tree consisting of one node can be created by writing

new (my_tree);
my_tree ↑ .info: = symbol;
my_tree ↑ .left: = **nil**;
my_tree ↑ .right: = **nil**

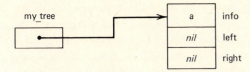

Figure 4.3 A binary tree with one element.

The first instruction allocates a record of type *binary_tree_node* and makes *my_tree* refer to it. The next three instructions initialize the field *info* with the value of a character valued variable *symbol*, and the two pointer fields to **nil**. The result is illustrated in Figure 4.3, assuming *symbol* is equal to *a*.

Appending a left tree to *my_tree* can be done as follows.

new (node_ref) {node_ref must be of type tree_ref};
node_ref ↑ .info: = 'b';
node_ref ↑ .left: = **nil***;*
node_ref ↑ .right: = **nil***;*
my_tree ↑ .left: = node_ref

The result is shown in Figure 4.4.

Pointers can be manipulated by assignment and comparison for equality and inequality. Such manipulations, however, are only legal if the operands point to objects of compatible type (see Section 4.5.2 for a definition). Unlike ALGOL 68, Pascal pointers can point only to unnamed data objects; in particular, they cannot point to the location associated with a variable that is allocated on the stack.

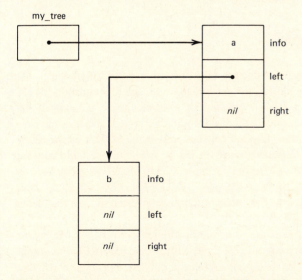

Figure 4.4 Binary tree of Figure 4.3 after adding a left subtree.

4.3.2.2.5 Packed Data In some applications—for example, in systems program-ming—the programmer might wish to use a high-level language but still preserve the ability of assembly languages to pack as much information as possible into a single machine word. In Pascal, data structures can be specified as packed by prefixing **array, set** or **record** by the keyword **packed**. Obviously, the semantics of the data structure is independent of whether the prefix **packed** does or doesn't exist, but the compiler can use this information to minimize the amount of storage allocated for the data structure. As we will see in Section 4.7, however, access procedures are slower on packed data structures.

Pascal treats strings as packed arrays of characters. Because they are arrays, however, they have a fixed maximum size during their lifetime.

4.3.2.2.6 The File Constructor A Pascal file is a sequence of elements of any type. The following sample declarations define *t*1 and *t*2 as file variables.

type *pattern* = **record** . . . **end;**
　　tape = **file of** *pattern;*
var *t1, t2: tape*

Automatically associated with each file is a buffer variable that contains the next element of the file. The program can read from or write into this buffer variable. The operations *get* and *put* read the next element into the buffer and append the contents of the buffer to the end of the file, respectively. Pascal files can only be processed sequentially; the current position within a file is implicitly updated by the operations *get* and *put*.

The type structure of Pascal can be summarized by the diagram in Figure 4.5, in which the hierarchy imposed by the language is illustrated clearly.

4.4 TYPE CONVERSION

It is often necessary to *convert* a value of one type to a value of another—as, for example, when we want to add the integer variable *v* to the real constant 3.753. In most languages, such conversion is implicit. For example, the evaluation of the above addition usually implies a conversion of *v* from integer to real and then the exe-cution of the floating-point addition. Implicit conversion is made explicit by the trans-lator, which generates conversion code based on the type of the operands and the type hierarchy of the language. For example, FORTRAN's hierarchy is COMPLEX > DOUBLE PRECISION > REAL > INTEGER. Given the operation *a op b,* the operand with a type lower in the hierarchy is converted to the type of the other operand before execution of *op*.

ALGOL 68 consistently applies the principle of implicit conversions (*coercions* in the ALGOL 68 jargon) to the extreme. The type of the value required at any point in an ALGOL 68 program can be determined from the context. For example, if the mode of *a* is **ref t**, the type of the value yielded by the right-hand side of an assignment

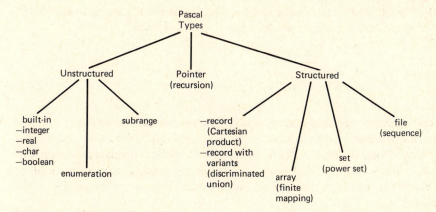

Figure 4.5 Pascal type structure.

$a:=$ . . . must be **t**. A set of rules are defined that effect the implicit coercion of values from a given type to the desired type. We have already seen the coercion of *dereferencing,* which causes a value to be automatically stripped of one **ref**. *Deproceduring* effects a procedure call and uses the returned value; *rowing* converts a single value to a row of a single value; *voiding* yields **empty** and discards the original value; *uniting* changes the mode to a desired united mode that must include the original mode; *widening* converts an **int** to a **real** and a **real** to a **compl**. There is no coercion from **real** to **int**. This conversion must be explicitly performed, using a cast, by the programmer. Examples of these coercions are shown in the following program segment.

int *i;* **real** *r;* *[1:1]* **int** *rowi;* **ref int** *refi;*
union (int,real) *ir;* **proc int** *p;*

.
.
.

r:= i/r;	¢ *widening of i* ¢
ir:= i;	¢ *uniting* ¢
ir:= r;	¢ *uniting* ¢
i:= p;	¢ *deproceduring* ¢
i:= refi;	¢ *dereferencing (twice)* ¢
p;	¢ *deproceduring followed by voiding* ¢
rowi:= 5;	¢ *rowing* ¢

It is interesting to consider the interaction of coercion rules with other constructs of the language. For example, united modes such as

mode wrong= union (int, ref int)

are not allowed, since for a variable v of this mode, sometimes it cannot be determined whether or not dereferencing is needed. For example, consider:

wrong $w;$
ref int $v;$
$w := v$

Should v be dereferenced or not? A united variable can take on values of different modes. But whether a value is dereferenced is determined by the mode of the value that is desired—for example, on the left-hand side. In the abovementioned assignment, these two rules would conflict, because the left-hand side can accept either an **int** or a **ref int**. Thus such united modes are not allowed (they are mnemonically called *incestuous*).

These elaborate notions of coercion in ALGOL 68 can be criticized on the ground that they lead to rather obscure programs. Automatic conversions weaken the ability of the translator to type-check the program, because they override the declared type of a variable with default automatic transformations. In general, the more the translator can perform implicitly, the less error-checking service it can provide, because the compiler may assume actual errors to be implicit requests for conversions.

4.5 PROBLEM AREAS AND SAMPLE SOLUTIONS

We have stressed the fact that programming languages are important not in themselves, but only as tools that help in the production of software. Therefore, we are interested not in the features that make a language ''more clever'' or fancier than another, but rather in how such features can support the production of software of overall good quality.

This section reviews the most debatable features of the previously discussed programming languages and shows how the discoveries of flaws have stimulated the definition of different and—one hopes—better features.

4.5.1 Strong Typing

One major effect of the introduction of types is the possibility of static type checking. The resulting programs are more likely to be correct, and also more efficient, because it is not necessary to have run-time type descriptors or to execute checks on them. A language is said to be *strongly typed* if it allows all type checking to be done statically.

By examining Pascal and ALGOL 68, we can conclude that Pascal is not strongly typed, and ALGOL 68 is, for the following reasons.

1. The type of a procedure or function parameter—that is, a procedure or function that is itself a parameter—is not determinable for Pascal at translation time. For example, the Pascal procedure

```
procedure who_knows (i,j: integer; procedure f);
    var k: boolean;
begin k: = j < i;
    if k then f (k) else f (j)
end
```

might contain one or two incorrect calls to the actual parameter associated with the formal *f*, because of type mismatch and/or difference in number of parameters. A compiler cannot foresee whether an error will arise at run-time, because the presence of error depends on the particular actual parameters with which procedure *who_knows* is called.

On the contrary, ALGOL 68 requires procedure parameters to specify the types (modes) of their parameters and their return values. For example, procedure *who_knows* might be written in ALGOL 68 as

```
proc who_knows = (int i, int j, proc (bool)void f) void:
begin bool k;
    k: = j<i;
    if k then f(k)
            else f(j) ¢ illegal call, caught by compiler¢
    fi
end
```

2. In Pascal, subranges cannot be checked statically. For example, in $a: = b+c$, where the variables are all declared as belonging to the subrange 1..10, it is not possible to state *a priori* whether the value of $b+c$ belongs to the subrange type; this can only be done at run-time. Since the index type of an array is part of the type of the array, every time the index belongs to the base type of the index type, access to an array element requires a run-time check to verify that the index lies within the bounds. ALGOL 68, on the other hand, considers the array bounds as part not of the type, but of the value. Subscripts of subscripted variables are ignored at translation time, and checks on values are inserted for run-time evaluation.

3. It is not possible to check the correct use of Pascal's variant records statically; and run-time checking is seldom provided, because of the severe impact on execution efficiency. Therefore, variant records provide a loophole that allows the programmer to short-cut the protection of the type structure of the language. In contrast, the ALGOL 68 union is completely safe: that is, the syntax of the language is such that all improper accesses can be caught at compile-time. Since any run-time checks are explicitly specified by the programmer, the costs are not hidden in the implementation.

4. There are no rigorously specified type-compatibility rules in the Pascal Report, whereas ALGOL 68 takes great pains to define the notion of

compatibility precisely (see Section 4.5.2). As a consequence, Pascal type checking is often based on shaky grounds, and its effect can vary on different implementations.

4.5.2 Type Compatibility

So far, we have been deliberately informal in our discussions as far as type-compatibility (or type-equivalence) rules are concerned. Such rules should give an exact specification of how the type checking mechanism should be applied. Consider the following Pascal declarations.

type *t* = **array** [*1..20*] **of** *integer;*
var *a, b:* **array** [*1..20*] **of** *integer;*
  c: **array** [*1..20*] **of** *integer;*
  d: t;
  e, f: **record** *a: integer;*
            b: t
  end

It is possible to define the following two notions of type compatibility.

1. *Name equivalence.* Two variables have compatible types if they have the same user-defined or built-in type name, or if they appear in the same declaration. Thus, *a* and *b* (and *e* and *f*) have compatible types, as do *d, e.b,* and *f.b*—but not *a* and *c*. The term "name equivalence" reflects the fact that two variables that are not declared together have compatible types *only if* their type name is the same.

2. *Structural equivalence.* Two variables have compatible types if they have the same structure. According to this definition, user-defined type names are just used as an abbreviation (or as a comment) for the structure they represent and do not introduce any new semantic features. To verify structural equivalence, user-defined type names are replaced by their definition. This process is repeated until no user-defined type names remain. The types are then considered to be structurally equivalent if they have exactly the same description. In the above example, *a, b, c, d, e.b,* and *f.b* have compatible types. This definition of structural equivalence can lead to an infinite loop when pointers are used to create recursive type definitions. Languages adopting structural equivalence take care of this problem by providing an appropriate rule (see Exercise 4.19).

Type compatibility is defined in ALGOL 68 via structural equivalence. The Pascal Report, on the other hand, does not specify the adopted notion of type compatibility and thus leaves this important issue to be decided by the implementation.

An unfortunate consequence is that a program accepted by one compiler might be rejected by another if the type-compatibility rules of the two implementations differ. In most cases, the original Pascal implementation used structural equivalence. The choice of name equivalence would have made it illegal, for example, to assign an integer value to a variable that is specified as a subrange of integers, unless appropriate conversions are defined by the language. Name equivalence is used for parameter passing.

The concept of type compatibility based on structural equivalence adopted by ALGOL 68 goes to the extreme of completely ignoring user-defined names. As a consequence, ALGOL 68 strong typing is based on a rather poor, purely syntactic notion of type. For example, the ALGOL 68 type declarations

mode celsius = int

and

mode fahrenheit = int

cause **celsius** and **fahrenheit** to be compatible types. As a consequence, the value of a variable representing a temperature in celsius degrees can legally be assigned to a variable representing a temperature in fahrenheit degrees, even though, presumably, this is not the programmer's intention.

Name equivalence is closer than structural equivalence to the concept of abstract data types. Although it does not associate operations to the type, it does prevent considering two data types compatible only because their structures happen to be identical. Commonality of properties can thus be specified by using the same type name, which would enhance the readability of programs. Name equivalence is also simpler to implement. In fact, implementing structural equivalence requires a pattern-matching procedure that can be quite complicated.

Both notions, however, can be regarded as mostly syntactic, rather than semantic. From a semantic point of view, what should be expressed is the notion of identical behavior under application of the same operations, rather than that of compatible representation structures; this, however, requires language facilities that support the definition of abstract data types.

4.5.3 Pointers

Pointers came under criticism in the mid 1970s. Just as unrestricted **goto**s broaden the context from which a labeled statement can be executed, unrestricted pointers broaden the context from which a data object can be accessed.

Pointers comprise the basic tool provided for representing recursively defined data objects. As a lower-level language construct, however, they can be used for purposes other than those originally intended. They make programs less understandable and, often, unsafe, for the following main reasons.

a. In some languages the use of pointers can lead to serious type violations, because pointers are not qualified by the type of data objects to which they may point. For example, pointers in PL/I are declared simply as pointers, rather than as pointers to a certain type. Variables declared as BASED are accessed only through pointers. For example, the declarations

DECLARE P POINTER,
    X FIXED BASED, /* INTEGER */
    Y FLOAT BASED; /* REAL */

declare P as a pointer, X as an integer, and Y as a real. Access to X is made through a pointer: that is, $P{\rightarrow}X$ indicates access to an integer data object X through a pointer P. A pointer to a based variable is set when the variable is (explicitly) allocated, as in

ALLOCATE X SET P;

However, since P is not qualified to point only to integers, we may also try to access Y through the same P, as in $P{\rightarrow}Y$.

At translation time, it is impossible to guarantee that the pointer being supplied is pointing to a variable of the correct type. In many implementations, dynamic checking is considered to be quite costly. The usual solution, therefore, is for the translator to assume that accesses are being made correctly. This can result in run-time errors that are very hard to find.

b. A pointer may be left dangling: that is, it can refer to a location that is no longer allocated for holding values. A classic PL/I example is the following.

BEGIN;
    DCL P POINTER;
    BEGIN; DCL X FIXED; /*ALLOCATE NEW X */
        P= ADDR(X); /*P NOW POINTS TO X*/
    END;
/* AT THIS POINT, X IS DEALLOCATED BUT */
/* P STILL POINTS TO ITS LOCATION! THE */
/* REAL CULPRIT IS THE FUNCTION ADDR */
/* WHICH ALLOWS THE ADDRESS OF ANY VARIABLE */
/* TO BE USED AS A VALUE */
END;

Both ALGOL 68 and Pascal bind each pointer value to a specific data type, and thus overcome problem **a** above. In terms of problem **b,** however, both languages have a number of insecurities.

b.1. The ALGOL 68 restriction that in an assignment to a pointer, the scope of the object being pointed to be at least as large as that of the pointer itself, can only be checked at run-time. For example, consider a procedure *p* with two formal parameters *x*—an integer—and *y*—a pointer to integers. Whether the assignment $y := x$ in the procedure is legal depends on the actual parameters and obviously is unknown at translation time. As usual, checking the error at run-time slows down the execution of the program, and not checking the error leaves dangling references uncaught. Pascal pointers do not give rise to such problems, because they can only be bound to unnamed, heap-allocated data objects.

b.2. The amount of heap storage allocated during execution of a program can become exceedingly large. As soon as an area of heap storage becomes unreferenced, however, it could be released and later allocated to new heap variables. To make this possible, many implementations of Pascal provide the standard procedure *dispose,* which explicitly deallocates heap storage. Unfortunately, the programmer can request deallocation of a heap variable while there are still pointers to it. Dangling references can therefore be created, unless incorrect use of *dispose* is checked at run-time. Both ALGOL 68 and SIMULA 67 avoid this problem by not allowing explicit deallocation of heap variables. Instead, they explicitly rely on a garbage collector that automatically reclaims unused heap storage. Garbage collection will be discussed in Section 4.7.4

c. Uninitialized (and **nil** valued) pointers can cause uncontrolled access to storage because the bit string found in the location bound to the pointer would be interpreted as a pointer value. To make run-time checking possible, pointers could be automatically initialized to **nil**, with the value of **nil** being an illegal address; accordingly, addressing with a **nil** value could be detected automatically by the hardware at run-time.

d. If the use of Pascal variant records is not checked at run-time, a field might be assigned an integer under one variant and be interpreted as a pointer under another. As a consequence, the program could randomly modify the contents of storage in an absolutely uncontrolled way. The following example illustrates this point.

```
type harmful = record . . .
              case tag : boolean of
                  true: (i: integer);
                  false: (ref: ↑ integer)
          end;
var trouble_maker: harmful; . . .
begin . . .
      while b do
```

```
begin trouble_maker.tag:= true;
      trouble_maker.i:= 000
      trouble_maker.tag:= false;
      trouble_maker.ref ↑ := 0
         . . .

end;
   . . .
end
```

An additional problem with Pascal pointers arises as a consequence of the previously discussed undefined notion of type compatibility. For example, after the declarations

```
type ptr = ↑ node; ref= ↑ node;
     node = record item: integer;
                         next: ptr
            end
```

it is not clear whether it is legal to assign a variable of type *ref* to a variable of type *ptr*, and vice versa.

Euclid solves this problem by introducing *collections*. Collections are special programming variables that denote a set of data objects of the same type. When a pointer is declared, it is bound to a collection. Several collections can have elements of the same type, and several pointers can point into the same collection; but each pointer can only refer to a specific collection. For example,

```
type nodes= record . . . end;
var my_nodes: collection of nodes;
type my_ref= ↑ my_nodes;
var my_ref1, my_ref2: my_ref;
```

declare *my_ref1* and *my_ref2* as references into the collection of nodes *my_nodes*. Variables *my_ref1* and *my_ref2* can point to nodes of the collection *my_nodes,* but no other pointers can, unless they are declared as bound to the same collection. There are no operations defined for collections; collections can only be passed as parameters, but cannot even be assigned. This view of pointers has strong analogies to array indices. A pointer is an index within the collection, and dereferencing is equivalent to indexing within the array. As happens with arrays, a pointer cannot be dereferenced within a given scope unless its collection is visible within that scope: that is, the collection is a global variable or it is passed as a parameter.

4.5.4   The Type Structure of Ada

The type structure of Ada is based largely on Pascal. We do not intend to provide a detailed and comprehensive view of Ada's type structure, but rather to show how such structure overcomes a number of the problems and insecurities presented above. Discussion of the Ada facilities for describing abstract data types will be delayed until Section 4.6.2.2

Ada carefully distinguishes between *static* and *dynamic* properties of types. Static properties are those that can (and must) be checked by an analysis of the program at translation time. Dynamic properties are those that can (in general) be checked only at run-time. Static properties of types are the applicable operations; dynamic properties are, for example, range constraints on integers, or index constraints on arrays. To make the distinction clear, Ada allows the programmer to specify a dynamic property on a type by defining a **subtype.** For example,

type FLAVOR **is** (CHOCOLATE, MINT, PEACH, STRAWBERRY, VANILLA,
            BLUECHEESE, CATSUP, GARLIC, ONION);
subtype ICE_CREAM_FLAVOR **is** FLAVOR **range** CHOCOLATE . .
        VANILLA;
subtype SMALL_INT **is** INTEGER **range** − 10 . . 10;
subtype SMALL_POS_INT **is** SMALL_INT **range** 1 . . 10;
subtype MY_INT_SET **is** INTEGER **range** A . . B;

A variable of a subtype such as ICE_CREAM_FLAVOR inherits all the properties from type FLAVOR, but has values that satisfy a certain constraint (they belong to the subset CHOCOLATE through VANILLA). The last example (MY_INT_SET) shows that constraints may involve expressions that cannot be evaluated statically; rather, they are assumed to be evaluated when the subtype declaration is elaborated at the entry of the scope where the declaration appears.

A similar approach is taken for arrays that, unlike Pascal, can be dynamic. An array type is characterized by the type of the components, the number of indices, and the type of each index; the values of the bounds are not considered as part of the array type. For example, consider the following declaration.

type MY_ORDERS **is array** (INTEGER **range** <>) **of** ICE_CREAM_
FLAVOR;
--Symbol <> stands for an unspecified range

Objects of type MY_ORDERS have components of type ICE_CREAM_ FLAVOR indexed by values in an unspecified range of integers. For any object of an array type, however, the bounds of each index must be specified. For example, we can write

subtype MONTHLY_ORDERS **is** MY_ORDERS (1 . . 31);
subtype ANNUAL_ORDERS **is** MY_ORDERS (1 . . 365);

and then declare

JULY_ORDERS, AUGUST_ORDERS: MONTHLY_ORDERS;
LAST_YEAR_ORDERS: ANNUAL_ORDERS;

Another way of instantiating the bounds is by initialization. For example, we can declare

SEPTEMBER_ORDERS: **constant** MY_ORDERS: = JUNE_ORDERS;

Variable SEPTEMBER_ORDERS denotes a read-only data object (because of the specification **constant**) that satisfies the same range constraints of and is initialized with the same values as JUNE_ORDERS.

An even more interesting way of instantiating the bounds is by parameter passing. For example, the following function receives an object LIST of type MY_ORDERS and an object CHOICE of type ICE_CREAM_FLAVOR, and evaluates how many times CHOICE appears in LIST.

```
function HOW_MANY (LIST: MY_ORDERS; CHOICE:
                         ICE_CREAM_FLAVOR) return INTEGER is
RESULT: INTEGER: = 0;
begin for I in LIST'FIRST . . LIST'LAST loop
      if LIST (I) = CHOICE
          then RESULT: = RESULT + 1;
      end if;
   end loop;
   return RESULT;
end HOW_MANY;
```

Variable RESULT is local to HOW_MANY, and it is initialized to zero when it is declared. Loop variables (e.g., I) are considered to be implicitly declared. The formal parameter LIST has (automatically) the same bounds as the actual parameter, and such bounds can be accessed by concatenating the attribute names FIRST and LAST to the name of the array. As a consequence, the function can be called with arrays of different sizes as parameters. For example,

```
A: = HOW_MANY (LAST_YEAR_ORDERS, VANILLA) +
     HOW_MANY (JULY_ORDERS, VANILLA);
```

It is also possible to declare, local to the procedure, an array whose bounds depend on the parameters; for example,

TEMPORARY: MY_ORDERS (LIST'FIRST . . LIST'LAST);

As in ALGOL 68, strings are viewed as arrays of characters and defined as follows:

```
subtype NATURAL is INTEGER range 1 . . INTEGER'LAST;
--INTEGER'LAST is the maximum representable integer
type STRING is array (NATURAL range <>) of CHARACTER;
```

Another interesting issue is how Ada defines discriminated unions. The Pascal example introduced in Section 4.3.2.2.2, in the discussion of variant records, can be written in Ada as follows.

```
type DEPT is (HOUSEWARE, SPORTS, DRUGS, FOOD, LIQUOR);
subtype MONTH is INTEGER range 1 . . 12;
type ITEM (AVAILABLE: BOOLEAN: = TRUE) is
    record
            PRICE: REAL;
            case AVAILABLE of
                when TRUE = > AMOUNT: INTEGER;
                              WHERE: DEPT;
                when FALSE = > MONTH_EXPECTED: MONTH;
            end case;
        end record;
```

Type ITEM has a discriminant, AVAILABLE, that defines the possible variants of ITEM. The default initial value of the discriminant is declared above to be TRUE.

It is possible to define subtypes in which the variant is frozen—for example,

```
subtype OUT_OF_STOCK is ITEM (FALSE);
```

In such a case, the amount of space to be reserved by the translator for variables of subtype OUT_OF_STOCK is exactly what is needed by the variant, and variables of the subtype cannot change their variant.

Variables of a discriminated-union type are handled by Ada in a safe way. In fact, the discriminant is mandatory and cannot be assigned directly. In the absence of default initial values for the discriminants, a discriminant constraint must be given for any object declaration, possibly supplying the name of a subtype that incorporates such a constraint. For example,

```
X: ITEM (FALSE);
```

or

```
Y: OUT_OF_STOCK;
```

The value of a discriminant can be changed only for objects that have not been explicitly constrained. Moreover, the discriminant can be changed only by assignment to the record as a whole, and not by assignment to the discriminant alone. This forbids the producing of inconsistent data objects. For example, after the declaration

```
COCA_COLA: ITEM ; -- AVAILABLE has the default initial value TRUE
```

we can write the following statement.

COCA_COLA: = Y; --the variant is set to false
                -- because Y is of subtype OUT_OF_STOCK

or the statement

COCA_COLA: = (PRICE = >1.99, AVAILABLE = >TRUE, AMOUNT = >
           1500, WHERE = >FOOD);
     --the right-hand side of the assignment is a record value specified field by
     --field

Finally, an access to a component such as

COCA_COLA.WHERE

is automatically converted by the compiler into the run-time test

if not COCA_COLA.AVAILABLE **then raise** CONSTRAINT ERROR
                 --raises a run-time error
end if;

which precedes the required manipulation of COCA_COLA.WHERE.

Type compatibility in Ada is based on name equivalence. Objects belonging to different subtypes of the same type are compatible. Constraints must be checked during translation wherever possible; otherwise, at run-time.

Pointers are defined in a way similar to that used in Pascal. Moreover, two pointers can refer to the same data object only if their types are compatible. Using the Euclid terminology, each pointer type has an implicitly associated collection. Two pointers of compatible types are associated with the same implicit collection; two pointers with noncompatible types are guaranteed not to point into the same collection.

Figure 4.6 shows the Ada type structure.

4.6 ABSTRACT DATA TYPES

The concept of type, as defined in Pascal and ALGOL 68, has been a major step toward achieving a language capable of supporting structured programming. However, these languages do not fully support a methodology—such as information hiding—in which programs are developed by means of problem decomposition based on the recognition of abstractions. The data abstraction useful for this purpose does not merely classify objects according to their representation structure; rather, objects are classified according to their expected behavior. Such behavior is expressible in terms of the operations that are meaningful on those data, and the operations are the only means for creating, modifying, and accessing the objects.

Starting with SIMULA 67, other programming languages, such as Concurrent Pascal, CLU, Mesa, Euclid, Modula, and Ada, allowed the programmer—to a varying

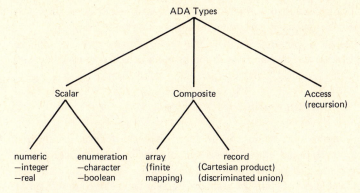

Figure 4.6   Ada type structure.

degree—to define an abstract data type by providing special language constructs for encapsulating both the *representation* and the *concrete operations* that implement the abstract view.

As we saw in Section 2.2, the existence of an encapsulating mechanism to enclose in a textual unit both the data structure that represents the objects and the procedures that represent the operations, improves the localization of modifications. A change to the data structure is likely to require a change in the access procedures, but the effect of these changes is confined within the boundaries of the encapsulating mechanism. Similarly, a change to the program that uses the data abstraction has no effect on the correctness of the program part enclosed within the encapsulating mechanism.

The possibility of parameterizing user-defined abstractions provides a still more flexible and powerful tool for expressing abstractions in a programming language. For example, the abstract data types ''integer queue'' and ''customer queue'' may display the same abstract behavior, independently of the (abstract) type of the items that are enqueued. A natural way of expressing this is by defining a *generic type* (or *type generator*) ''queue'' where the type of storable items is a parameter.

Section 4.6.1 reviews the concept of **class** as originally proposed in SIMULA 67 and evaluates its power and flexibility in defining abstract data types. A modification of the SIMULA 67 **class** mechanism will be justified and further detailed in Section 4.6.2, along with a presentation of the features provided by CLU and Ada.

4.6.1   The SIMULA 67 Class Mechanism

SIMULA 67, a general-purpose programming language, was defined as an extension to ALGOL 60, for systems description and simulation. The most important departure from ALGOL 60 is in the concept of **class**, which, initially inspired by the particular requirements of discrete simulation, was later recognized as a general tool for designing programs organized in levels of abstractions. Its generalization to concurrent programming led to the Concurrent Pascal concept of *monitor*. Similarly, classes originated the idea of *abstract data types,* as provided by Concurrent Pascal (with the

class construct) and CLU (with the **cluster** construct); and, more generally, they suggested how to provide language constructs for information hiding modules.

SIMULA 67 has a conventional ALGOL-like nested structure. A class can be declared in the declaration list that appears in the heading of a block, together with procedures and variables. A class declaration has the general form

$$<class\_heading> \; ; \; <class\_body>$$

$<class\_heading>$ contains the name of the class and the formal parameters. $<class\_body>$ is a conventional block: that is, it can contain local declarations of variables, procedures, and classes and executable statements.

For example, the concept of complex numbers in polar form can be described by the following class declaration. Parameters x and y denote the components of the complex number in Cartesian form, and local variables *angle* and *radius* denote the components in polar form. Functions *sqrt* and *arctan* are built-in, whereas *error* (which is left unspecified) is a procedure accessible from the class. Global variable *epsilon* denotes a positive **real** value that is used as an approximation of zero. Global **real** variable *pi* represents the value of π.

```
class complex (x,y); real x,y;
begin real angle,radius;
        radius: = sqrt (x**2 + y**2);
        if abs (x) < epsilon
           then begin if abs (y) < epsilon
                         then error
                         else begin if y > epsilon
                                       then angle: = pi/2;
                                       else angle: = 3*pi/2
                            end
                end
           else angle: = arctan (y/x)
end complex;
```

As with the type declarations of ALGOL 68 and Pascal, a class declaration defines a *prototype*, or *template*, of a class of data objects. Each *instance* of the class is a manipulable data object.

Class instances (called objects in SIMULA terminology) can be created dynamically in an arbitrary number, and can be individually referred to only via a pointer. For example, in the following pair of statements, c is declared to be a pointer to a *complex* in the first statement and is made to point to a newly created such object in the second statement.

```
ref (complex) c;
c: − new complex (1.0, 1.0)
```

(":−" is the reference assignment symbol and is read "denotes"). The effect of these statements is illustrated in Figure 4.7.

The *attributes* of a class instance are instances of the variables declared local to the class body and of the parameters listed in the class heading. Like the fields of a Pascal record, the attributes of a class instance are accessible from outside the class through the use of the dot notation. For example, after the above-listed statements have caused the generation of the class instance pointed by *c,* the execution of the statements

my_angle: = *c.angle;*
my_radius: = *c.radius;*
my_x: = *c.x;*
my_y: = *c.y*

yields the following values.

my_angle = 0.78, *my_radius* = 1.42, *my_x* = 1.0, and *my_y* = 1.0

Class declarations somehow resemble the ALGOL 68 or Pascal **record** type declarations. Actually, SIMULA 67 does not have an explicit Cartesian product constructor; the class can be used for this purpose. Unlike in ALGOL 68 or Pascal, however, in SIMULA 67 access is available only via reference variables, and class instances have no name. Also, each instance of the class must be generated explicitly via a **new** statement. Finally, an instance of a class is an initialized object, since the class body is automatically executed by the **new** statement.

More generally, however, classes are encapsulating mechanisms that support the definition of abstract data types. A class may enclose the procedures that implement the operations on data. For example, procedures *add* and *multiply,* for adding and multiplying complex numbers, can be enclosed within the body of class *complex.* These operations are also attributes accessed via the dot notation—*c.add, c.multiply*— and they may take parameters. For example, the headings of procedures *add* and *multiply* enclosed within **class** *complex* are

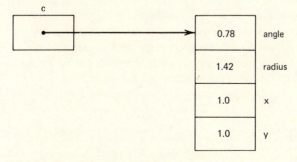

Figure 4.7   An instance of class *complex.*

procedure *add (operand);* **ref** *(complex) operand;*

and

procedure *multiply (operand);* **ref** *(complex) operand;*

Addition between the complex numbers referenced by $c1$ and $c2$ can be expressed as

cl.add (c2)

That is, $c2$ is passed as a parameter to the *add* procedure associated with $c1$.

This notation is rather awkward for binary operations on variables of an abstract type, however, since the same operation could also be expressed as

c2.add (cl)

That is, $c1$ is passed as a parameter to the *add* procedure associated with $c2$.

A more serious problem is that the dot notation provides access to all attributes of an object, and so, for example, one is not forbidden from writing

cl.angle:= c2.angle;
cl.radius:= c2.radius + c3.radius

to make $c1$ denote the result of the addition of the complex numbers denoted by $c2$ and $c3$, if the angles of $c2$ and $c3$ are known to be equal. In other words, *add* and *multiply* are not the only operations that can manipulate complex data objects, because direct access to the representation also is permitted.

SIMULA 67 contains also a special feature that allows the programmer to specify discriminated unions of types, as well as generic abstract-data types. The particular feature used for this purpose, the *subclass,* in fact has a more general applicability and is intended to provide a general tool in the organization of systems in levels of abstraction. It is achieved by *prefixing* a class with the name of another class.

Suppose we want to define the abstraction ''stack of elements'' (of possibly nonhomogeneous type). The operations on a stack should allow the programmer to reference the first element (*top*), to insert a new element in the first position (*push*), to eliminate the first element (*pop*), and to check whether the stack is empty (*empty*). Such operations are independent of the particular types of the elements that are stacked together. We first describe as follows the class of items that can be stacked.

class *stack_member;*
begin ref *(stack_member) next_member;*
    next_member:− **none**
end

This specifies that the only property shared by all stackable objects is the existence of an attribute that is a reference to the next item in the stack. Each instance of *stack_member* has the attribute *next_member* initialized to **none**, the null pointer value. The class *stack* can be described separately, specifying only the operations applicable to all stackable objects.

```
class stack;
begin ref (stack_member) first;
        ref (stack_member) procedure top;
            top: − first;
        procedure pop;
            if ¬ empty then first: − first.next_member;
        procedure push (e); ref (stack_member) e;
        begin if first = / = none
                then e.next_member: −first;
            first: − e
        end push;
        boolean procedure empty;
            empty: = first = = none;
        first: − none
end stack
```

Procedure *top* returns the topmost element—that is, a **ref** (*stack_member*)—of a nonempty stack. Symbol "¬" in procedure *pop* stands for "not." Symbol "=/=" in procedure *push* stands for "not equal." Procedure *empty* returns a **boolean;** symbol "= =" stands for "equal." Each instance of class stack is initialized as an empty stack, because attribute *first* is set to **none**.

Having defined the two classes *stack_member* and *stack,* we can now create stackable objects of a particular type—for example, *complex*—by prefixing class *complex*.

stack_member **class** *complex (. . .)*

        .

        .

        .

        end *complex*

specifies that the objects generated by

new *complex*

have all the attributes of *stack_member,* as well as the attributes of *complex*. In other words, they are complex numbers that can be stacked. *Complex* is called a subclass of *stack_member*—it is more specialized than *stack_member*.

If *s* is declared of type **ref** (*stack*), we can create a stack of complex numbers by doing *s:* − **new** *stack;*

Stack *s* currently contains no elements, so that *s.empty* returns **true.** If we have several complex objects, *c*1, *c*2, *c*3, we may insert them in the stack in the following way.

s.push (c1);
s.push (c2);
s.push (c3).

We can look at the top element by doing *s.top,* which returns a reference; and we may remove the top element by *s.pop.*

Note that because *first* is available for access from the outside, the user is not protected from accidentally modifying *s.first* and thus losing the entire stack (see Exercise 4.10).

Class *stack_member* can be viewed as a union of the types corresponding to all its subclasses. For example, if the following declaration appears in the program—

stack_member **class** *vector (. . .)*

.

.

.

        end *vector;*

—a variable of type **ref** (*stack_member*) can reference both a complex *stack_member* and a vector *stack_member*.

In fact, vector objects and complex objects may be inserted in the same stack. All that stack cares about is that an attribute *next_member* of type **ref** (*stack_member*) exists in the object it is manipulating. All subclasses of *stack_member* include such an attribute.

· This freedom also causes insecurities. For example, if we insert two vector objects, *v*1 and *v*2, in the above stack—that is, *s.push (v1); s.push (v2)*—a future *pop* may yield either a vector or a complex object. It is therefore possible to try to access an attribute in an object that does not have that attribute—for example, *v.angle*. Although SIMULA 67 provides facilities for examining the type of an object (**if** *v* **is** *vector* **then** . . .) the programmer is not forced to use them. In other words, the language does not automatically enforce protection. In particular, if the goal is to define *stack* as a generic type, one must be careful not to push stack members of different types onto the same stack instance.

Another interesting feature of the SIMULA class is the ability to create class instances that work in quasiparallel—that is, in an interleaved—fashion. The class bodies can in fact be activated as coroutines. This subject is treated in Chapter 5.

In conclusion, the SIMULA 67 class combines many interesting concepts:

a. It allows grouping of related, highly dependent programming objects into an encapsulating construct (**class**).

b. It provides a useful linguistic construct (subclass) for hierarchical system decomposition.

c. It views abstract objects as entities that can only be accessed via references and provides explicit facilities to manipulate references.

d. It allows the specification of quasi-concurrency of execution of class instances.

4.6.2 Abstraction and Protection: CLU and ADA

The initial design of SIMULA 67 did not provide any form of protection on classes, whose attributes could be (perhaps inadvertently) manipulated outside the class.

Invisibility of the representation of abstract data types is a major issue of newer languages such as Concurrent Pascal and CLU. In other recent languages, such as Mesa, Euclid, Modula, and Ada, the encapsulating construct is not restricted to hiding the implementation of one abstract data type, but, more generally, acts as a filter for which it is possible explicitly to control which internal details of the encapsulated unit are made visible to the outside (i.e., are *exported*). In some cases, it is also possible to specify the external information that is made visible within the module (i.e., *imported* by the module). This view of modules as information hiding devices provides a powerful system-structuring language tool that can be especially valuable for large, complex programs. Sections 4.6.2.1 and 4.6.2.2 review the constructs provided by CLU and Ada for describing data abstractions.

4.6.2.1 CLU

CLU makes it possible to define abstract data types by means of the *cluster* construct, which is illustrated below, along with some other features of the language, in an example.

We want to define the abstract data type *complex* number, with the following operations.

- *create:* receives a pair of real numbers as parameters and generates a complex number having the two parameters as real and imaginary part, respectively (CLU data objects must be created explicitly).

- *add:* receives a pair of complex numbers as parameters and delivers the result of their addition.

- *equal:* receives a pair of complex numbers as parameters and if they are equal, delivers a true result; otherwise, a false result.

The cluster implementing the data type is described below.

```
complex =  cluster is create, add, equal
    rep =  record [x,y:real]
    create =  proc (a,b:real) returns (cvt)
                return (rep $ {x:a,y:b})
    end create
    add =  proc (a,b:cvt) returns (cvt)
                return (rep $ {x:a.x + b.x,y:a.y + b.y})
    end add
    equal =  proc (a,b:cvt) returns (bool)
                return (a.x = b.x and a.y = b.y)
    end equal
end complex
```

The cluster heading (**cluster is** . . .) lists what operations are available on the data type *complex*. The data structure chosen to give a concrete representation to objects of the abstract type is specified by the **rep** clause. In the example, it is a record with two fields: one for the real part and the other for the imaginary part. The procedures that implement the operations (as well as other possible local procedures not listed in the cluster heading) follow the **rep** clause. In the example, they are procedures *create, add,* and *equal*.

The keyword **cvt**, which can only be used within a cluster, denotes a change of viewpoint. For example, in procedure *add* the parameters *a* and *b* are of type *complex* when viewed from outside the cluster but are "converted" to their representation type (here, **record** . . .) inside the *add* procedure. As a consequence, it is legal to write *a.x* within procedure *add*. Similarly, the returned data object of the representation type that holds the result of the addition is "converted" to the abstract type *complex* at procedure exit. The meaning of **return** (**rep** $ . . .) is that an object of the representation type (i.e., a **record**) is returned; the value stored in the record is specified within curly brackets in a self-explanatory notation. The **cvt** in the **returns** clause causes a change to the abstract representation after return to the caller.

An important semantic issue that makes CLU somewhat unusual is the way the language views variables and data objects. First, scope and lifetime are disjoint issues: that is, variables are declared within units, as

p: complex

but they are explicitly created, as

p: = *complex* $ *create* (*h,k*)

The symbol "$" is similar to the dot notation of SIMULA 67. Therefore, operation *create* enclosed within cluster *complex* is invoked with *h* and *k* as actual parameters. The **return** statement executed by procedure *create* generates an object (a complex number whose real and imaginary parts are *h* and *k,* respectively). The returned object is assigned to *p*.

Second, CLU variables are uniformly viewed as references to data objects, and an assignment such as *x:= e*

causes *x* to refer to the data object resulting from the evaluation of *e.* Therefore, the assignment does not modify the data object referenced by *x,* but rather makes *x* refer to a different data object and leaves the original data object unmodified. The original data object may still be referenced by other variables, or, if no such variables exist, may become inaccessible. This form of assignment is called *assignment by sharing.*

Parameter passing in CLU is defined in terms of assignments. For example, the call

. . . *complex* $ *add* (*x,y*) . . .

assigns *x* and *y* to the formal parameters *a* and *b,* respectively, which act as local variables. Consequently, the same data object becomes shared by *x* and *a* and by *y* and *b,* respectively.

CLU procedures and clusters can be *generic*: that is, they may be parameterized by a type. A generic procedure or cluster must explicitly state which procedures the parameter type must provide. For example, a cluster implementing sets of components of type *t* might have the following heading.

set = **cluster** [*t:***type**] **is** *create, insert, delete, is_in*
           where *t* **has** *equal:* **proctype** *(t, t)* **returns** *(bool)*

This means that type *set* is characterized by the operations *create, insert, delete,* and *is_in* (membership test); type *t* must have an operation *equal,* which returns a boolean when applied to two parameters of type *t.* This information about parameters of type **type** allows the type-checking mechanism to verify that only the listed operations are used on objects of the parameter type within the cluster.

Declaration of a *set* variable must specify the type of the components as a parameter—for example,

s: set [**integer**]
t: set [**bool**]

Similarly, operations on such sets must be written as

set [**integer**] $ *create* (. . .)
set [**bool**] $ *create* (. . .)
etc.

4.6.2.2   Ada

The Ada encapsulating mechanism is the *package.* A program unit has a typical ALGOL-like nested structure. As in Pascal, nesting is achieved through declarations: that is, a declaration of a subprogram or a package can contain a declaration of local variables, procedures, and packages.* Nesting can also be achieved by defining new blocks in sequences of statements, as in ALGOL 60.

Packages can be used for a variety of applications, ranging from the declaration of a set of common entities—variables, constants, types—to grouping a set of related subprograms (e.g., a mathematical package for the solution of differential equations) or describing abstract data types.

An example of the first case is the following.

```
package COMPLEX_NUMBERS is
     type COMPLEX is
          record
               RE: INTEGER;
               IM: INTEGER;
          end record;
     TABLE: array (1 . . 500) of COMPLEX;
end COMPLEX_NUMBERS;
```

The above declaration is processed as if it were the declaration of the enclosed variables and types; therefore, such variables and types have the same scope and lifetime as the variables and types declared in the declarative part, where the declaration of package COMPLEX_NUMBERS appears. The names declared within the package can be used within the scope of the package by using the dot notation (*à la* SIMULA 67), as in

COMPLEX_NUMBERS.TABLE (K)

When grouping a set of related subprograms, or describing an abstract data type, it is often necessary to hide some local entities within the package. In the case of the set of related subprograms, the hidden local entities might be local variables and/or local procedures; in the case of abstract data types, they will include the concrete representation and perhaps some internal auxiliary variables and procedures. The lack of this capability, as we have seen, is a weakness in SIMULA 67. Ada has overcome this problem rather nicely.

The general structure of a package is composed of two parts: the *package specification* and the *package body*. The package specification contains exactly all the information that is exported by the module, whereas the package body contains all the hidden details of the implementation and an initialization section that is executed upon activation of the unit that contains the package declaration.

As a first example, the following package exports the following two related functions.

- BELONGS_TO (X): gives a boolean result if X belongs to a certain (ordered) set of integers;

---

*Tasks are another kind of unit that can be hierarchically nested (see Section 5.2.4.3).

- POSITION (X): gives the ordinal position of X in the set.

The structure and the contents of the ordered set of integers is hidden within the package; the operations BELONGS_TO and POSITION are the only available manipulations on integer sets.

```
package INT_SET_PACK is
        function BELONGS_TO (X: INTEGER) return BOOLEAN;
        function POSITION (X: INTEGER) return INTEGER;
end INT_SET_PACK;
package body INT_SET_PACK is
        STORED_INT: array (1 . . 10) of INTEGER;
        function BELONGS _TO (X: INTEGER) return BOOLEAN;

                        .
                        .
                        .
        end BELONGS_TO;
        function POSITION (X: INTEGER) return INTEGER;

                        .
                        .
                        .
        end POSITION;
                --now comes the initialization of array
                --STORED_INT, i.e., the initialization of the set
                .
                .
                .
end INT_SET_PACK;
```

As a second example, the following package defines the abstract data type *complex* number that we have already described in CLU.

```
package COMPLEX_NUMBERS is
        type COMPLEX is private;
        procedure INITIALIZE (A, B: in REAL; X: out COMPLEX);
        function ADD (A, B: in COMPLEX) return COMPLEX;
private
        type COMPLEX is
            record R, I: REAL;
            end record;
end COMPLEX_NUMBERS;
package body COMPLEX_NUMBERS is
        procedure INITIALIZE (A, B: in REAL; X: out COMPLEX) is
        begin X.R: = A;
                X.I: = B;
        end INITIALIZE;
```

```
        function ADD (A, B: in COMPLEX) return COMPLEX is
        TEMP: COMPLEX;
        begin TEMP.R: = A.R + B.R;
              TEMP.I: = A.I + B.I;
              return TEMP;
        end ADD;
end COMPLEX_NUMBERS;
```

In the example, type COMPLEX exported by the module is **private**: that is, the details of the representation enclosed within the portion **private** . . . **end** COMPLEX_NUMBERS of the package specification are not visible outside the package. Variables of type COMPLEX can only be manipulated by using the subprograms INITIALIZE and ADD exported by the package. The predefined operations of assignment and test for equality/inequality are also permitted.

Exported variables can also be described as **limited private**. In such a case, assignments and tests for equality/inequality would not be automatically defined for the type. If they are needed, they must be explicitly provided by the package as additional procedures.

One difference from CLU is that no explicit *create* operation must be provided by the Ada package, because creation is automatically performed when the units that declare variables of type COMPLEX are activated. Package COMPLEX_NUMBERS, however, provides an explicit procedure for initialization.

In the example, parameters to procedures are specified as either **in** or **out**. The specification **in** denotes an unmodifiable input parameter. The specification **out** specifies an output parameter whose value is set by the procedure. Parameter passing in Ada is discussed in Section 5.2.1.1.

Packages (and procedures) can be **generic,** in which case they must be instantiated before being used, as shown below. For example, a package describing sets of a predefined maximum cardinality may have the following specification part.

```
generic
        type COMPONENT is private
package SET_MANIPULATION is
        type SET is limited private;
        procedure INSERT (S: in out SET; ELEM: in COMPONENT);
        procedure DELETE (S: in out SET; ELEM: in COMPONENT);
        function IS_IN (S: in SET; ELEM: in COMPONENT) return BOOLEAN;
private
        type SET is
                record STORE: array (1 . . MAX_CARDINALITY) of
                                        COMPONENT;
                       CARDINALITY: INTEGER range 0 . .
                       MAX_CARDINALITY: = 0;
                end record;
end SET_MANIPULATION;
```

Procedure INSERT (DELETE) can be used to insert a new element into (delete an existing element from) a set. Function IS_IN returns a boolean value that is true if an element ELEM is in a set, and false otherwise. The data structure used to represent sets comprises an array whose component type is a parameter specified in the **generic** clause that prefixes the package. The size of sets is fixed by the value of global variable MAX_CARDINALITY.

Type COMPONENT is **private**: that is, the only operations permitted on components within the package are assignments and tests for equality and inequality. Additional operations, if necessary, can be provided as additional generic parameters. The field CARDINALITY of type SET is used to record the number of elements that are stored in a set; it is initialized to zero.

Instantiation of a generic module requires a specification of the actual generic parameters. For example,

package INTEGERS **is new** SET_MANIPULATION (INTEGER);
package FLAVORS **is new** SET_MANIPULATION (FLAVOR);

where type FLAVOR is the one defined in Section 4.5.4. Semantically, the two instantiations can be viewed as the declarations of two distinct packages, which happen to have the same internal structure (and thus are described by the same generic module). In the scope of such instantiations, it is possible to write the declarations

A, B: INTEGERS.SET. --A and B are of type SET instantiated by INTEGERS
C: FLAVORS.SET: --C is of type SET instantiated by FLAVORS

4.7 IMPLEMENTATION MODELS

This section reviews the basic implementation models for data objects. The description is intended to be rather language-independent, but the examples given and the emphasis of the discussion are Pascal-oriented. Our representation models are not intended to provide a detailed description of efficient techniques for representing data objects within a computer, which can be highly dependent on the hardware structure. Rather, the most straightforward solutions will be presented, along with some comments on alternative, more efficient representations.

Following the discussion of Chapter 3, data will be represented by a pair consisting of a descriptor and a data object. Rather than use a concrete data structure, we will describe the descriptor abstractly as a set of attributes of the data object. The main reason for this procedure is that descriptors are usually kept in a table during translation, and, as we have seen, only a subset of the attributes stored therein needs to be saved at run-time. Therefore, the format of descriptors—free versus fixed format, number of fields, and so on—is highly dependent on the overall structure of the table, and the number of attributes stored in a descriptor can vary from translation-time to run-time.

4.7.1 Built-in Types and User-Defined Unstructured Types

Integers and reals are hardware-supported on most conventional computers that provide fixed- and floating-point arithmetic. Integer and real variables are often represented as shown in Figures 4.8 and 4.9.

Values in a subrange can be represented as if they were in the base type, so that transfer of values between the subrange and the basic type does not require any conversion, only run-time checks. The descriptor must contain the values of the subrange bounds; such values are needed at run-time to make bounds-checking possible.

Values of an enumeration type t can be mapped into the integer values 0 to n-1, n being the cardinality of t. This mapping does not introduce any possibility of mixing up values of type t with values of any other enumeration type, if all run-time accesses are routed via a descriptor containing the type information. The use of descriptors is of course not necessary for typed languages.

Booleans and characters can be viewed as enumeration types and implemented as above. To save space, characters can be stored in storage units smaller than a word (e.g., bytes), if such units are addressable by the hardware directly. It is also possible to pack several booleans declared in the same unit into the same word (or byte), each boolean being represented by a particular bit. In this case, accessing an individual boolean (i.e., a bit) within the collection (i.e., a word or a byte) would be less efficient on machines that do not have bit addressing.

4.7.2 Structured Types

4.7.2.1 Cartesian Product

The standard representation of a data object of a Cartesian product type is a sequential layout of the components. The descriptor contains the Cartesian product type name and one set of triples (name of the selector, type of the field, reference to a data object) for each field.

Figure 4.10 illustrates this representation for a variable of the Pascal type

type $t =$ **record** *a: real;*
                    b: integer
      end

Each component of the Cartesian product occupies an integral number of addressable storage units (e.g., words), and can be referenced within the program by

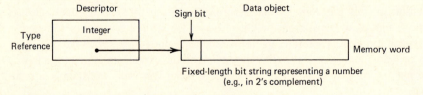

Figure 4.8 Representation of an integer variable.

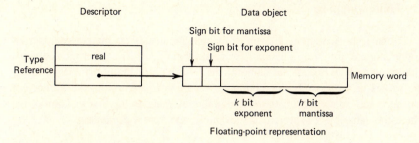

Figure 4.9 Representation of a real variable.

giving the field name. Field names cannot be held by variables. In a strongly typed language, therefore, descriptors need not be saved at run-time, and the reference to each field within the activation record of the unit to which the Cartesian product is local can be evaluated by the translator.*

In a language such as Pascal, the user can direct the translator to use storage in an efficient way by explicitly stating the **packed** option. In such a case, more than one component might be packed into an addressable storage unit. In doing so, the user is trading processing time for the saving in storage.

For example, variables of the type

packed record *a: char;*
           b: 0 . . 7
     end

could be represented by two bytes of a single word.

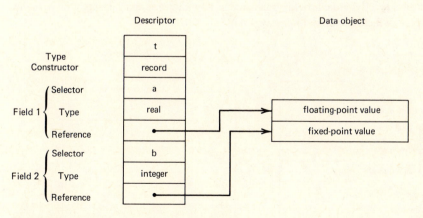

Figure 4.10 Representation of a Pascal record.

---

*This is true for Pascal records. For simplicity's sake the possibility of having dynamic arrays as components of a Cartesian product (as in ALGOL 68) is ignored here.

4.7.2.2 Finite Mapping

A conventional representation of a finite mapping allocates an integral number of addressable storage units (e.g., words) for each component. The descriptor contains the finite-mapping type name; the name of the base type of the domain type, along with the values of the bounds; the codomain type name, along with the number of locations necessary to store each element; and the reference to the first location of the area where the data object is stored. For example, the Pascal declaration

type $a =$ **array** $[0 . . 10]$ **of** *real*

could be represented as in Figure 4.11.

Since indexing into the array can be done by subscripting with a variable, the array bounds should be saved in a run-time descriptor in order to perform bounds checking at run-time.

A reference to $a[i]$ is computed as an offset from the address (b) of the first component of the array (within the activation record of the unit in which the array is local). If the domain type is a subrange $m . . n$ and the number of words occupied by each element is k, then the offset to be evaluated for accessing $a[i]$ is $k(i-m)$. Thus, a reference to $a[i]$ can be expressed as $b + k(i - m) = (b - km) + ki = b' + ki$, where b' is a constant that can be evaluted at compile-time.

As per the discussion presented in Section 3.6.2, in a language that supports dynamic arrays, the descriptor can be split into a static part and a dynamic part. The static part contains the information that is used only at translation time (such as the type of the array components) and a reference to the dynamic part. The dynamic part is allocated at run-time within the activation record of the unit that declares the array at an offset known at translation time. It contains a reference to the array data object (which, in general, can only be evaluated at run-time) and the values of the bounds. Any access to a dynamic array is translated as an indirect address through the dynamic descriptor (which is called a *dope vector*).

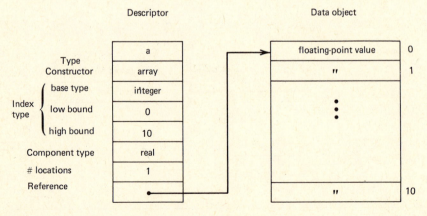

Figure 4.11 Representation of a Pascal array.

4.7.2.3 Sequences

Both sequences of characters (strings) and sequences of records on a backup storage are represented in a variety of ways, depending both on the semantics of the language and—especially in the case of files—on certain architectural aspects of the machine.

In Pascal, strings are nothing more than a packed array of characters; therefore, their lengths are statically determinable and cannot be changed. In Ada, strings are nothing more than dynamic arrays of characters; therefore, the length generally is unknown at translation time, and becomes known upon entry to the unit in which the string variable is declared. In both languages, strings can be represented as other arrays (Section 4.7.2.2).

In other languages, such as SNOBOL4 and ALGOL 68, strings may vary arbitrarily in length, having no programmer-specified upper bound. As we have seen, strings of this kind are dynamic variables and must be allocated on a heap. Figure 4.11 shows an example of a possible representation for a string of length 5. As before, the descriptor is split into a static part and a dynamic part; the dynamic part is allocated on the execution stack and contains the current string length (useful for dynamic type checking) and a reference to the head of the string. The string is allocated on the heap as a linked list of words, each word containing one or more characters. The number of characters stored in a word depends on the word size; Figure 4.12 assumes that each word contains two characters.

4.7.2.4 Discriminated Union

A variable of discriminated union type is not bound to any particular variant, but the variant can vary as a consequence of assignments. Therefore, the amount of space to be allocated for the variable should be sufficient to hold values of the variant requiring the most space.

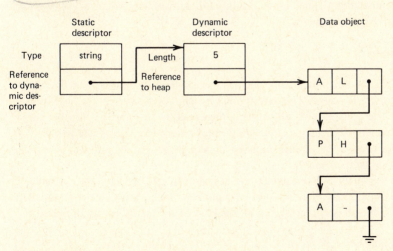

Figure 4.12   Representation of a variable-length string.

Ada provides the option of binding a variable to a specific variant. In such a case, the amount of space to be allocated can be exactly that required by the variant.

Figure 4.13 shows the representation of a variable of the following discriminated union type.

type *v* = **record** *a: integer;*
                case *b: boolean* **of**
                      true: (c: integer);
                      false: (d: integer;
                            e: real)
      end

The tag field has an entry in the descriptor that points to a case table. For each possible value of the tag, the case table contains a reference to a descriptor for the associated variant.

4.7.2.5   Powerset

It is possible to implement powersets efficiently, both in terms of access and manipulation time and in terms of storage, provided that a machine word has at least as many bits as there are potential members in a set. The presence of the ith element of the base type in a certain set S is denoted by a "1" as the value of the ith bit of the word associated with S. The empty set is represented by all zeros in the word. The union between two sets is easily performed by an *or* between the two associated words, and the intersection by an *and*. If the machine does not allow bit-level access, test for membership requires shifting the required bit into an accessible word position (e.g., the sign bit), or using a mask.

The existence of such an appealing representation for powersets is responsible for the implementation-defined limits for the cardinality of sets, which is usually equal to the size of a memory word.

4.7.2.6   Pointers

A pointer variable holds as a value the absolute address of an object of the type to which the pointer is bound. The description of such type appears in the descriptor of the pointer. The pointer value **nil** can be represented by an address value that causes a hardware-generated error trap to catch an inadvertent reference via a pointer with value **nil**. For example, the value might be an address beyond the physical addressing space into a protected area.

Pointer variables are allocated on the execution stack, like any other variable. In Pascal, data objects that are referred to via a pointer variable are allocated in the heap. A sketchy view of this is represented in Figure 4.14 for the following declaration.

type *T* = ↑ *integer;*
var *t: T*

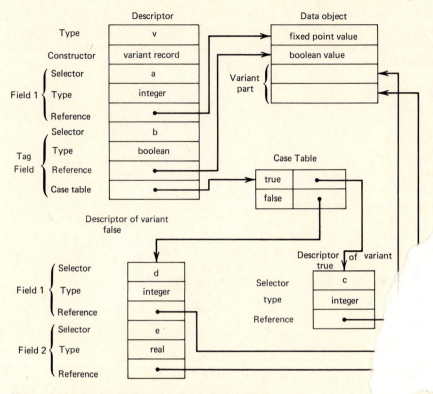

Figure 4.13 Representation of a discriminated union.

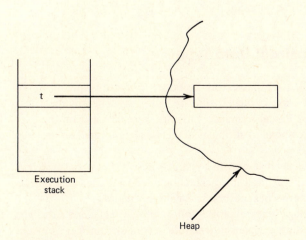

Figure 4.14 Run-time view of a Pascal pointer.

In general, structured types can be formed by aggregating unstructured types in arbitrarily complex structures. As a consequence, descriptors of variables of a structured type can be organized as trees, with each component type being described by a subtree. For example, a data object of the following type t

type $t =$ **record** *a: real;*
$\qquad\qquad\qquad$ *b: t1;*
$\qquad\qquad\qquad$ *c: integer*
$\qquad$ **end**

where

$t1 =$ **array** $[0 \ . \ . \ 3]$ **of** *integer*

can be represented as in Figure 4.15.

Similarly, a two-dimensional array variable of the type

type $t2 =$ **array** $[0 \ . \ . \ 2]$ **of** $t4$

where

$t4 =$ **array** $[0 \ . \ . \ 5]$ **of** *integer*

can be represented as in Figure 4.16.

Each component of type $t4$ of an array of type $t2$ is represented by six consecutive floating-point values. Each elementary component of the array can be indexed by a pair (i,j)—i being a value in the subrange $0 \ . \ . \ 2$ that selects a component of type $t4$ and j being a value in the subrange $0 \ . \ . \ 5$ that selects an integer within this component. If b is the starting address of the array within its activation record, the reference to the component is given by the expression $b + 6i + j$.

4.7.3 Classes and Abstract Data Types

The implementation of SIMULA 67 classes can be rather straightforward, if we do not consider the possibility of class instance bodies to run quasi-concurrently. Class references, like ALGOL 68 or Pascal reference variables, are allocated on the execution stack; variables that correspond to attributes of a class are allocated on the heap (see Exercise 4.11).

Other programming languages that contain constructs derived from the SIMULA 67 class have a different behavior as far as the generation of encapsulated data objects is concerned. Two opposite approaches are briefly mentioned below.

The first approach is the more static approach followed by Modula and Ada. The basic idea is that the encapsulating mechanism (**module** in Modula; **package** in Ada) should simply package a set of highly related declarations and provide suitable ini-

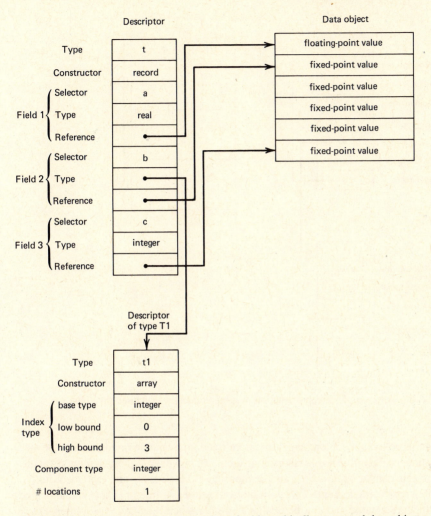

Figure 4.15 An example of representation of a hierarchically structured data object.

tialization. The encapsulating mechanism does not introduce a new template of a unique, structured object to be dynamically created, but rather introduces a set of (partially visible) declarations. Among the exported entities can be types, but the variables of such types behave like any other program variables.

The CLU approach is more dynamic. All CLU data objects are allocated in a heap and are accessible at run-time via a (stack-allocated) reference. In conventional programming languages, a variable can be viewed at run-time as a holder for the value of a data object. All CLU variables, however, are references to objects. Once created, objects continue to exist forever, but they can become inaccessible if no variables refer to them. The only way to reuse space previously allocated is to have a garbage collector to reclaim storage occupied by unreferenced data objects.

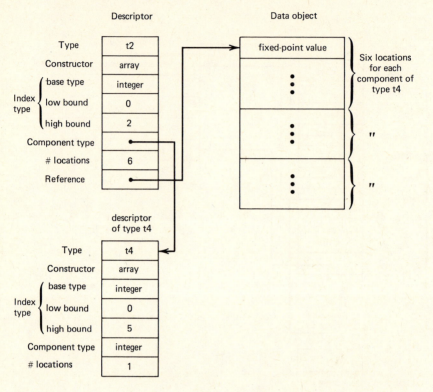

Figure 4.16   An example of representation of a hierarchically structured data object.

The more dynamic a language, the more freedom available in controlling the size and lifetime of data objects. Memory management, however, becomes more difficult. Heap objects cannot be allocated and deallocated at block entry and exit according to a simple, easily implemented, first-in/first-out strategy. Rather, they are allocated when they are created and can be deallocated only when they have no references.

Since explicit storage deallocation performed by the programmer can generate dangling references—as we have seen in Section 4.5.3 for the Pascal primitive *dispose*—efficient techniques for garbage collection become a critical factor in the run-time performance of a heap-based programming language. Garbage collection techniques are discussed in the next section.

4.7.4   Garbage Collection

A garbage collector is a run-time language support system that acquires the portions of heap storage that have previously been allocated but are no longer used by the program. Usually, the garbage collector is automatically invoked when the space set aside for the heap is nearly full.

Garbage collection is reasonably easy when

   i. The heap data objects have fixed size.

   ii. It is known *a priori* which fields of a heap object contain pointers to other heap data objects.

   iii. It is possible to find all the pointers into the heap.

Free fixed-size storage elements can be chained together in a *free list*; the garbage collector is automatically called when a request for a new heap element is issued and the free list is empty.

The following two-step method for garbage collection can be implemented easily.

1. Mark all reachable heap data objects, starting from the references stored in the stack. To do so, a temporary stack T may be used. Initially, T contains the stack references in the heap. Every time the top element E is popped, the object referenced by E is marked, and E is replaced by the references to the node(s) referenced by E, if they are not marked. When T becomes empty, all reachable heap data objects have been marked.

2. Insert all unmarked data objects into the free list.

This simple method presents a number of problems in practice.

a. Heap objects are of variable size and contain pointers to other heap objects in different positions. As a consequence, the identification of unreferenced data objects can proceed in a way similar to the homogeneous-size case outlined above, provided that the heading of each data object contains coded information (i.e., a run-time descriptor) about the fields of the data object that contain references to other heap objects and about the size of the object.

b. The stack and the heap are often implemented as growing from the two sides of a fixed-size main memory area (Figure 4.17). In such a case, the garbage collector is called when the two areas meet, because the heap must be compacted in order to allow the stack to grow. Implementation of this method, however, requires that some space be set aside for the additional stack used by the marking algorithm. This stack can be implemented in an area within the heap, but its size is very critical. If it is large, space for the heap is lost; if it is small, there is a chance of overflow during execution of the marking algorithm.

An alternative method that does not require an additional stack is described in (Schorr and Waite 1967). Starting from a reference into the heap stored into the stack, a chain of heap objects is traversed to the end. As each heap element is reached, the element is marked and the pointer is reversed. When the end of the chain is reached, the algorithm follows the reversed pointers. As a side chain is encountered, a new traversal is accomplished in a similar manner.

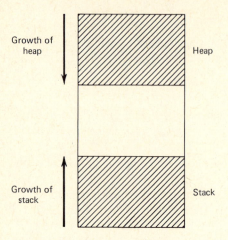

Figure 4.17 Organization of main memory.

c. As a consequence of the variable size of heap objects, the free-list solution is not adequate, because of memory fragmentation. There might be no blocks of consecutive storage locations that can hold a new heap data object while the *total* amount of fragmented free space is larger than the requested amount. Free-storage compaction is thus necessary. The main difficulty is that pointers to active heap objects must be readjusted when heap objects are shifted to different locations.

The main problem with garbage collection is that "useful" processing time is lost every time the garbage collector is invoked. This can be particularly dangerous in real-time systems, because an urgent request for service might arrive from the environment just after the garbage collector has started its rather complex activity.

Garbage collection can be distributed more uniformly over processing time by using a *reference counting* scheme. In such a scheme, each allocated data object keeps track of how many other data objects reference it. When the count reaches zero, the storage area allocated for it can be relinquished. Unfortunately, this method does not work in the case of circularly linked heap objects. When there are no references from the stack to the circular structure, reference counts associated with each node of the list are not zero, but equal one. Solutions to this problem are cited in the Suggestions for Further Reading section at the end of the chapter.

Finally, we would like to mention that garbage collection can also be viewed as a process that is concurrently active with the program under execution. Parallel garbage-collection techniques might become of practical interest with the advent of new multiprocessor architectures. A multiprocessor dedicated to the execution of a high-level, heap-based programming language might reserve a processor to perform on-line garbage collection. The decreasing cost of processors will probably make this solution appealing in the future.

SUGGESTIONS FOR FURTHER READING AND BIBLIOGRAPHIC NOTES

The systematic view of data aggregates and the classification of data structuring methods presented in Section 4.2 are taken from C. A. R. Hoare in (Dahl et al. 1972). Hoare defines Cartesian products, finite mappings, sequences, discriminated unions, recursive data structures, and powersets. He also discusses implementation models for each data structuring mechanism.

A critical comparison of ALGOL 68 and Pascal, with particular attention to their type structures, is presented by (Tanenbaum 1978) and by D. M. Berry in (Wegner 1979). (Habermann 1973), (Lecarme and Desjardins 1975), (Welsh et al. 1977), and (Tennent 1978) contain several comments on Pascal and, in particular, show the insecurities of its type structure. (Fischer and LeBlanc 1980) discuss implementation issues of type checking for Pascal programs.

Abstract data types were introduced in (Liskov and Zilles 1974). Formal approaches to the specification of abstract data types are presented in (Liskov and Zilles 1975), (Wulf et al. 1976), (Guttag 1977), (Goguen et al. 1978), and (Guttag et al. 1978). (Gries and Gehani 1977) contains several insights into the concept of generic data type. The conference proceedings (ACM-SIGPLAN 1976) contains many papers on data types and data abstraction. An overview of programming language concepts related to data types can be found in the survey paper by P. Wegner in (Wegner 1979).

Besides CLU and Ada, other languages provide data abstraction facilities—for example, Euclid, Gypsy, Modula, Mesa, Alphard, and Russell. Alphard (Shaw et al. 1977), (Wulf et al. 1976) and Russell (Demers and Donahue 1980**a**), (Demers and Donahue 1980**b**) are particularly interesting.

Implementation models for data objects are analyzed in the aforementioned paper by C. A. R. Hoare in (Dahl et al. 1972), as well as in most compiler design textbooks—including (Gries 1971), (Aho and Ullman 1977), and (Barrett and Couch 1979)—and in other programming language textbooks, such as (Pratt 1975). Garbage collection is studied in (Schorr and Waite 1967), (Knuth 1973), and (Deutsch and Bobrow 1976). (Pratt 1975) contains a survey of garbage collection techniques for heap-based programming languages. The paper by U. Hill in (Bauer and Eickel 1976) presents a detailed discussion of special run-time techniques for ALGOL 68. Parallel garbage collection is discussed in (Steele 1975) and (Dijkstra et al. 1978).

Exercises

4.1 What are the differences between Pascal's (and ALGOL 68's) type-definition facilities and abstract data types?

4.2 What is strong typing, and what are its benefits?

4.3 Give simple examples that show that Pascal is not strongly typed.

4.4   Design simple test programs to assess the type-compatibility rules adopted by your Pascal compiler.

4.5   Design simple test programs to verify the security of variant records in your Pascal implementation.

4.6   Design simple test programs to evaluate the security of pointers in your ALGOL 68 implementation.

4.7   Design simple test programs to evaluate the security of pointers in your Pascal implementation.

4.8   Discuss the problematical issues of Pascal enumerations according to the criticisms raised in (Welsh et al. 1977) and (Tennent 1978). Give simple programs to illustrate your points.

4.9   Is the mode

union (int, ref int)

legal in ALGOL 68? Why? Does a similar problem arise in Pascal?

4.10   The class *stack* declared in Section 4.6.1 has an attribute *first*, which is used to point to the first stack element, and the four attributes *pop, push, top,* and *empty,* which are used to operate on the stack instance. We discussed the problem that *first* is directly accessible from outside the class and thus unprotected. All variables and procedures declared in the outer block of a class are accessible from the outside. Why is it not possible to make *first* inaccessible by declaring it as a variable local to an inner block in the class? Can it be made local to one of the procedures?

4.11   Classes can be implemented by associating an activation record with each class. For each attribute, the activation record contains enough storage for its value if it is a variable, and a pointer to the code segment if it is a procedure. The code segment corresponding to the class implements the initialization code. The execution of a **new** statement causes the allocation of an activation record for the class and the execution of the initialization code.
   a.   Can activation records for classes be allocated on a stack?
   b.   Does each instance of a class require its own copy of the procedures that are attributes of the class?

4.12   How can discriminated unions be implemented in SIMULA 67? How can the INSPECT statement of SIMULA 67 be used to deal with discriminated unions in a safe way? What are the differences between this statement and the ALGOL 68 conformity clause?

4.13   What are the differences between SIMULA 67's classes and abstract data types?

4.14   What are the basic semantic differences between the CLU cluster and the Ada package?

4.15   Two CLU clusters with the following headings are given:

STACK = **cluster is** CREATE, PUSH, POP, TOP, EMPTY
QUEUE = **cluster is** CREATE, ENQUEUE, DEQUEUE, FIRST, EMPTY

Cluster STACK defines LIFO data structures. Cluster QUEUE defines FIFO data structures. Both abstract data types can store elements of the same type (say, integers).

a. Design a function SAME that gives a true result if the sequence of items extracted from a stack (via operation TOP) and from a queue (via procedure FIRST) are the same.

b. Function SAME would be more efficient if it had direct access to the data structures (e.g., arrays) used to represent stacks and queues. How can an Ada implementation solve this problem?

4.16 Let X be a n-dimensional Pascal array declared in procedure P, and let o be its offset within P's activation record. Let lb_1, lb_2, . . . lb_n and ub_1, ub_2, . . . , ub_n be the lower and upper bounds, respectively, of the n subscripts. How can the address of X [i_1, i_2 . . . i_n] be evaluated at run-time? (**Hint:** suppose that X is stored in row-major order).

4.17 How can mode **bits** of ALGOL 68 be used to implement powersets?

4.18 Assume that X is a subclass of Y: that is, X has been declared as Y **class** X **begin**. . .**end**. Given the two declarations

ref (X) a;
ref (Y) b;

SIMULA 67 allows both of the following assignment statements.

a: − b;
b: − a;

One of these two assignment statements can be used to show that SIMULA 67 is not strongly typed. Which one? (**Hint:** consider accessing attributes of the class after each of the assignments.) Propose a rule that would prevent such assignments. Are there reasons not to use your rule?

4.19 ALGOL 68 and Euclid adopt structural type equivalence. As mentioned in Section 4.5.2, recursively defined types might cause the type-checking algorithm to loop forever. How do these languages take care of the problem?

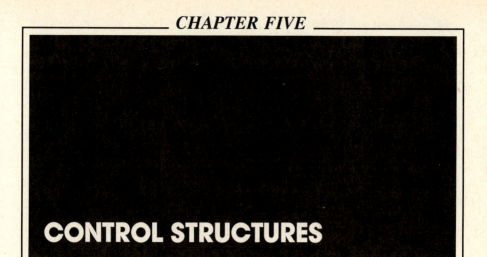

CHAPTER FIVE

CONTROL STRUCTURES

This chapter is devoted to a detailed analysis of control structures—the mechanisms by which programmers can specify the flow of execution among the components of a program. In Section 2.3, we distinguished between unit-level control structures and statement-level control structures. For simplicity, we will start our analysis with the latter category. Unit-level control structures and their implementation models will be studied in Section 5.2.

5.1 STATEMENT-LEVEL CONTROL STRUCTURES

There are three kinds of statement-level control structures: sequencing, selection, and repetition. We analyze each of these separately, in Sections 5.1.1 through 5.1.3.

Statement-level control structures strongly contribute to the readability and maintainability of programs. In fact, for the intellectual manageability of programming it is crucial that instructions be connected according to sufficiently simple, natural, and well-understood schemes.

5.1.1 Sequencing

Sequencing is the simplest structuring mechanism available in programming languages. It is used to indicate that the execution of a statement (B) must follow the execution of another statement (A). This is usually written as

$A;B$

where ";" (which can be read as "and then") denotes the sequencing control operator. Languages that adopt a line-oriented format (e.g., FORTRAN) use the end of the line implicitly to separate instructions and superimpose a sequencing mechanism among

129

them. It is possible to group together statements of a sequence to form a unique *compound* statement. Several languages (e.g., ALGOL 60 and Pascal) use the bracketing keywords **begin**, **end** for this purpose. For example: **begin** A; B; . . . **end**.

5.1.2 Selection

Selection control structures allow the programmer to specify that a choice is to be made among a certain number of possible alternative statements.

The logical IF statement of FORTRAN is an example of a selection statement that specifies the execution of a statement according to a boolean expression. For example, the FORTRAN statement

IF (I.GT.0) I= I−1

decreases the value of *I* by one if *I* is positive.

More general and powerful is the **if** statement of ALGOL-like languages, in which the presence of an **else** branch allows the programmer to choose between two control paths as a consequence of a test. Here, unlike in FORTRAN, a branch can be any statement (e.g., a compound statement). For example, the program fragment

```
if i = 0
  then i := j
  else begin i := i + 1;
            j := j − 1
       end
```

sets *i* to the value of *j* if $i=0$; otherwise, it sets *i* to $i+1$ and *j* to $j-1$. If the keywords **begin**, **end** were omitted, $j:=j-1$ would have been considered as a statement following the selection, and thus also executed in the case $i = 0$.

The selection construct of ALGOL 60 raises a well-known ambiguity problem. In the example

if $x>0$ **then if** $x<10$ **then** $x:= 0$ **else** $x:= 1000$

it is not clear whether the **else** branch is part of the innermost conditional (**if** $x<10$ . . .) or part of the outermost conditional (**if** $x>0$ . . .). The execution of the above statement with $x=15$ would assign 1000 to x under one interpretation, and leave it unchanged under the other. To eliminate ambiguity, the ALGOL 60 syntax requires an unconditional statement in the **then** branch of an **if** statement. Thus, the above fragment must be replaced either by

(i) **if** $x>0$ **then begin if** $x<10$ **then** $x:= 0$ **else** $x:= 1000$ **end**

or by

(ii) **if** *x>0* **then begin** *if x<10* **then** *x:= 0* **end else** *x:= 1000*

according to the desired interpretation.

The same problem is solved in PL/I and Pascal by automatically matching an **else** branch to the closest conditional without an **else.** Thus, the brackets **begin, end** would be unnecessary in case *(i)*. This disambiguation rule is explicitly stated in the language definition. Even though the rule removes the ambiguity, deeply nested conditional structures are difficult to read, especially if the program is written without careful indentation. It thus may be useful to use the brackets **begin, end** to make the desired interpretation explicit.

A syntactic variation that avoids this problem is adopted by ALGOL 68, which uses the keyword **fi** as an enclosing final bracket of the **if** statement. A sequence of statements is allowed between the keywords **then** and **else**, and between **else** and **fi**. This makes it unnecessary to use the brackets **begin, end** to construct a compound statement. Thus, the above examples may be coded in ALGOL 68 as

if *i=0*
  then *i:= j*
  else *i:= i+1;*
     j:= j−1
fi

and

if *x>0* **then if** *x<10* **then** *x:= 0* **else** *x:= 1000* **fi fi**

or

if *x>0* **then if** *x<10* **then** *x:= 0* **fi else** *x:= 1000* **fi**

according to the desired interpretation. A similar solution was adopted by Ada, which uses the keyword **end if** to close a selection.

Both ALGOL 68 and Ada allow the programmer to use an abbreviation if more alternatives can be chosen, depending on different conditions. For example, the awkward program fragment

if *a*
  then S_1
  else if *b*
      then S_2
      else if *c*
           then S_3
           else S_4
        fi
    fi
fi

can be written in ALGOL 68 by using the contraction **elif** (Ada uses **elsif**) and eliminating the **fi** (**end if** in Ada) of the inner clauses.

if *a*
   then S_1
elif *b*
   then S_2
elif *c*
   then S_3
   else S_4
fi

PL/I has recently adopted the special construct SELECT in order to specify selection among two or more branches. The above example can be coded in PL/I as

```
SELECT;
        WHEN (A) S₁;
        WHEN (B) S₂;
        WHEN (C) S₃;
        OTHERWISE S₄;
END;
```

Multiple-choice selection constructs are expressed in other languages, such as ALGOL 68, Pascal, and Ada, using the **case** statement, which specifies selection of a branch based upon the value of an expression. For example, the following Pascal fragment evaluates *result* by manipulating *operand1* and *operand2* according to a boolean operator specified by a character-valued variable *operator*.

var *operator: char;*
   operand1, operand2, result: boolean;
   .
   .
   .
   case *operator* **of**
       '.': *result:= operand1* **and** *operand2;*
       '+': *result:= operand1* **or** *operand2;*
       '=': *result:= operand1 = operand2*
   end

In ALGOL 68, selection of a **case** branch can only be based on the value of an integer expression. The value of such an expression—say, *i*—selects the *i*th branch for execution. Pascal selection, on the other hand, can be based on the value of an expression of any ordinal type, and branches are explicitly labeled by one or more values that can be evaluated by the expression. As a consequence, the order in which the branches appear in the text is immaterial.

The rich expressive power of the Pascal **case** unfortunately suffers from the possibility of producing unsafe programs. The language does not specify the effect of a value of the selecting expression that is out of the range of values explicitly listed, nor does it allow the programmer to specify in the construct which actions should be executed in this case. In ALGOL 68, an optional **out** clause can be specified; it is executed when the value of the selecting expression is not in the stated set of values. If the **out** clause is absent, it is equivalent to an **out** clause with a **skip** statement—which is equivalent to a null statement.

The Ada multiple-selection combines the positive aspects of ALGOL 68 and Pascal. First, branch selection can be done by using expressions of both enumeration and integer types. Second, it is required that all possible values of the type of the discriminating expression be provided in the selections. Third, the abbreviation **others** can be used to represent values that are not explicitly listed. Therefore, the multiple selection of the previous example might be coded in Ada as follows.

```
case OPERATOR of
    when "." => RESULT: = OPERAND1 and OPERAND2;
    when "+" => RESULT: = OPERAND1 or OPERAND2;
    when "=" => RESULT: = OPERAND1 = OPERAND2;
    when others => . . .produce error message . . .
end case;
```

A simple and powerful mechanism for specifying selection has been proposed by Dijkstra (Dijkstra 1976). The general form of the construct is

```
if B1 → S1
▯ B2 → S2
  - - -
▯ BN → SN
fi
```

where Bi, $1 \leqslant i \leqslant N$, is a boolean expression called a *guard* and $Si, 1 \leqslant i \leqslant N$ is a statement list. $Bi \rightarrow Si$, $1 \leqslant i \leqslant N$, is called a guarded command. The semantics of the **if** statement is that any Si for which the guard Bi evaluates to true, can be nondeterministically chosen for execution. If no guard evaluates to true, the program aborts; therefore, the programmer is forced to list all the possible choices.

The most interesting and novel feature of Dijkstra's construct is the abstraction that nondeterminism can provide. The programmer is not forced to overspecify programs when it is irrelevant which of a certain set of choices is actually chosen. For example, the maximum of two numbers A and B can be evaluated elegantly as

```
if A≥B → MAX: = A
▯  A≤B → MAX: = B
fi
```

As we will see in Section 5.2.4.3, Ada contains a specialized form of the guarded **if** statement.

5.1.3 Repetition

Most useful computations involve repetition of a number of actions. Consequently, all high-level languages provide control structures that allow the programmer to specify looping over a certain set of instructions.

FORTRAN provides the DO statement, with which a fixed number of iterations can be specified by introducing a counter (the *loop control variable*) that assumes values over a finite integer set. For example,

```
  DO 7 I = 1,10
      A(I) = 0
      B(I) = 0
7 CONTINUE
```

sets to zero the elements of index 1 through 10 of arrays *A* and *B*. Counter-driven iterative control structures are very useful and have been adopted by most programming languages, including COBOL, ALGOL 60, and PL/I. Pascal allows counter-driven loops where the counting variable is of any ordinal type, as shown in the following example.

type *day* = *(sunday, monday, tuesday, wednesday, thursday, friday, saturday);*
var *week_day: day;*

```
        -
        -
        -
```

    for *week_day:* = *monday* **to** *friday* **do**
```
        -
        -
        -
        -
```

Scanning days in reverse order can be written as

for *week_day:* = *friday* **downto** *monday* **do**. . .

Pascal also prescribes that the control variable and its lower and upper bounds not be altered in the loop. The value of the variable also is assumed to be undefined outside the loop. These restrictions, far from placing arbitrary constraints on the programmer, contribute to the readability and maintainability of the resulting programs by limiting the scope of the loop counter.

Repetition over a finite set of values can be used to model the frequent case in which the number of repetitions is known in advance, such as in the processing of arrays. Often, however, one does not know the number of repetitions in advance. For example, a program that processes all records in a file usually does not know the number of file elements. For this reason, most programming languages defined after FORTRAN provide condition-driven repetition structures: that is, repetition structures in which new iterations are executed until the value of a boolean expression is changed.

Pascal supports two condition-driven loop constructs. The first (**while** loop) describes any number of iterations, including zero. The second (**until** loop) describes loops with at least one iteration. The file processing program mentioned above can be written in Pascal as outlined below.

while not *eof(f)* **do**
    begin
        "read item from file f";
        "process item"
    end

The end-of-file condition *eof* is evaluated for file *f* before executing the body of the loop, and the loop is exited if **not** *eof* (*f*) is false. Therefore, the program also works correctly in the case of an empty file.

The **until** loop is similar, except that the exit condition is tested at the end of the loop body. In the above example, if the file always contains at least one element we could write

repeat
    "read item from file f";
    "process item"
until *eof* (*f*)

In this fragment, the loop is repeated as long as the condition *eof* (*f*) is false.

The counter-driven and the condition-driven control structures of Pascal are combined by PL/I and ALGOL 68 into a single form, which is composed of various, optional parts. The general form of the ALGOL 68 loop can be written as follows.

for *i* **from** *j* **by** *k* **to** *m* **while** *b* **do** . . . **od**

where **do** and **od** enclose the loop body and the **for**, **from**, **by**, **to**, and **while** clauses are all optional. If the **for** clause is omitted, there is no explicit loop-control variable. If the **from** clause is omitted, 1 is implicitly assumed as the starting value of the control variable. If the **by** clause is omitted, the value that increases the counter after each iteration is 1.

For example,

to 10 **do** *a*: = *a* + 2 **od**

adds 20 to *a*.

Leaving out **for, from, by,** and **to** gives a condition-driven loop; leaving out the **while** also gives an endless loop that must be exited explicitly from within the loop.

The control variable of the loop in ALGOL 68 cannot be modified within the loop (as in Pascal), and its scope is defined to be the loop body. Thus, it is inaccessible outside the loop. The values of the expressions following **by** and **to** can be altered within the loop. However, these expressions are evaluated only once, before the loop execution starts; any change to their operands within the loop does not affect the loop termination condition.

Ada has only one loop structure, with the following form.

iteration specification **loop**
      loop body
end loop

where iteration specification is either

while *condition*

or

for *counting_variable* **in** *discrete_range*

or

for *counting_variable* **in reverse** *discrete_range*

In addition, the loop can be terminated by an unconditional exit statement:

exit;

Or by a conditional exit statement:

exit when *condition*;

If the loop is nested within other loops, it is possible to exit an inner loop and any number of enclosing loops, as illustrated below.

MAIN _LOOP:
      loop
          .
          .
          .
          loop . . .
                  . . .
                  exit MAIN_LOOP **when** A = 0;

        end loop;
.
.
.

end loop MAIN_LOOP;
-- after the exit statement, execution continues from here

In the example, control is transferred to the statement following the end of MAIN_LOOP when *A* is found to be equal to zero in the inner loop.

    The **exit** statement is used to specify the premature termination of a loop. It has the same effect as the PL/I LEAVE statement.

    An interesting example of looping structures is provided by PLZ. The loop body is enclosed by the brackets **do, od**. An **exit** statement allows the programmer to specify an exit from any of the enclosing loops. A **repeat** statement can be used to terminate the current iteration of any of the enclosing loops and restart its execution from the first instruction of the loop body. An **exit** or **repeat** statement that does not specify the label of a loop, by default refers to the immediately enclosing loop. For example, a program that evaluates the number of times (n) a row (of length m) of a two-dimensional $k \times m$ array a equals, element by element, a one-dimensional array b (of length m), can be written as follows.

```
i: = 0
n: = 0
main: do
    i: = i+1
    if i>k then exit fi
    j: = 0
    do
        j: = j+1
        if j>m then exit fi
        if a [i,j] = b [j] then repeat from main fi
    od
    n: = n+1
od
```

The programming language C contains similar constructs.

    Using the Dijkstra's guarded commands notation, loops are specified by bracketing the commands by the keywords **do, od**.

```
do B1 → S1
 ▯   B2 → S2
     - - -
 ▯   BN → SN
od
```

The semantics of the statement is that at each iteration a statement Si is executed, whose guard Bi is true, $1 \leq i \leq N$. If two or more guards are true, a choice is made nondeterministically. If none is true, the loop terminates. Selection and repetition statements based on guarded commands encourage the production of well-structured and elegant algorithms. Moreover, as we will show in Section 6.4, programs written by using such notation are amenable to the formal reasonings of program correctness. This notation, however, has not been adopted by any existing programming language.

5.1.4   An Appraisal of Statement-Level Control Structures

Sequencing, selection, and repetition represent the programmer's basic control-structuring tools for organizing control flow among statements. Sequencing is an abstraction over the sequential fetch of instructions provided by the computer's program counter. Selection and repetition are abstractions over the very simple, but overly powerful, control mechanism provided by the hardware to modify explicitly the value of the program counter: that is, conditional and unconditional jumps.

There are several reasons why abstract control structures are preferred over the lower-level mechanisms of explicit control transfer. First, they are more problem-oriented, and thus programmers can more easily express their intentions by using the general patterns of sequencing, selection, and repetition. Second, by using explicit jumps, programs can easily assume the well-known unreadable spaghettilike structure shown in Figure 5.1. Higher-level control structures, obviously, ultimately will be translated into the conditional and unconditional jumps of the machine code of a traditional computer, but this fact should not concern the programmer. The burden of producing efficient machine code should rest entirely with the translator.

There is now widespread consensus that even in applications in which the efficiency of programs is the primary goal, obscurity engendered by the use of machine-level control structures is too high a price to be paid. There have been proposals for adding higher-level control structures into existing machine-level languages; more recently, there has been a move toward higher-level languages for systems software applications (e.g., Bliss, C, PLZ, Euclid, Ada).

As we have seen in Sections 5.1.2 and 5.1.3, however, a large variety of control structures have been proposed, and there is still no consensus on which are the best for inclusion in a programming language. Even though sequencing, selection (**if then else**), and repetition (**do while**) theoretically provide a sufficient set of control structures to code all the possible algorithms for a computer (Böhm and Jacopini 1966), using only these three control structures is often unnatural, and it results in awkward programs. Additional control structures, such as multiple selection (**case**), counter-driven loops (**for**), and condition-driven **until** loops, though theoretically redundant, can enhance the writability and readability of programs.

A typical case of the practical inadequacy of the above-cited restricted set of control structures arises when it is necessary to exit from the middle of a loop. As an example, suppose that a program processes a deck of cards, each card containing n integer values. The sum of the n values is zero for the last card of the deck. If the

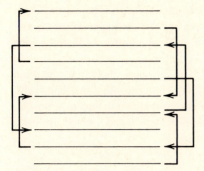

Figure 5.1   Spaghettilike structure produced by explicit jumps.

sum is not zero, the *n* values are "valid" and are further processed in an unspecified manner. The simplest solution to this problem can be abstractly written as follows.

do
read the *n* values and evaluate the sum;
if the sum is zero terminate the loop;
process the *n* valid values
od

Expressing the program in terms of a **while** loop leads to an undesirable duplication of parts, as shown below.

read *n* values and evaluate the *sum*;
while *sum* ≠ 0 **do**
    begin process the *n* values;
            read *n* values and evaluate the *sum*
    end

Similarly, expressing the program in terms of a **repeat until** loop leads to an unnecessary reevaluation of conditions:

repeat read *n* values and evaluate the *sum*;
      if the *sum* is not zero
          then process the *n* values
until the *sum* is zero

The initial solution, which uses an explicit control transfer to break the loop in the middle, is more natural to write, easier to understand, and more efficiently implementable.

Loops with exits in the middle can be easily coded with a **goto** statement. Since the unrestricted use of the **goto** statement can lead to badly structured programs but restricted uses of it are desirable in cases such as exit from a loop, several languages (e.g., Ada) provide a specific construct (**exit**) mirroring this case. The **exit** provides a restricted (and safe) form of forward **goto** that can only be used to terminate loops. A more general form of the **exit** statement, but one still more restricted than the **goto** statement, is given in Exercise 5.4.

There are also cases in which one would like to terminate the current iteration of a loop based on some condition that is discovered while executing the loop body. This can be coded in PLZ (or C) with a **repeat** (or **continue**, in C) statement. Consider the following example, in which the current iterations of loops B and A must terminate, and a new iteration of Loop A started, when x is true.

```
A: do . . .
      . . .
   B: do . . .
         if x then repeat from A
            . . .
      od
      . . .
      . . .
od
```

This example can be coded in Ada as

```
A: loop . . .
      . . .
   B: do . . .
         exit when x;
      end loop;
      if not x then
         . . .
         . . .
      end if
end loop
```

The Ada solution leads to an unnecessary reevaluation of the exit condition immediately after exiting the inner loop; to avoid this, a programmer might decide to code a solution that uses the **goto** statement.

This phenomenon is quite general. The lack of specialized control structures to solve a problem may lead to unnatural and inefficient solutions, if the **goto** statement is not available. On the other hand, we do not know exactly which specialized control structures should be provided to cover all programming needs. Most programming languages provide a rich set of disciplined control structures. Often, they also provide an unrestricted **goto** statement. Whether or not this is a good language-design choice is controversial. If programs are designed in a disciplined way, the usefulness of the **goto** statement arises only occasionally. However, when the **goto** statement is available, there is no way to enforce a restricted use of it, and programmers can easily produce spaghettilike programs. The only, partial solution consists of adopting a programming standard that relies on **goto**s only for synthesizing "legitimate" control structures when the language does not provide them. Legitimacy can be defined based on the needs of the application.

To summarize, many factors influence the choice of the set of control structures to be included in a language, and it is difficult to argue in absolute terms the merits of different solutions. For example, minimality of the set of control structures, which appears to be a reasonable goal as far as the ease of learning of a language is concerned, conflicts with other goals, such as expressive power.

5.1.5   User-Defined Control Structures

An interesting property of the Pascal counter-based loop is that the control variable can be of any ordinal type, not just a subset of integers. Further abstraction is provided by languages such as CLU, Alphard, and Euclid, which allow the programmer to have control variables of any abstract data type and provide constructs for specifying how the sequence of values of such control variables is to be produced. Such languages can be viewed as *extensible*, because the user can augment the base language by defining new (abstract) data types, new operations (via procedures), and also new control structures. Our presentation of user-defined control structures will be based on the constructs provided by CLU.

In the CLU program fragment

for *atom : node* **in** *list (x)* **do**
    perform an action on atom

atom, the loop control variable, is of user-defined type *node*, and *list* is an *iterator*, which is a particular program unit yielding the sequence of values the **for** loop is to span. These instructions are meant to retrieve and manipulate all the nodes belonging to a list *x*.

The elements of the collection (a list, in the above example) are provided by the iterator one at a time. The policy that selects the next element of the collection is hidden to the user of the iterator and implemented by the iterator. The iterator used above can be specified by a module that takes a parameter of abstract type *linked_list* and delivers a parameter of abstract type *node*.

list = **iter** *(z: linked_list)* **yields** *(node)*
                -
                -
                -
        yield *(n)*
                -
                -
                -
    end *list*

At each iteration of the above loop (**for** *atom* . . .), module *list* is activated, and a node yielded by it—by the operation **yield**—is assigned to *atom* (remember that CLU has an assignment by sharing—Section 4.6.2.1—and therefore *atom* denotes the same object delivered by *list*). As a consequence of yielding, the iterator is suspended, its local environment is retained, and control flows back to the loop invocation. At each loop iteration, the iterator is resumed in the saved local environment, much like a coroutine. When the iterator indicates that the sequence of objects is exhausted, the **for** statement terminates.

CLU iterators are called only by **for** statements and each **for** statement invokes exactly one iterator. Thus, active invocations are always nested and can be implemented easily via a stack policy, as shown below.

5.1.5.1   Implementation Model for Iterators

We can distinguish among the following four actions associated with an iterator.

- Calling an iterator, corresponding to the first activation of an iterator caused by the initiation of a **for** loop.

- Resuming an iterator, corresponding to any activation of the iterator after the first iteration.

- Yielding: that is, the action of transferring control back from the iterator to the program executing the **for** statement.

- Returning from an iterator, when the **end** of the iterator is reached.

The iterator's activation record contains two return points and a dynamic link. The first return point (*normal return point*) is the address of the first instruction of the body of the **for** loop that calls the iterator. The second return point (*final return point*) is the address of the first instruction after the **for** loop: that is, the instruction to be executed upon termination of the iterator. The dynamic link points to the activation record of the unit that executes the loop. The activation record of that unit contains an additional entry (the *resume link*), which is used to chain together in an *iterator chain* the information necessary to resume suspended iterators invoked by the current module (if any).

Calling an iterator resembles a conventional subprogram call: the activation record of the iterator is stacked, and the return points and the dynamic link (to the calling unit's activation record) are set.*

Yielding is different from the usual return from a procedure, because the activation record of the iterator remains on the stack. First, a *resume frame* is pushed onto the stack. The resume frame contains the information necessary to resume the iterator on the next iteration: that is, the address of the instruction where control will go after the iterator is resumed (*return point*) and a reference to the activation record

---

*CLU modules are not statically nested and have no global variables. Therefore there is no static link. Other languages with an ALGOL-like structure can be accommodated easily in this scheme.

of the iterator (*iterator link*). Second, resume frames are linked together via a resume link to form the iterator chain of the calling module, as explained below. Finally, the yielded value is assigned (by sharing) to the loop control variable of the invoking **for**, and control is transferred to the normal return point specified in the iterator's activation record.

The iterator chain is a last-in/first-out data structure. After the body of a loop is executed, the resume frame of the iterator to be resumed is the one last inserted into the iterator chain for the current activation record. Such a resume frame is removed from the chain, and the information contained in it is used to resume the iterator.

Finally, returning from an iterator is identical to the normal return from a subprogram: the iterator's activation record is removed from the stack, and control transfers to the final return point specified therein.

The following example illustrates these mechanisms. Suppose that a module *M* contains the following nested loops.

for . . . **in** *iter1* . . . **do**
    for. . . **in** *iter2*. . . **do**
       -
       -
       -

Also, suppose that module *iter2* contains the following loop.

for . . . **in** *iter3*. . . **do**
    -
    -
    -

When *M* calls *iter*1, the activation record IR1 is pushed on top of the stack. Yielding then pushes the resume frame RF1, and the resume link from *M*'s activation record (*M*R) is set to point to RF1. A call to *iter2* caused by the execution of *M*'s inner loop then pushes IR2 on top of the stack. A subsequent call to *iter3* from *iter2*, followed by yielding from *iter3*, pushes IR3 and RF3 on top of the stack, and the resume link from IR2 is set to point to RF3. Finally, yielding from *iter2* to *M* pushes RF2 on top of the stack, and inserts RF2 into the iterator chain originating in *M*R. After this action, the resume link from *M*R points to RF2, and the resume link from RF2 points to RF1. Figure 5.2 sketches the configuration of the execution stack at this point. Details of the structure of activation records are omitted for simplicity; only that information necessary to manage the execution stack is shown explicitly.

5.2 UNIT-LEVEL CONTROL STRUCTURES

This section discusses programming language mechanisms for specifying control flow among program units. The simplest mechanism is exemplified by the ALGOL 60 block, which creates a new referencing environment and is executed when it is en-

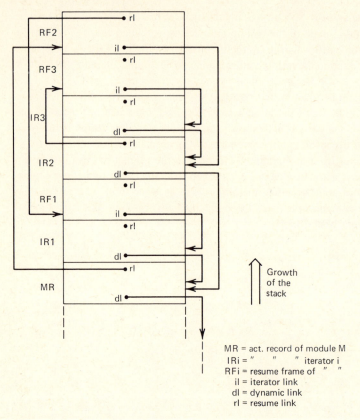

RF2 — rl
il — rl
RF3 — rl
il — rl
IR3 — dl — rl
IR2 — dl — rl
RF1 — rl
il — rl
IR1 — dl — rl
MR — dl

Growth
of the
stack

MR = act. record of module M
IRi = "   "   " iterator i
RFi = resume frame of "   "
il = iterator link
dl = dynamic link
rl = resume link

Figure 5.2   Configuration of the execution stack in the presence of iterators.

countered during the sequential progression of execution. More powerful mechanisms allow the programmer to transfer control from one unit to another by means of explicit *unit calls.*

In most cases, the called unit is subordinate to the caller. In other words, the caller explicitly names its subordinate unit, whereas such a unit simply transfers control back to the caller: that is, to an implicitly specified unit. This is the case of *subprograms,* in which control is transferred back by executing a *return* operation. The unit being returned to is implicit. There are cases in which the called unit is also implicit, such as for *exception handlers.* A unit may raise an exception and implicitly activate an exception handler bound to that exception. Units can also be organized in a symmetrical scheme as a set of *coroutines,* in which case both units explicitly activate one another. The units proceed in an interleaved fashion. Finally, units can be organized as a set of *concurrent* (or *parallel*) *units* (*processes*). With concurrent processes, there is no notion of control being passed back and forth between units. Each is considered an autonomous unit.

The following sections contain a discussion of unit-level control structures according to the classification scheme given above.

5.2.1 Explicitly Called Subordinate Units

This class covers the case of subprograms from FORTRAN subroutines and functions to Ada procedures. The basic run-time modeling issues of unit activation and return have been presented in Chapter 3. In this section we will cover in particular one important point deliberately left out of our previous discussion: passing parameters across subprograms.

Parameter passing allows for the communication of data among program units. Unlike communication via global environments, parameters allow for the transfer of different data at each call and provide advantages in terms of readability and modifiability.

Most programming languages use a positional method for binding actual to formal parameters in subprogram calls. If the procedure is declared as

subprogram *S (F1,F2, . . . Fn);*

.
.
.

end *S*

and the subprogram call is

call *S (A1,A2, . . . An)*

then the positional method implies that the formal parameter Fi is to be bound to actual parameter Ai, $i = 1,2, . . . n$. The positional method has some disadvantages in terms of readability when the parameter list is long. An alternative form of parameter passing (optional, in Ada) is known as *keyword method*. Procedure calls explicitly list the correspondence between actual and formal parameters. For example, a subprogram *init* with formal parameters *table* and *value*, intended to initialize all components of the integer array *table* to the value of *value*, can be called by writing (in a hypothetical syntax)

init (*table* **is** *x, value* **is** *v*)

where *x* and *v* are the actual parameters corresponding to *table* and *value*, respectively.

The keyword method is particularly valuable if the language allows default bindings to be specified for formal parameters. In such a case, a subprogram call can specify simply a subset of the actual parameters. In the example, if the subprogram heading specifies 0 as a default value for *v*, inserting all zeroes into array *b* can be written as

init (*table* **is** *b*)

We can divide program entities that can be passed as parameters into three classes: data, subprograms, and types. Passing a type to a generic procedure involves the issues described in Section 4.7.3 for generic abstract data types. We will study data parameters in the next section and subprogram parameters in Section 5.2.1.2.

5.2.1.1 Data Parameters

There are different conventions for passing parameters to subprograms. It is important to know which convention is adopted by a language, because the choice affects the semantics of the language. The same program may produce different results under different data parameter passing conventions (see, for example, Exercise 5.5).

Three conventions for data parameter passing are described in Sections 5.2.1.1.1 through 5.2.1.1.3.

5.2.1.1.1 Call by Reference (or by Sharing)   The calling unit passes to the called unit the address of the actual parameter (which is in the calling unit's environment). A reference to the corresponding formal parameter in the called unit is treated as a reference to the location whose address is so passed. A variable that is transmitted as an actual parameter is thus shared—that is, directly modifiable by the subprogram. If an actual parameter is an expression, the subprogram receives the address within the calling unit's activation record of a temporary location that contains the value of the expression.

In terms of the model presented in Chapter 3, addresses of parameters can be stored in specific locations of the activation record of the called unit, and references to the parameters within the called unit can be treated as indirect references through these locations. Since a subprogram has a fixed number of parameters, the required number of such locations and their offsets are fixed statically.

5.2.1.1.2 Call by Copy   In call by copy—unlike in call by reference—formal parameters do not share storage with actual parameters; rather, they act as local variables. Thus, call by copy protects the calling unit from inadvertent modifications of actual parameters. It is possible further to classify call by copy into three modes, according to the way local variables corresponding to formal parameters are initialized and the way their values ultimately affect the actual parameters. These three modes are call by value, by result, and by value-result.

In *call by value*, the calling unit evaluates the actual parameters, and these values are used to initialize the formal parameters, which act as local variables in the called unit. Call by value does not allow any flow of information back to the caller, since assignments to formal parameters do not affect the calling unit.

In *call by result*, local variables corresponding to formal parameters are not set at subprogram call, but their value, at termination, is copied back into the actual parameter's location within the environment of the caller. Call by result does not permit any flow of information to the called unit.

In *call by value-result*, local variables denoting formal parameters are both initialized at subprogram call (as in call by value) and delivered upon termination (as in call by result).

5.2.1.1.3 Call by Name As in call by reference, a formal parameter, rather than being a local variable of the subprogram, denotes a location in the environment of the caller. Unlike with call by reference, however, the formal parameter is not bound to a location at the point of call; rather, it is bound to a (possibly different) location each time it is used with the subprogram. As a consequence, each assignment to a formal parameter can refer to a different location. Basically, in call by name each occurrence of the formal parameter is considered to be replaced textually by the actual parameter. This apparently simple rule can lead to unsuspected complications. For example, the following procedure, which is intended to interchange the values of *a* and *b* (*a* and *b* are by-name parameters)

procedure *swap (a,b: integer);*
var *temp: integer;*
begin *temp:= a;*
      a:= b;
      b:= temp
end *swap;*

can produce unexpected and incorrect results when invoked by the call

swap (i, a [i])

The replacement rule specifies that the statements to be executed are

temp:= i;
i:= a [i];
a [i]:= temp

If $i = 3$ and $a [3] = 4$ before the call, $i = 4$ and $a [4] = 3$ after the call (*a* [3] is unaffected)!

    Another trap is that the actual parameter that is (conceptually) substituted into the text of the called unit belongs to the referencing environment of the caller, not to that of the called unit activation. For example, suppose that procedure *swap* also counts the number of times it is called and that it is embedded in the following fragment.

procedure *x. . .*
var *c: integer;*
. . . . . .
    procedure *swap (a, b: integer);*
    var *temp: integer;*
    begin *temp:= a; a:=b;*
        b:= temp; c:= c+1
    end *swap*

```
procedure y . . .
var c, d: integer;
    . . . . . . .
    swap (c, d);
    . . . . . . .
end y;
```
end *x;*

When procedure *swap* is called by procedure *y*, the replacement rule specifies that the statements to be executed are

temp:= c; c:= d;
d:= temp; c:= c+1

However, the location bound to name *c* in the last statement belongs to procedure *x*'s activation record, whereas the location bound to the previous occurrences of *c* belong to *y*'s activation record. Notice that the problem is not the identification of the actual parameter—that can be done easily at translation time. The problem is the difficulty encountered by the programmer in foreseeing the run-time binding of actual and formal parameters.

Call by name, therefore, can easily lead to programs that are hard to read. It is also hard to implement. The basic implementation technique consists of replacing each reference to a formal parameter with a call to a subprogram (traditionally called *thunk*) that evaluates a reference to the actual parameter in the appropriate environment. One such thunk is created for each actual parameter. Obviously, the burden of run-time calls to thunks makes call by name costly.

Call by reference is the standard parameter passing mode of FORTRAN. Call by name is standard in ALGOL 60, but, optionally, the programmer can specify call by value. SIMULA 67 provides call by value, call by reference, and call by name.

Pascal allows the programmer to pass parameters either by value or by reference. For example, the heading of the procedure

procedure *x (y: integer;* **var** *z: newtype)*

specifies that *y* is passed by value, whereas *z* (of type *newtype*) is passed by reference (indicated by the keyword **var**). The choice whether to pass a parameter by value or by reference can be dictated by several considerations, such as the desire to avoid unwanted side-effects caused by inadvertent modification of formal parameters, or efficiency of implementation. In general, passing parameters by reference can be costly in terms of processing time if the formal parameters are used very often within the subprogram, because each access requires indirect addressing. However, if objects are large and/or are accessed only a few times, call by copy can be costly both in terms of storage and in terms of processing time.

ALGOL 68 has a single parameter-passing mechanism, which is similar to call by value. However, a parameter can be of type **ref m**: that is, its value is a reference to a data object of type **m**. Therefore, it is also possible to achieve the effect of call by reference.

More precisely, the meaning of the call

p (*i*)

on procedure

proc *p* = *(***int** *a)* **void**:
    (. . .body. . .)

is stated to be the same as

*(***int** *a* = *i;*
(. . .body. . .))

Therefore, *a* is set identically equal to *i*: that is, it acts as a constant integer within the scope of the call. So the parameter is almost like call by value, except that it cannot be changed.

Had the procedure been declared

proc *p* = *(***ref int** *a)* **void**:
    (. . .body. . .)

then the call *p* (*i*) would have been (conceptually) expanded to

*(***ref int** *a* = *i;*
(. . .body. . .))

which enables the procedure to access the actual parameter *i* through the reference *a*. This is, exactly, call by reference. The rich type structure and the orthogonality of ALGOL 68 are thus exploited to obtain a uniform parameter passing mechanism.

Call by result can model the so-called function subprograms provided by languages such as Pascal, where the name of the function subprogram acts as a local variable that will ultimately contain the value produced by the function subprogram itself.

Ada provides three parameter-passing conventions: **in**, **out**, and **in out**. By default, an unspecified convention is taken as **in**. An **in** formal parameter acts as a local constant whose value is provided by the corresponding actual parameter and cannot be modified by the subprogram. An **out** formal parameter acts as a local variable whose value is assigned to the corresponding actual parameter upon exit from the subprogram. An **in out** formal parameter acts as a local variable and permits access and assignment to the corresponding actual parameter. The Ada definition does not say whether parameter passing must be implemented by sharing or by copy. The choice between the two implementations is left entirely to the translator, which may choose on the basis of efficiency. Ada programs that would produce different results under the two implementations of parameter passing are called "erroneous." Unfortunately, however, the translator cannot catch erroneous programs, and therefore such programs may produce different results when moved to a different installation. The reason for the possible discrepancy between the two implementations is that in passing parameters by copy, the local variable associated with a formal parameter occupies a fresh local storage. Call by reference, on the other hand, creates a new access path to a location that may be accessible by the same subprogram via other access paths (e.g., a global name). This issue is analyzed in more detail in Section 6.2.

5.2.1.2   Subprogram Parameters

Passing subprograms as parameters is useful in many practical situations. For example, a subprogram S that evaluates analytic properties of functions of a single variable in a given interval $a..b$ can be written without knowledge of the function and can be used for different functions, if the values of the function are produced by a subprogram that is sent to S as a parameter. As another example, if the language does not provide explicit features for exception handling, one can transmit the exception handler as a subprogram parameter to the unit that may raise the exception.

   Although useful, subprogram parameters can easily promote the creation of obscure programs, because of the difficulties in understanding their referencing environments—as the following discussion will show. To simplify matters, we will restrict our attention here to languages with static scope rules, à la ALGOL.

   Transmitting a subprogram as a parameter requires at least passing a reference to the code segment of the actual parameter. However, the subprogram being passed can also access nonlocal variables, and thus it is also necessary to pass information about the nonlocal environment of the actual subprogram parameter. In ALGOL-like languages, the nonlocal environment that can be accessed by a subprogram P, which is sent as parameter in a call such as $X(P)$, is the one that is bound to P when $X(P)$ is issued. In other words, if Y is the subprogram that makes the call $X(P)$, the nonlocal environment associated with parameter P is determined by the static chain originating in the activation record that contains a definition of P, and that is visible when Y is executed. Consequently, subprogram parameters can be represented by a pair: a pointer pc to the code segment; and a pointer pa to the activation record of the unit that contains the subprogram definition. A call to the subprogram parameter requires installing the activation record on top of the stack, setting the static link to the value of pa, and transferring control to the code specified by pc.

   For example, consider the following fragment.

procedure *main* . . .

   . . . .

```
      procedure a . . .
            . . . . . . . .
      end a;
      procedure b (procedure x);
      var y: integer;
            procedure c . . . .
                  . . . . . . .
                  y: = . . . . ;
                  . . . . . . . .
            end c ;
            x;
            b (c);
            . . . . .
      end b;
      . . . . . .
      b (a);
      . . . . .
end main;
```

Procedure *main* calls *b* with procedure *a* as a parameter. The call to *x* issued by procedure *b* activates procedure *a*. Procedure *b* is then called recursively, with procedure *c* as a parameter. The execution stacks before and after this call are shown in Figures 5.3**a** and 5.3**b**, respectively. (For simplicity's sake, variable names are used in the activation records, although according to the discussion of Section 3.6 this is not necessary.) The execution of a new call to *x* at this point activates procedure *c* (figure 5.3**c**). This example shows that when procedure parameters are used in a program, nonlocal variables visible at a given point are not necessarily those of the latest allocated activation record of the unit where such variables are locally declared. For example, the assignment to *y* performed by procedure *c* modifies the contents of a location that is not in the topmost activation record for *b*, but in the next one (Figure 5.3**c**).

5.2.2 Implicitly Called Units

This section analyzes units that are called implicitly when an exception condition arises. The concept of "exception condition" can hardly be stated in absolute terms. Programs are often required to behave "reasonably" under a wide range of circumstances, even in the presence of a failure of the underlying hardware/software supports, or of events that happen so infrequently as to be considered anomalous, or of invalid input data. However, what is considered to be a "normal" processing state is a design decision taken by the designer, and it depends on the nature of the application. As a consequence, an "anomalous" processing state (or *exception*) does not necessarily mean that we are in the presence of a "catastrophic" error, but rather that the unit

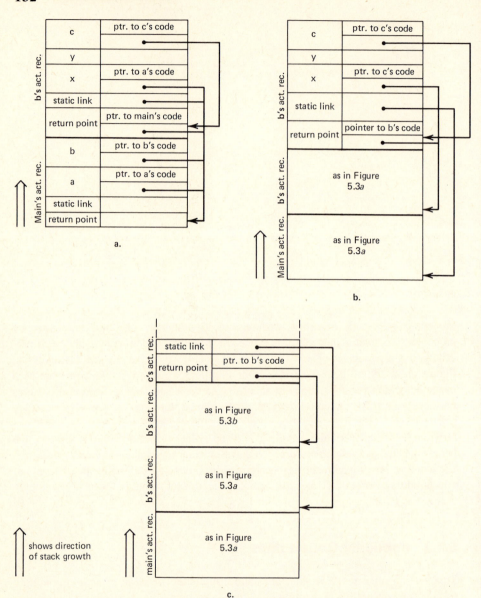

Figure 5.3 Evolution of the execution stack in the presence of procedure parameters.

executing is unable to proceed in a manner that leads to normal termination. The inability of the program to trap anomalous processing states and to handle them appropriately can produce software that works only under certain circumstances; it is not *fault-tolerant*.

Traditional programming languages (except PL/I) offer no special help in properly handling anomalous processing states. A number of more recent languages, however, provide *ad hoc* exception-handling features. With these features, the concern for anomalies may be moved out of the main line of program flow, so as not to obscure the basic algorithm.

The central issues raised by exception handling schemes are

1. How is an exception declared, and what is its scope?

2. How is an exception raised?

3. How do we specify the units intended to be executed when exceptions are raised (*exception handlers*)?

4. How is a raised exception bound to a handler?

5. Where does control flow after an exception is handled?

We examine question 5 first, because its solution has a strong impact on the power and the usability of the mechanism. The basic language design choice is whether, after execution of the appropriate exception handler, to allow control to return to the point where the exception was raised. In such a case, the exception handler can perform some repairing actions and terminate, so that normal execution can continue. This point of view has been adopted by PL/I and Mesa. The resulting mechanism is very powerful and flexible, but it turns out to be difficult to master for inexperienced programmers. In fact, it can promote the unsafe programming practice of removing the symptom of an error without removing the cause. For example, the exception raised for an unacceptable value of an operand could be handled by arbitrarily generating an acceptable value.

The other solution consists of terminating the execution of the unit that raises the exception and then transferring control to the exception handler. Conceptually, this means that the action that raised the exception cannot be resumed. From an implementation point of view, this means that the activation record of the signaling unit can be deleted. Bliss, CLU, and Ada adopt this simpler scheme.

We will now review the exception handling features offered by a number of languages.

5.2.2.1 Exception Handling in PL/I

Exceptions are called CONDITIONS in PL/I. Exception handlers are declared by ON statements:

ON CONDITION (*exception_name*) *exception_handler*

where *exception_handler* can be a simple statement or a block. An exception is explicitly raised by the statement

SIGNAL CONDITION (exception_name);

The language also defines a number of built-in exceptions and provides system-defined handlers for them. Built-in exceptions are automatically raised by the execution of some statements (e.g., ZERODIVIDE is raised when, during the evaluation of an expression, the denominator of a division is found to be zero). The action performed by a system-provided handler is specified by the language. This action can be redefined, however, as with user-defined exceptions:

```
ON ZERODIVIDE BEGIN;
                . . .
        END;
```

When an ON unit is encountered during execution, a new binding takes place between an exception and a handler. Once this association is established, it remains valid until it is overridden by the execution of another ON statement for the same exception, or until termination of the block in which the ON statement is executed. If more than one ON statement for the same exception appears in the same block, each new binding overrides the previous one. If a new ON statement for the same exception appears in an inner block, the new binding remains in force only until the inner block is terminated. When control exits a block, the bindings that existed prior to block entry are reestablished.

When an exception is raised (either automatically, or by a SIGNAL statement), the handler currently bound to the exception is executed as if it were a subprogram invoked explicitly at that point. Therefore, unless otherwise specified by the handler, control subsequently will return to the point that issued the SIGNAL.

We see from the above discussion that the binding is highly dynamic between an exception raised in a certain point of the program and the exception handler that is invoked. As a consequence, PL/I programs that use these constructs can be rather awkward—difficult to write and to understand. Moreover, the language does not allow the programmer to pass parameters from the point raising the exception to the exception handler. Consequently, the necessary information flow can only be established by using global variables, which can be an unsafe programming practice. Furthermore, use of global variables is not always possible. For example, when a STRINGRANGE exception is raised, indicating an attempt to access beyond a string's bounds, there is no practical way for the exception handler to know which string is involved if two or more strings are visible in the scope. Such situations often make the PL/I exception handling useless.

PL/I exception handling mechanisms can be complicated further by explicitly *enabling* and *disabling* built-in exceptions; user-defined exceptions cannot be disabled, because they must be explicitly signaled anyway. Most built-in exceptions are enabled by default and bound to the standard system-provided error handler. Enabling a previously disabled exception (or an exception that is not enabled by default) can be specified by prefixing a statement, block, or procedure with the exception name. For example,

```
(ZERODIVIDE): BEGIN;
                 . . . .
         END;
```

The scope of the prefix is static; it is the statement, block or procedure to which it is attached. An enabled exception can be explicitly disabled by prefixing a statement, block, or procedure with NO*exception_name*. For example,

(NOZERODIVIDE): BEGIN;

. . . .

END;

5.2.2.1.1 Implementation Model   We will now outline an implementation of the PL/I exception handling mechanism. When an ON unit is encountered during exe-cution, the condition name and the reference to the handler's code are saved in an entry of the current unit's activation record. All entries of established ON units for a given unit activation U are made accessible through a fixed location in U's activation record. When a condition is raised, ON unit entries are searched, starting from the most recent, until an established ON unit for that condition is found. If none is found, the default action is taken. The main disadvantage of this implementation is that the search may take a significant amount of time. That search only takes place, however, when an exception is raised. We can increase the efficiency of the search by adding to the cost of block exit and ON-unit processing. In particular, we can keep a table for all conditions that a program may raise. The entry for a condition C is a pointer to a stack of pointers to established ON-unit activation records for C. All stacks are empty initially. When an ON-unit is encountered during execution, a new entry is inserted on top of the appropriate stack. When a block activation terminates, all stacks pushed during that activation may be popped.

5.2.2.2   Exception Handling in CLU

CLU's exception handling features are less powerful than those provided by PL/I, but they are easier to use and seem to provide effective ways of handling anomalous situations.

Exceptions can only be raised by procedures. The exceptions that a procedure may signal are declared in the heading of the procedure. An exception is explicitly raised by means of a *signal* instruction. Built-in operations can raise a known set of exceptions; for example, a division can signal that the value of the denominator is zero.

When an exception is raised, the procedure returns to its immediate caller, which is responsible for providing a handler for the exception. Unlike PL/I, the procedure that raises the exception cannot be resumed, even after performing some recovery actions. Furthermore, the exception handler is statically bound to the point of call.

Exception handlers are bound to statements by means of **except** clauses in the syntactic form

⟨*statement*⟩ **except** ⟨*handler_list*⟩ **end**

where ⟨*statement*⟩ can be any (compound) statement of the language. If the execution of a procedure invocation within ⟨*statement*⟩ raises an exception, control transfers to ⟨*handler_list*⟩. A ⟨*handler_list*⟩ has the following form.

when ⟨*exception_list_1*⟩: ⟨*statement_1*⟩

⎯

⎯

when ⟨*exception_list_n*⟩: ⟨*statement_n*⟩

If the raised exception belongs to ⟨*exception_list_i*⟩, then ⟨*statement_i*⟩ (the handler body) is executed. When execution of the handler is completed, control passes to the statement following the one to which the handler is attached. If ⟨*statement_i*⟩ contains a call to a unit, another exception can be raised. In such a case, control flows to the **except** statement that encloses ⟨*statement*⟩. If the raised exception is not named in any exception list, then the process is repeated for the statically enclosing statements. If no handler is found within the procedure that issued the call, the procedure implicitly signals a language-defined exception **failure** and returns.

Another notable difference from PL/I is that exceptions can return parameters to their handlers, thus avoiding unnecessary global variables. A typical example is the **failure** exception whose return value is a string denoting the uncaught exception.

By deliberate choice, the design of CLU does not provide mechanisms for disabling exceptions. The argument is that unless an exception is proven not to occur, it would be unsafe to disable it. Also, disabling exceptions that can be proven not to occur can be done by an optimizing compiler, which would then save in both time spent in trying to detect impossible exceptions and in space used for handlers.

5.2.2.2.1 Implementation Model   The implementation of CLU's exception handling is rather straightforward: when an exception is signaled, control returns to its caller as if it were a normal return—the only difference here being that the return point is not the instruction that follows the call, but the closest exception handler.

The implementation of CLU associates each procedure with a (fixed-contents) *handler table*, which stores information about all the handlers provided by the procedure. Each entry of the table contains

a.   The list of exceptions handled by the handler.

b.   A pair of pointers to the portion of text of the calling procedure to which the handler is attached (the scope of the handler).

c.   A pointer to the code for the handler.

When an exception is raised within procedure P, the address of the instruction that issued the call is found in the caller's activation record, and this value is used to find the appropriate return point by searching P's handler table.

5.2.2.3   Exception Handling in Ada

Ada's exception handling features have similarities to the schemes used in Bliss and Gypsy. They also show resemblances to the CLU approach.

A program unit can explicitly raise an exception, as in

raise HELP;

Exception handlers can be attached to a subprogram body, a package body, or a block, after the keyword **exception**. For example,

begin . . .
exception when HELP => . . .
   when DESPERATE => . . .
end;

  If the unit that raises the exception provides a handler for the exception, control is transferred immediately to that handler: the actions following the point at which the exception is raised are skipped, the handler is executed, and then the unit terminates. If the currently executing unit U does not provide a handler, the exception is propagated. If U is a block, its execution terminates and the exception is implicitly reraised in the enclosing unit. If U is a subprogram body, the subprogram returns and the exception is implicitly reraised at the point of call. If U is a package body, it acts like a procedure that is implicitly called when the package declaration is processed. If there is no handler associated with the package body, the exception is propagated to the unit that contains the package declaration.

  Ada's exception handling mechanism is multilevel, as opposed to the single-level mechanism of CLU. In other words, in Ada the exception raised by a unit may also be handled by units other than its immediate caller. The CLU restriction can be justified on the basis of methodical programming. In particular, CLU views a procedure as the implementation of an abstract action. The caller of a procedure wants the procedure to execute its abstract action, and need not know about its internal workings. The exceptions that a procedure may raise characterize the abstract behavior of the procedure, and thus must be known to the caller. However, the caller should not know about the exceptions raised by procedures that are (locally) used in the implementation of an abstract action. Obviously, a multilevel scheme can be explicitly programmed in CLU by having the caller signal the same exception as is raised by the invoked procedure. However, in such a case the exception would be explicitly part of the caller's abstraction. The same reasoning also explains why a CLU procedure must return upon an exception and cannot be resumed. To handle the exception in a way that allows the called unit to continue, requires the caller to know about the internal structure of the called unit.

  Again in contrast to Ada, CLU does not allow the unit that raises the exception to handle it. The justification for this is that by definition, exceptions are anomalous conditions that the signalling procedure is unable to handle. The Ada choice on this point, however, seems to be preferable, because it allows the programmer to specify easily some cleanup actions that the called unit might wish to execute before returning. CLU would require passing parameters back to the caller's handler in order to let it do the cleanup. This is probably one reason why Ada does not provide parameter passing to exception handlers.

5.2.2.3.1 Implementation Model The implementation of Ada's exception handling scheme can be accomplished by using the handler table concept of the CLU implementation. The basic difference is that the exception handler is not necessarily provided by the immediate caller; therefore, it might be necessary to traverse the dynamic chain of procedure invocations to locate an entry for the required handler.

5.2.3 Symmetrical Units: Coroutines in SIMULA 67

Symmetrical units (coroutines) can be viewed as a group of program units that activate one another explicitly. As we saw in Section 2.3, when control is transferred to a unit, its execution resumes at the place following where it last terminated. As a consequence, units run in an interleaved fashion, according to a predefined pattern of behavior.

This section provides a simplified view of the SIMULA 67 mechanism for instantiating symmetrical units and for switching control from one coroutine to another.

A SIMULA 67 coroutine is an instance of a **class** whose general form is the following.

class *x (parameters);*
        parameter declarations;
begin
        declarations;
        statement_list_1;
        detach;
        statement_list_2
end

If variables *y*1 and *y*2 are *references* to *x,* we can write

*y*1: − **new** *x* (. . .); *y*2: − **new** *x* (. . .)

When **new** is encountered, a new instance of the class is created and the class body is executed. As soon as **detach** is encountered, control is transferred back to the unit that issued the **new**. As a consequence of **detach**, the unit activation now behaves as a coroutine that can be resumed and, in turn, can resume other coroutines.

For example, a four-player card game, in which all players use the same strategy, can be described as follows.

begin boolean *gameover;* **integer** *winner;*
        class *player (n, hand);* **integer** *n;*
                                integer array *hand (1:13);*

        begin ref *(player) next;*
                detach;
                while ¬ *gameover* **do**
                begin *execute a move;*
                        if *gameover* **then** *winner:= n*
                                else *resume(next)*

```
            end
    end;

    ref (player) array p (1:4); integer i;
    integer array cards (1:13);

    for i:= 1 step 1 until 4 do
    begin generate the cards for the hand of player i in array cards;
            p (i):= new player (i, cards)
    end;

    for i:= 1 step 1 until 3 do
        p (i).next:– p (i+1);
    p (4).next:– p (1);

    resume p (1);
    print the winner's name
end
```

The first loop of the program (**for** $i:=$ **step** 1 **until** 4 **do** . . .) creates the four players. They are subsequently linked together by the next loop (**for** $i:=$ 1 **step** 1 **until** 3 **do** . . .), and then player number 1 is resumed. From this point on, players resume each other according to the ordering established by the links. When the execution of the move (a procedure that is not detailed in the above program) sets *game-over* to **true,** the identity of the winner is assigned to variable *winner,* the execution of the coroutine instance terminates, and control flows back to the program that activated the set of symmetrical units. The main program then prints the name of the winner and stops.

5.2.3.1 Implementation Model

The stack model of execution discussed in Chapter 3 is unable to support coroutines. When a coroutine A issues a **resume** to a coroutine B, one must save (in A's activation record) the pointer to the instruction following the instruction **resume** (B). Moreover, A's activation record is not deallocated. Each coroutine may enter inner blocks and procedures during execution. Consequently, each coroutine requires an activation record stack that can grow and shrink independently of the other stacks. Thus, the creation of a set of coroutines can be viewed as the creation of a new execution stack, one for each coroutine. The run-time organization of the memory can be viewed as a *tree of stacks* (Figure 5.4)—a so-called "cactus stack."

5.2.4 Concurrent Units

As we saw in Section 2.4, there are cases in which the system we want to design can be characterized abstractly as a set of processes that proceed concurrently and interact only occasionally. A correct interaction can be guaranteed by the proper use of the

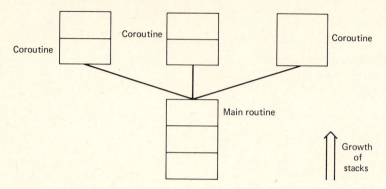

Figure 5.4 A tree of stacks.

synchronization statements (or *primitives*) provided by the programming language. This section reviews and evaluates three basic synchronization mechanisms: semaphores, monitors, and rendezvous. We have selected these three from among the many proposals that have appeared in the literature because they represent the historical evolution of the concept of synchronization of concurrent units, and because they have been incorporated into existing programming languages.

5.2.4.1 Semaphores

Semaphores were invented by Dijkstra and later introduced as synchronization primitives into ALGOL 68. A semaphore is a data object that can assume an integer value and can be operated upon by the primitives *P* and *V*. ALGOL 68 uses the names **down** and **up**. The semaphore is initialized to a certain integer value when it is declared.

The definitions of *P* and *V* are

$P(s)$: **if** $s>0$ **then** $s:= s-1$
            else *suspend current process*

$V(s)$: **if** *there is a process suspended on the semaphore*
            then *wake up the process*
            else $s:= s+1$

The primitives *P* and *V* are assumed to be indivisible, atomic operations: that is, no two processes can be executing *P* and/or *V* operations on the same semaphore at the same time. This must be guaranteed by the underlying implementation, which should make *P* and *V* behave like elementary machine instructions.

The semaphore has (1) an associated data structure where the identity of processes suspended on the semaphore is recorded and (2) a policy for selecting one process to be woken up when required by the primitive *V*. Usually, the data structure is a queue served on a first-in/first-out basis. However, we might want to assign priorities to processes and devise more complex policies based on such priorities.

The simple producer-consumer example of Section 2.3 can be solved by using semaphores as shown below (using an arbitrary, self-explanatory Pascal-like notation).

const $n = 20;$
shared var *buffer of length n, with primitives append and remove which update t, total number of buffered items;*

semaphore *mutex:= 1;*   {*to guarantee mutual execution*}
            in:= 0;   {*number of items in buffer*}
            spaces:= n; {*number of free spaces in buffer*}

process *producer;*
         var *i: integer;*
         repeat
              produce (i);
              P (spaces);   {*wait for free space*}
              P (mutex);   {*wait for buffer availability*}
              append i to buffer;
              V (mutex);   {*finished accessing buffer*}
              V (in)   {*one more item in buffer*}
         forever
end *producer;*

process *consumer;*
         var *j: integer;*
         repeat
              P (in);   {*wait for item in buffer*}
              P (mutex);   {*wait for buffer availability*}
              remove item from buffer into j;
              V (mutex);   {*finished accessing buffer*}
              V (spaces);   {*one more space in buffer*}
              consume (j)
         forever
end *consumer*

The keywords **process** and **end** enclose the segments of code that can proceed concurrently, and **shared var** declares the variable(s) that can be accessed by the processes concurrently. Semaphores *spaces* and *in* are used to guarantee the logical correctness of the accesses to the buffer. In particular, *spaces* (number of available free positions in the buffer) suspends the producer when it tries to insert a new item into a full buffer. Similarly, *in* (number of items already in the buffer) suspends the consumer if it tries to remove an item from an empty buffer.

Semaphore *mutex* is used to enforce mutual exclusion of accesses to the buffer. This is necessary under the assumption that operations *append* and *remove* concurrently modify the value of *t* (total number of buffered items). Note, however, that variable *t* has been introduced in Section 2.3.2.4 for the sole purpose of explaining the problem of mutual exclusion. Operations *append* and *remove* can be implemented easily in such a way that no need for mutual exclusion arises, provided that (as happens in our case) the logical correctness of accessing the buffer is ensured (see Exercise 5.14).

Programming with semaphores requires the programmer to associate one semaphore with each synchronization condition. Our example shows that semaphores are a very simple but rather low-level mechanism; their use can be awkward in practice, and the resulting programs are often difficult to design and to understand. Moreover, little checking can be done statically on programs that use semaphores. For example, a compiler would not be able to catch the incorrect use of a semaphore, such as the one resulting from a change of V (*mutex*) into P (*mutex*) in the above *producer* process (see Exercise 5.12). Catching such an error is impossible because it would require the translator to know the semantics of the program: that is, that the operations on the buffer are to be executed in mutual exclusion, and that *mutex* is used exactly to guarantee such mutual exclusion. Therefore, semaphores require considerable self-discipline on the part of the programmer. For example, one should not forget to execute a P before accessing a shared resource, or neglect to execute a V in order to release it.

Using semaphores for synchronization purposes other than mutual exclusion is even more awkward. In the producer/consumer example, process *consumer* suspends itself by executing P (*spaces*) when the buffer is full. The programmer should not forget to write a V (*spaces*) after each consumption, lest the producer becomes blocked forever.

PL/I was the first language to allow concurrent units—called *tasks* in PL/I. A procedure may be invoked as a task, in which case it executes concurrently with its caller. Tasks can also be assigned priorities. Synchronization is achieved by the use of events, which are similar to semaphores but can only assume one of two values: '0'B and '1'B. A P operation on a semaphore is represented by a WAIT operation on the completion of an event E: WAIT (E). A V operation is represented by signaling the completion of the event: COMPLETION (E) = '1'B. PL/I extends the notion of semaphores by allowing WAIT operation to name several events and an integer expression e. The process will be suspended until any e events have been completed. For example,

WAIT (E1, E2, E3) (1);

indicates the waiting for any one of the events $E1$, $E2$, or $E3$.

ALGOL 68 allows one to describe concurrent processes in a parallel clause whose constituent statements are elaborated concurrently. Synchronization can be provided by semaphores, which are data objects of mode **sema.**

5.2.4.2 Monitors

Monitors describe abstract data types in a concurrent environment. Mutual exclusion in accessing the operations that manipulate the data structure is guaranteed automatically by the underlying implementation. Cooperation in accessing the shared data structure must be programmed explicitly by using the monitor primitives **delay** and **continue**.

Using the notation of Concurrent Pascal, the following program illustrates the use of monitors in the producer/consumer example.

```
type fifostorage =
monitor
      var    contents:       array [1 . . n] of integer; {buffer contents}
             tot: 0 . . n;   {number of items in buffer}
             in,             {position of item to be added next}
             out: 1 . . n;   {position of item to be removed next}
             sender, receiver: queue;
      procedure entry append (item: integer);
      begin if tot = n then delay (sender);
             contents [in]: = item;
             in: = (in mod n) + 1;
             tot: = tot + 1;
             continue (receiver)
      end;

      procedure entry remove (var item: integer);
      begin if tot = 0 then delay (receiver);
             item: = contents [out];
             out: = (out mod n) + 1;
             tot: = tot - 1;
             continue (sender)
      end;
begin
      tot: = 0; in: = 1; out: = 1
end
```

An instance of the monitor (i.e., a buffer) can be declared as

var *buffer*: *fifostorage*

and can be created by the statement

init *buffer*

The **init** statement allocates storage for the variables encapsulated within the monitor definition (i.e., *contents*—the contents of the buffer—, *tot*—the total number of buffered items—, and *in* and *out*—the positions at which the next items will be appended and removed, respectively) and executes the initialization statement (which sets *tot* to zero and *in* and *out* to one).

The monitor defines the two procedures, *append* and *remove*. They are declared with the keyword **entry**, meaning that they are the only exported procedures that can be used to manipulate monitor instances. Cooperation between the producer and the consumer is achieved by using the synchronization primitives **delay** and **continue**. The operation **delay** (*sender*) suspends the executing process (e.g., the *producer*) in the queue *sender*. The process loses its exclusive access to the monitor's data structure and is delayed until another process (e.g., the *consumer*) executes the operation **continue** (*sender*). Similarly, a *consumer* process is delayed in the queue *receiver* if the buffer is empty, until the *producer* resumes it by executing the instruction **continue** (*receiver*). The execution of the **continue** operation makes the calling process return from the monitor call. If there are processes waiting in the specified queue, one of them immediately will resume the execution of the monitor procedure that previously delayed it.

The structure of a Concurrent Pascal program that uses the abovementioned monitor to represent cooperation between a producer and a consumer is given below.

```
const n = 20;
type fifostorage = . . . as above. . . ;
type producer =
process (storage: fifostorage);
var element: integer;
begin cycle
        —
        —
        —
    storage.append (element);
        —
        —
        —
    end
end;

type consumer =
process (storage: fifostorage);
var datum: integer;
begin cycle
        —
        —
        —
    storage.remove (datum);
        —
        —
        —
    end
end;
```

```
var meproducer: producer;
    youconsumer: consumer;
    buffer: fifostorage;
begin
        init buffer, meproducer (buffer), youconsumer (buffer)
end
```

Processes are described here as nonterminating, cyclic activities (**cycle** . . . **end**). Two particular instances (*meproducer* and *youconsumer*) are declared as bound to an instance of the resource type *fifostorage* and subsequently activated as concurrent processes by the **init** statement.

Monitors were proposed by Brinch Hansen and Hoare as a high-level synchronization mechanism. They have been implemented in the programming languages Concurrent Pascal and Modula.

5.2.4.3 Rendezvous

Rendezvous is the mechanism provided by Ada for describing synchronization of concurrent processes (*tasks*, in the Ada jargon). We will concentrate on the basic properties of the mechanism; additional features, as well as the interaction with other facilities provided by the language (such as scope rules and exception handling), will be ignored for the sake of simplicity.

An Ada task is a program unit that is executed concurrently with other tasks. Its structure is very similar in form to a package module. For example, the following task describes a process that handles the operations *append* and *remove* on a buffer.

```
task BUFFER_HANDLER is
    entry APPEND (ITEM: in INTEGER);
    entry REMOVE (ITEM: out INTEGER);
end;

task body BUFFER_HANDLER is
    N: constant INTEGER: = 20;
    CONTENTS: array (1 . . N) of INTEGER;
    IN, OUT: INTEGER range 1 . . N: = 1;
    TOT: INTEGER range 0 . . N: = 0;
 begin loop
    select
       when TOT < N = >
          accept APPEND (ITEM: in INTEGER) do
                CONTENTS (IN): = ITEM;
          end;
       IN: = (IN mod N) + 1;
       TOT: = TOT + 1;
```

```
    or
      when TOT > 0 =>
          accept REMOVE (ITEM: out INTEGER) do
          ITEM:= CONTENTS (OUT);
          end;
        OUT:= (OUT mod N) + 1;
        TOT:= TOT − 1;
    end select;
  end loop;
end BUFFER_HANDLER;
```

The visible part of task BUFFER_HANDLER specifies APPEND and REMOVE as *entries*. Entries can be called by other tasks in the same way as procedures. Unlike procedures, however, entry bodies are not executed immediately after the call, but only when the task owning the entry is ready to accept the call by executing a corresponding **accept** statement. At this point the calling and the called tasks can be viewed as meeting together in a *rendezvous*. If the calling task issues the call before the called task executes an **accept**, the calling task is suspended until the rendezvous occurs. Similarly, a suspension of the called task occurs if an **accept** statement is executed before the corresponding call. Note that a task can accept calls from more than one task; as a consequence, each entry potentially has a queue of tasks calling it.

The **accept** statement is similar to a procedure. After a repetition of the heading of the entry, the **do** . . . **end** part (**accept** body) specifies the statements to be executed at the rendezvous. Once a match between an entry call and the corresponding **accept** occurs, the caller is suspended until the **accept** body is executed by the called task. The **accept** body is the only place at which the parameters of the entry are accessible. Possible **out** parameters (as in the case of REMOVE) are passed back to the caller at the end of the rendezvous: that is, when the execution of the **accept** body is completed. Thereafter, the two tasks that met in the rendezvous can proceed in parallel.

The bodies of tasks PRODUCER and CONSUMER, which interact with BUFFER_HANDLER in the producer/consumer example, are sketched below.

```
PRODUCER
loop
    produce a new value V;
    BUFFER_HANDLER.APPEND (V);
    exit when V denotes the end of the stream;

end loop

CONSUMER
loop
    BUFFER_HANDLER.REMOVE (V);
    consume V;
    exit when V denotes the end of the stream;
end loop
```

In the BUFFER_HANDLER example, **accept** statements are enclosed within a **select** statement. The **select** statement is similar to the guarded **if** statement of Dijkstra's language (Section 5.1.2) and specifies several alternatives, separated by **or**, that can be chosen in a nondeterministic fashion. The Ada selection is specified by an **accept** statement, possibly prefixed (as in our example) by **when** *condition*. Execution of the select statement proceeds as follows.*

a. The conditions of the **when** parts of all alternatives are evaluated. Alternatives with a true condition, or without a **when** part, are considered open; otherwise, they are considered closed. In the example, both alternatives are open if $0 < TOT < N$.

b. An open alternative can be selected if a rendezvous is possible (i.e., an entry call has already been issued by another task). After the alternative is selected, the corresponding **accept** body is executed.

c. If there are open alternatives but none can be selected immediately, the task waits until a rendezvous is possible.

d. If there are no open alternatives, an error condition is signaled by the language-defined exception SELECT_ERROR.

5.2.4.4   A Comparison

Semaphores, monitors, and rendezvous are all primitives for modeling concurrent systems. We have already pointed out that semaphores are rather low-level mechanisms: programs are difficult to read and write, and no check on their correct use can be done automatically. Monitors, on the other hand, are a higher-level structuring mechanism. In a language such as Concurrent Pascal, system structuring proceeds by identifying (1) shared resources as abstract objects with suitable access primitives and (2) processes that cooperate through the use of resources. Resources are encapsulated within monitors. Mutual exclusion on the access to a shared resource is guaranteed automatically by the monitor implementation, whereas cooperation must be enforced by explicitly suspending and signaling processes via **delay** and **continue** statements. The distinction between active and passive multiprogramming entities (processes and monitors, respectively) disappears in Ada. Shared resources to be used cooperatively are represented by Ada tasks: that is, by active components representing resource managers. A request to use a resource is represented by an entry call, which must be accepted by the corresponding resource manager. A system structured via monitors and processes can easily be structured via Ada tasks, and vice versa; the choice between the two schemes is largely dependent on personal taste. The Ada scheme probably mirrors more directly the behavior of a concurrent system in a distributed architecture, in which remote resources are actually managed by processes that behave as guardians of the resource.

---

*We are ignoring several of Ada's features that would complicate the implementation (and our presentation).

5.2.4.5 Implementation Issues

In a concurrent system, processes either are suspended on some synchronization condition or are potentially active: that is, there are no logical obstacles to their execution. In general, only a subset of the potentially active processes can be running, unless there are as many processors as there are potentially active processes. In the common case of a uniprocessor, only one of such processes can be running at a time. It is thus customary to say that processes can be in one of the following states (see also Figure 5.5).

- Waiting.

- Ready (i.e., potentially active, but presently not running).

- Running.

In concurrent programming, the programmer has no direct control over the speed of execution of the processes. In particular, the user is not responsible for changing the state of a process from ready to running (operation of selection in Figure 5.5), which is done by the underlying implementation. Figure 5.5 shows that a process can leave the running state and enter the ready state as a consequence of the action of *preemption*.

Preemption is an action performed by the underlying implementation, which forces a process to abandon its running state even if, from a logical point of view, it could safely continue to be executed. A process can be preempted either after it performs a synchronizing statement that makes another suspended process enter the ready state (e.g., a *V* on a semaphore) or when some other condition occurs, such as the expiration of a specified amount of time (*time slice*). After the preemption of one process, one of the ready processes can enter the running state. This kind of implementation allows the programmer to view the system as a set of activities that proceed in parallel, even if they are all executed by the same processor. Only one process at a time can be executed by the processor, but each process runs only for a limited amount of time, after which control is given to another process. Note, however, that it is possible to have nonpreemptive implementations of concurrency. In this case,

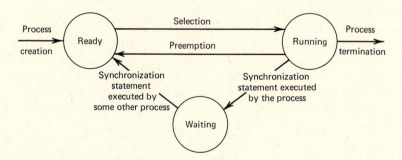

Figure 5.5 State diagram for a process.

execution switches to another process only when the currently executing process deliberately suspends itself or requires the use of an unavailable resource.

The portion of run-time support of a concurrent language responsible for the implementation of the state transitions shown in Figure 5.5, is called the *kernel*. To illustrate the basic features of a kernel, consider the case of a single processor shared by a set of processes. For the sake of simplicity, we will ignore the problems of synchronizing processes with I/O devices and concentrate our attention on the interactions among internal processes. More complete discussions of these issues are traditionally (and perhaps more properly) addressed in textbooks on operating systems. Here we provide only a glimpse of the basic problems that are relevant to understanding concurrency features of programming languages.

The information about a process needed by the kernel is represented in a *process descriptor,* one for each process. The descriptor for a process is used to store all the information needed to restore the process from a waiting or blocked state to the running state. This information (called *process status*) includes the process priority (if priorities are used) and all information required to instruct the processor about the identity and point of execution of the process—notably, the contents of machine registers (program counter, index registers, accumulator, etc.). Saving the status of the process when the process becomes suspended, and restoring the status when the process becomes running, is one of the kernel's jobs.

The kernel can be viewed as an abstract data type: it hides some private data structures and provides procedures that provide the only ways to use these data structures. The kernel's private data structures are organized as queues of process descriptors. The descriptors of ready processes are kept by the kernel in READY_QUEUE. There is also one CONDITION_QUEUE for each condition that might suspend a process: that is, there is one queue for each semaphore and one for each object declared to be of type queue in a monitor. Each such queue is used to store the descriptors of all processes suspended on the semaphore or delayed in the queue by the monitor. A variable RUNNING denotes the descriptor of the running process. A typical snapshot of the kernel's data structures is shown in Figure 5.6.

Time slicing is implemented by a clock interrupt. Such an interrupt activates the following kernel operation, which suspends the most recently running process into READY_QUEUE and transfers a ready process into the running state.

Operation Suspend-and-Select

1. Save status of running process into RUNNING.

2. Enqueue RUNNING into READY_QUEUE.

3. Move a descriptor from READY_QUEUE into RUNNING.

4. Restore the contents of machine registers with the values found in RUNNING.

5.2.4.5.1 Semaphores If semaphores are provided by the language, primitives *P* and *V* can be implemented as calls to kernel procedures. A suspension on condition

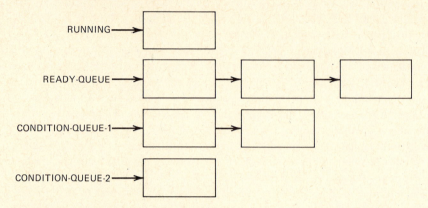

Figure 5.6 Data structures of the kernel.

c caused by a P operation is implemented by the following private operation of the kernel.

Operation Suspend-on-Condition

1. Save status of running process into RUNNING.
2. Enqueue RUNNING into CONDITION_QUEUE_c.
3. Move a descriptor from READY_QUEUE into RUNNING.
4. Restore the contents of machine registers with the values found in RUNNING (this step is used to activate the process).

Awakening a process waiting on condition c, caused by a V operation, is implemented by the following private operation of the kernel.

Operation Awaken

1. Save status of running process into RUNNING.
2. Enqueue RUNNING into READY_QUEUE.
3. Move a descriptor from CONDITION_QUEUE_c into READY_QUEUE.
4. Move a descriptor from READY_QUEUE into RUNNING.
5. Restore the contents of machine registers with the values found in RUNNING.

In order to guarantee indivisibility of primitives P and V, the corresponding kernel procedures are executed with the clock-interrupt disabled. This is not necessary when operation *Suspend-and-select* is invoked by the clock interrupt, because the operation may be assumed to terminate within a fraction of the time slice and hence is intrinsically indivisible. It would be necessary even in such a case too, and also in general, if I/O interrupts are used to wake up processes awaiting I/O operations.

5.2.4.5.2 Monitors   In the case of monitors, a simple way to implement the required mutual exclusion consists of disabling the clock interrupt when a monitor procedure is called and enabling it on return from the call (Exercise 5.16 suggests an alternative implementation). We are assuming that interrupts are enabled and disabled by a single machine instruction, and further, that a special machine register determines whether interrupts are enabled or disabled. This register is part of the process status and must be saved in the process descriptor when the process is suspended. For the sake of simplicity, we also are assuming that monitor procedures do not contain calls to other monitor procedures. When a process calls a monitor procedure, the value of the return point from the call is saved in an entry of the process descriptor. Operations **delay** and **continue** can be implemented by kernel procedures. In particular, **delay** is implemented by operation *Suspend-on-Condition*, whereas **continue** is implemented by the following operation.

Operation Continue

1.   Save status of running process into RUNNING.

2.   Set status of interrupts in RUNNING to *enabled;*

3.   Set the image of the program counter in RUNNING to the return point from the monitor call.

4.   Enqueue RUNNING into READY_QUEUE.

5.   Let CONDITION_QUEUE_c be the queue mentioned by the **continue** statement. If CONDITION_QUEUE_c is not empty, then move a descriptor from CONDITION_QUEUE_c into RUNNING. Otherwise, move a descriptor from READY_QUEUE to RUNNING.

6.   Restore the contents of machine registers with the values found in RUNNING.

Note that several steps of the kernel operations (e.g., step 3 of *Suspend-and-Select* and step 3 of *Suspend-on-Condition*) have been written deliberately to imply nondeterminism. These steps are exactly the points at which the implementation must select a suitable policy for making a deterministic choice. The part of the kernel responsible for this policy is called the *scheduler*. The scheduler can be very simple (e.g., all queues are handled as FIFO queues) or rather sophisticated (e.g., waiting times and priorities are taken into account).

5.2.4.5.3 Rendezvous   We discuss here some implementation issues of Ada's rendezvous. There is one queue of ready tasks (READY_QUEUE). Each entry has a descriptor that contains the following fields.

- A boolean value O describing whether the entry is open (O = true indicates that the task owning the entry is ready to accept a call to this entry).

- A reference W to a queue of descriptors of tasks whose calls to the entry are pending (*waiting queue*).

- A reference T to the descriptor of the task owning the entry.

- A reference I to the first instruction of the **accept** body (to simplify matters, we assume that no two **accept** statements for the same entry can appear in a **select** statement). This reference is significant only if the task owning the entry is ready to accept a call to the entry (that is, O = true).

We assume for simplicity's sake that the implementation of the synchronization statements is done by kernel operations that are noninterruptible: that is, interrupts are disabled and enabled by the kernel before and after executing such statements. The problem of passing parameters across tasks is ignored for the same reason.

The implementation of an entry call can be done by the kernel as follows.

1. Save status of running task into RUNNING.

2. Enqueue RUNNING into the queue associated with the entry.

3. If the entry is open, then close (i.e., set field O to false) all the open entries of the called task and move the descriptor of the called task into RUNNING; update the value of the program counter stored in RUNNING with the value stored in field I of the entry's descriptor. Otherwise, move descriptor from READY_QUEUE into RUNNING.

4. Restore the contents of machine registers with the values found in RUNNING.

When the **end** of the body of an **accept** statement is reached, the following kernel actions complete the rendezvous.

1. Save status of running task into RUNNING.

2. Move descriptor of caller referenced by field T of the entry's descriptor into READY_QUEUE.

3. Enqueue RUNNING into READY_QUEUE.

4. Move a descriptor from READY_QUEUE into RUNNING.

5. Restore the contents of machine registers with the values found in RUNNING.

The actions to be executed as a consequence of an **accept** statement (not embedded in a **select** statement) are

1. If the waiting queue of the entry is empty, then
    1.1 Set field *O* of the entry's descriptor to true and save the address of the first instruction of the **accept** body into field *I* of the entry's descriptor.
    1.2 Save the status of the running task into the task's descriptor and set field *T* of the entry's descriptor to reference the task's descriptor.
    1.3 Move a descriptor from READY_QUEUE into RUNNING.
    1.4 Restore the contents of machine registers with the values found in RUNNING.

2. If the waiting queue is not empty, then accept the rendezvous immediately: that is, continue the execution of the running task until the end of the **accept** body is reached.

In order to execute a **select** statement, a list of the open entries involved in the selection is first constructed. If this list is empty, then the exception SELECT_ERROR is raised. Otherwise, the following kernel actions are required.

1. If one or more entries of the list have a nonempty queue, then
    1.1 Arbitrarily choose one.
    1.2 Accept the rendezvous immediately: that is, continue to execute the **accept** body of the selected alternative.

2. If all entry queues are empty, then
    2.1 Switch the status of all such entries to "open" and save the address of the first instruction of each open alternative's **accept** body into field *I* of the corresponding entry's descriptor.
    2.2 Save the status of the running task into the task's descriptor and set field *T* of the entry's descriptor to reference the task's descriptor.
    2.3 Move a descriptor from READY_QUEUE into RUNNING.
    2.4 Restore the contents of machine registers with the values found in RUNNING.

SUGGESTIONS FOR FURTHER READING AND BIBLIOGRAPHIC NOTES

Statement-level control structures were actively researched in the early 1970s. (Dijkstra 1968a) was the first paper to stress the need for discipline in programming, and the influence of the **goto** statement on the production of obscure programs. Much of the subsequent research on "structured programming" was aimed at uncovering suitable control structures that could promote the writing of well-organized, readable programs. (Böhm and Jacopini 1966) provides a formal justification to these works by showing that a limited subset of control structures (sequencing, **if then else**, **do while**) is sufficient to write any program. (Knuth 1974) provides a comprehensive view of statement-level control structures and an in-depth comparison of many language proposals. Examples of extensions to machine-level languages to incorporate suitable high-level control structures are described in (Wirth 1968) and (Van der Poel and Maarsen 1974).

The user-defined statement-level control structures of CLU are described in (Liskov et al. 1977). An implementation model is presented in (Atkinson et al. 1978).

Parameter passing is studied in (Gries 1971), (Pratt 1975), and (Organick et al. 1978). The latter uses the descriptive model proposed by (Johnston 1971) to analyze the problem. The keyword method of parameter passing is discussed in (Francez 1977).

Exception handling is the linguistic feature that describes how programs can trap and handle undesired events in order to improve reliability. (Randell 1975) and (Parnas and Würges 1976) discuss program reliability and fault tolerance.

Exception handling is studied in (Goodenough 1975) and (Levin 1977). (MacLaren 1977) discusses exception handling in PL/I. Exception handling in CLU is presented in (Liskov and Snyder 1979), along with a comparison with other language proposals. CLU's implementation of exception handling is described in (Atkinson et al. 1978).

The first description of coroutines comes from (Conway 1963). (Knuth 1973) and (Wegner 1968) provide an introductory view of coroutines. (Marlin 1980) is a comprehensive text on coroutines that contains a survey of languages, a detailed semantic description, and a discussion of programming methodologies.

Concurrency in progamming languages is traditionally studied as a branch of operating systems. The reader can refer to (Brinch Hansen 1973), (Brinch Hansen 1977), and (Haberman 1976) for a study of operating system theory. The concept of semaphore was introduced by (Dijkstra 1968b) and (Dijkstra 1968c). Monitors were proposed by (Brinch Hansen 1973) and (Hoare 1974). Monitors were introduced in the programming languages Concurrent Pascal (Brinch Hansen 1975) and (Brinch Hansen 1977), Modula (Wirth 1976b), and CSP/k (Holt et al. 1978a). The new synchronization primitives presented by (Hoare 1978) and (Brinch Hansen 1979) have strongly influenced the rendezvous concept of Ada. These proposals are aimed at providing synchronization primitives for processes in distributed systems. Distributed systems are composed of a number of largely autonomous processors connected by a communication medium. Distributed systems, such as local networks of small computers (e.g., microprocessors), are likely to become increasingly popular in the future, and much research effort is being devoted to them.

Exercises

5.1 You must design a program part that reads a sequence of integer values. The length of the sequence is unknown. The sequence is terminated by a "special value" (e.g. zero). All values read (except for the terminator) must be processed in an unspecified manner. The following Pascal-like program fragment provides a solution.

read *item;*
while *item* ≠ *special value* **do**
begin *process item;*
  read new item
end

The same algorithm can be written in PLZ as

do *read item;*
 if *item* = *special value* **then exit**;
process item
od

Briefly compare the two solutions in terms of readability and writability.

5.2 ALGOL 68 does not provide a **repeat** . . . **until** loop.

 a. Describe how you can simulate it. (**Hint**: you can write a loop with an empty loop body; the **while** clause can be a sequence of statements that delivers a boolean value!)

 b. Discuss this solution from readability and writability points of view.

5.3 Rewrite the PLZ program of Section 5.1.3 in ALGOL 68, Pascal, and Ada. Comment on the readability and writability of the program in the different languages.

5.4 (Zahn 1974) proposes two new kinds of ''event driven'' control structures. Their general form is specified below, with some syntactic changes.

 (A) **begin** **quit on** *event1, event2, . . . , eventn;*
    statement_list_0
  then *event1: statement_list_1;*
    event2: statement_list_2;

    .

    .

    eventn: statement_list_n
  end

 (B) **do** **quit on** *event1, event2, . . . , eventn;*
    statement_list_0
  then *event1: statement_list_1:*
    event2: statement_list_2;

    .

    .

    eventn: statement_list_n
  od

Case *A* specifies the execution of the list of statements *statement_list_0*. Case *B* specifies repetition of *statement_list_0*.

There is a new statement **raise** *eventname*, which signals the occurrence of an event. Such a statement can occur within the part *statement_list_0* of cases *A* and *B*, provided that *eventname* is declared in the **quit-on** clause of the statement. The effect of **raise** *eventname* is a control transfer to the statements that follow *eventname* in the **then** clause.

1. Rewrite the program of Exercise 5.1 and the PLZ program of Section 5.1.3 using Zahn's loop.

2. Translate an **if then else** and a **case** selection into Zahn's statement *A*.

3. Translate the Pascal **do while** and **repeat until** into Zahn's statement *B*.

5.5 Manually execute the following ALGOL-like program by assuming (**a**) call by reference, (**b**) call by value, (**c**) call by result, (**d**) call by value-result, (**e**) call by name. Show the results produced by each call in array *a* and variable *i*.

```
program parameter_passing;
    var i: integer; a: array [1 . . 3] of integer;
    procedure mess (v: integer);
        begin v: = v+1;
            a [i] := 5;
            i: = 3;
            v: = v+1
        end mess;
        for i: = 1 to 3 do a [i]: = 0;
        a [2]: = 10;
        i: = 2;
        call mess (a [i])
end parameter_passing
```

5.6 The following subprogram is supposed to interchange the contents of two integer variables.

```
subprogram swap (a,b: integer),
var temp: integer;
begin temp: = a; a: = b; b: = temp
end swap
```

If *a* and *b* are parameters called by name, *swap* may not be commutative (i.e., the effect of *swap* (*c,d*) can be different from that of *swap* (*d,c*)). Prove this fact by examining the effect of *swap* (*i,a* [*i*]), where *a* is an integer array.

What happens if *a* and/or *b* are passed by value? By value-result?

5.7   Show how the effects of CLU iterators could be implemented in a language that supports coroutines but not iterators.

5.8   Describe how history-sensitive FORTRAN subprograms can be used to simulate coroutines.

5.9   One way to handle exceptions raised in procedures in a programming language that does not provide specific exception handling features is to return a special code indicating the raised exception (Section 2.3.2). Another way is to transmit the recovery procedure as a parameter (Section 5.2.1.2). What are the differences between these two methods?

5.10   The implementers of CLU mention the following alternative implementation to the one described in Section 5.2.2.2.1. Instead of having a unique handler table for a procedure, a branch table is constructed for each invocation. Each entry of the branch table corresponds to an exception that can be raised by the called procedure.

    1.   Explain why the branch table (for each call) can be constructed at translation time. Could the same be done for a PL/I-like exception handling scheme?

    2.   Show how a **signal** can be implemented.

    3.   Compare the branch table method with the handler table method in terms of speed and space.

    4.   The implementation criteria for exception handling mechanisms stated by the CLU implementers are
      • Normal-case execution efficiency should not be impaired at all.

      • Exceptions should be executed quickly, but not necessarily as fast as possible.

      • Use of space should be reasonably efficient.

    According to these criteria, why is the handler table method to be preferred over the branch table method?

5.11   Consider an Ada subprogram that terminates abnormally after raising an exception. Why can an implementation of parameter passing by copy produce different results from an implementation that passes parameters by reference?

5.12   In the producer/consumer example implemented with semaphores in Section 5.2.4.1, suppose that V (*mutex*) is incorrectly written as P (*mutex*) in process *producer*. How does the system behave?

5.13   When semaphores are used to implement mutual exclusion, it is possible to associate a semaphore SR with each resource R. Each access to R can then be written as

P (*SR*);
access R;
V (*SR*)

How should SR be initialized?

5.14 The producer/consumer example of Section 5.2.4.1 uses a semaphore for enforcing mutual exclusion on access to the buffer. Can you write an implementation of operations *append* and *remove* such that no need for mutual exclusion arises? (**Hint**: Try to write a solution that does not use variable *t*).

5.15 Some computers (e.g., the IBM 360) provide an indivisible machine-instruction test and set (TS) that can be used for synchronization purposes.

Let X and Y be two boolean variables. The execution of the instruction

$TS(X,Y)$

copies the value of Y into X and sets Y to false.

A set of concurrent processes that must execute a set of instructions in mutual exclusion can use a global boolean variable PERMIT, initialized to true, and a local boolean variable X in the following way.

repeat TS (X, PERMIT)
until *X;*
    instructions to be executed in mutual exclusion;
    PERMIT: = true

1. In this case, processes do not suspend themselves; they are always ready (this is called *busy waiting*). Compare this solution to one based on semaphores in which P and V are implemented by the kernel.

2. Describe how to implement P and V on semaphores by using the test and set primitive in a busy wait scheme.

5.16 We implemented mutual exclusion of monitor procedures by disabling interrupts. An alternative solution uses a semaphore for each monitor and performs a P on the semaphore before entering a monitor procedure, and a corresponding V upon exit. Detail this implementation and compare the two solutions.

5.17 Show how an Ada task can be used to implement a semaphore.

CHAPTER SIX

PROGRAM CORRECTNESS

"... curing sick programs or ... producing healthy programs?" (Wegner 1979)

We have seen in Chapters 1 and 2 that correctness and reliability have become prominent software production goals. In the early days of computing, these were only implicit and obvious goals. Today that view is regarded as quite naive. It is now recognized that if one hopes to come close to achieving such goals, special care and painstaking measures must be taken. The evolution of correctness considerations from tangential to central has affected the development of both software methodologies and programming languages. The effect on programming languages has also been felt indirectly through the new methodologies. This chapter traces the development of correctness ideas in programming languages.

6.1 CORRECTNESS AND RELIABILITY

Our first task is to define precisely the terms we have been using informally so far. A program is *correct* if it meets its specifications. In contrast, a program is *reliable* if it is highly probable that when we demand a service from the system, it will perform to our satisfaction. As such, reliability is hard to quantify, because it is related to the quality of the system as perceived by the user. Often, situations in which the service from the system is needed urgently weigh more in this perception than those in which demands are routine. Moreover, a system is often considered reliable even if the strict notion of correctness is not satisfied. This can happen because

1. The error does not impair the usability of the system and is easily detected and corrected by the user. For example, a spelling error in a message such as

PRAMETER N. 3 OUT OF RANGE

does not impair the reliability of the system. In contrast, signaling an incorrect parameter number might impair reliability.

2. The error does not manifest itself very often or it does not occur in critical cases. For example, in a message switching system, in peak situations, the (infrequent) loss of a packet of characters belonging to a long text, received on a certain input line, may be tolerated. In contrast, the loss of data can be unacceptable if the data are used to monitor a nuclear plant in real-time, and emergency situations are to be handled as soon as critical data are received by the computer.

On the other hand, software whose correctness has been rigorously assessed can be unreliable. In fact, correctness is defined relative to the specification, so that a program may be correct even if it does not achieve the user's needs. The basic reasons:

1. The specifications incorrectly or incompletely reflect the requirements. For example, the requirements may specify that a certain authorization is required for reading the amount of deposits of each customer of a bank, but the specifications fail to specify how and when such authorization is to be checked.

2. The specifications do not state what the system is supposed to do in "anomalous" cases such as failures of the underlying hardware/software supports or errors in input data. Therefore, the system behaves correctly if several assumptions about the environment hold, but unexpected (and undetected) input data might cause serious violations of system correctness, because no exception handlers are provided.

Although reliability is the ultimate goal, it is hard to quantify, and correctness is often used as an approximation in the hope that the specifications adequately capture the desired properties of the system. Moreover, correctness can be stated in precise terms, and suitable methodologies have been devised for proving program correctness. The remainder of this chapter will mainly discuss correctness issues.

The process undertaken to guarantee (certify) the correctness of the program is called *certification*. A program may be certified in any number of ways, including program testing and program verification or a combination of the two. The desire to ease program certification has influenced language designs to the extent that, for example, the languages Euclid and Gypsy have as their specific goals the verifiability of programs. Reliability is also listed as a design goal for Ada. We will be discussing the effects of these goals on programming languages.

These effects can be seen at several levels. The most global—and the most important—effect is on the program structuring techniques provided by the language. Large programs are complex and unwieldy objects. The only possible way to conquer this complexity is to divide the program into small pieces, each of which can be certified separately. The next task is then to certify that these pieces indeed combine to make the desired whole.

At another level, correctness concerns have focused attention on individual features used to write the small pieces. At still another level, the combination of these features have come under scrutiny.

We will examine the latter two levels in this chapter. Program structuring techniques will be examined in the next chapter.

6.2 REASONING ABOUT PROGRAMS

Having written a program, how do programmers know that it is the program they meant to write? In other words, how do they convince themselves, let alone other people, that they have produced a correct program? The process they follow in doing this has come to be known as "reasoning about programs." It is easier to show the correctness of some solutions and programs than of others—that is, some programs are easier to reason about. Below, we informally discuss some language features that make reasoning about programs difficult. More formal approaches will be studied in Sections 6.3 and 6.4.

It is important to realize, however, that assessing the correctness of software should not be confined to the programming phase. Actually, several experimental studies show that the cost of fixing errors at the coding stage is much higher than that of fixing them at the design phase. Suitable techniques have been proposed, and are now commonly used in practice, to allow project managers to monitor a project through all the phases of its development, in order to catch all possible errors as soon as possible.

A *walk-through* is one such technique. In the design phase, the person responsible for the design being reviewed presents documents and orally describes the design decisions to a group of people knowledgeable about the project. In this way, vague specifications or misunderstandings are likely to be discovered. The same technique, when applied at the programming stage, is referred to as *code inspection*. In this case, one or more programmers other than the author of the program go through the program in an attempt to find errors. Often, when a reader fails to understand some aspects of the program and asks for an explanation, the author discovers the presence of an error. It is clear that the programming language can help in this process to the extent that it supports the writing of programs that are easily readable.

Language features that complicate reasoning about programs are reviewed in Section 6.2.1. Section 6.2.2 analyzes the features introduced by recent languages to facilitate the reasoning process.

6.2.1 Harmful Language Features

The **goto** statement is the best-known example of a harmful language feature. In his famous letter about the effect of the **goto** statement (Dijkstra 1968**a**), Dijkstra stated that programs that contain many **goto**s also tend to contain many errors. Dijkstra's argument goes deeper than merely proposing the abolition of the **goto** statement. The reason why the **goto** statement is bad is that it makes reasoning about the program difficult. It does so by breaking the sequential continuity of the program statements and violating the requirement that the solution structure should be reflected in the program structure.

The **goto** statement, of course, is not the only such statement. Two other language features that can make reasoning about programs difficult are side effects and aliasing. Both of these features allow a program statement to have effects that are not evident from examining the statement alone. Such a statement obviously reduces the readability of the program. Side effects and aliasing are discussed separately in Sections 6.2.1.1 and 6.2.1.2.

6.2.1.1 Side Effects

Section 3.4 defined side effects as modifications of the nonlocal environment. Side effects are used principally to provide a method of communication among program units. Communication can be established through global variables. However, if the set of global variables used for this purpose is large, and each unit has unrestricted access to it, the program becomes difficult to read and understand. Each unit can potentially reference and modify every variable in the global environment, perhaps in ways other than those intended for the variable. The problem is that once a global variable is used for communication, it is difficult to distinguish between desired and undesired side effects. For example, if unit $u1$ calls $u2$, and $u2$ inadvertently modifies a global variable x used for communication between units $u3$ and $u4$, the invocation of $u2$ produces an undesired side effect. Such errors are difficult to find and remove, because the symptom is not easily traced to the cause of the error. (Note that a simple typing error could lead to this problem.) Another difficulty is that examination of the call instruction alone does not reveal the variables that can be affected by the call. This reduces the readability of programs, because, in general, the entire program must be scanned to understand the effect of a call.

Communication via unrestricted access to global variables is particularly dangerous when the program is large and is composed of several units that have been independently developed by several programmers. One way to reduce these difficulties is to route communication among units via parameters. The overhead caused by parameter passing, however, might make this solution unacceptable in time-critical applications. Alternatively, it must be possible to restrict the set of global variables held in common by two units to exactly those needed for the communication between the units. Also, it can be useful to specify that a unit can only read, but not modify, some variables. These and other problems will be discussed further in the next chapter.

Side effects also are used in passing parameters by reference, where a side effect is used to modify the actual parameter. The programmer must be careful not to produce undesired side effects on actual parameters by modifying the corresponding formal parameters. The same problem arises with call by name. A more substantial source of obscurity in call by name is that each assignment to the same formal parameter can affect different locations in the environment of the calling unit. Such problems do not arise in call by copy.

The effect of side effects on function subprograms can be particularly disturbing. Function subprograms are invoked by writing the subprogram name within an expression, as in

$$w := x + f(x,y) + z$$

In the presence of side effects—in Pascal, for example—the call to f might produce a change to x or y (if they are passed by reference), or even to z (if z is global to the function) as a side effect. This reduces the readability of the program because one cannot rely on the commutativity of addition in general. In the example, if f modifies x as a side effect, the value produced for w is different if x is evaluated before or after calling f.

Besides affecting readability, side effects can prevent the compiler from generating optimized code for the evaluation of certain expressions. In the example

$$u := x+z+f(x,y)+f(x,y)+x+z$$

one cannot evaluate function f and subexpression $x+z$ just once.

6.2.1.2 Aliasing

Two variables are *aliases* if they denote (*share*) the same data object during a unit activation (see Section 3.4). A modification of the data object under one variable name is automatically visible by all variables that share the object. An example is illustrated by the FORTRAN EQUIVALENCE statement. For instance, the statements

EQUIVALENCE (A,B)
A = 5.4

bind the same data object to A and B and set its value to 5.4. Consequently, the statements

B = 5.7
WRITE (6,10) A

would print 5.7, even though the value explicitly assigned to A is 5.4. The assignment to B affects both A and B.

Aliasing may arise during the execution of a procedure when parameters are passed by reference. Consider the following Pascal procedure, which is supposed to interchange the values of two integer variables without using any local variables.

procedure *swap (***var** *x,y: integer);*
begin   *x:= x+y;*
              y:= x−y;
              x:= x−y
end

Before proceeding, the reader is invited to reason about the procedure, trying to understand whether or not it works properly.

The answer is "generally yes"; in fact, the procedure works properly except when the two actual parameters are the same variable, as in the call

swap (a,a)

In this case, the procedure sets *a* to zero, because *x* and *y* become aliases and thus any assignments to *x* and *y* within the procedure affect the same location. The same problem may arise from the call

swap (b [i], b [j])

when the index variables *i* and *j* happen to be equal.

Pointers can create problems too. In fact, the call

swap (p ↑ , q ↑)

does not interchange the values pointed at by *p* and *q* if *p* and *q* happen to point to the same data object.

The above aliases occur because of the following two conditions.

1.   Formal and actual parameters share the same data objects.

2.   Procedure calls have overlapping actual parameters.

Aliasing may also occur when a formal (by reference) parameter and a global variable denote the same or overlapping data objects. For example, if procedure *swap* is rewritten as

procedure *swap (***var** *x: integer):*
begin   *x:= x+a;*
              a:= x−a;
              x:= x−a
end

where *a* is a global variable, the call

swap (a)

generates an incorrect result, because of the aliasing between x and a. It is interesting to note that aliasing does not arise if parameters are passed by copy; such parameters act as local variables within the procedure and the corresponding actual parameters become affected only at procedure exit.

Pointers are intrinsically generators of aliasing, as the following Pascal program fragment shows.

var $p, q : \uparrow T;$

   .

    .

     .

  new (p);
  q:= p

Pointers p and q point to the same object. It is thus possible to change the value of $p \uparrow$ by an assignment to $q \uparrow$, and vice versa. ALGOL 68 can generate further aliasing by pointing to named stack objects. This feature, as we have seen, has been ruled out by Pascal and several other languages.

The disadvantages of aliasing affect programmers, readers, and implementers. Subprograms are hard to understand, because, occasionally, different names denote the same data object. This phenomenon cannot be discovered by inspecting the subprogram; rather, discovery requires examining all the units that may invoke the subprogram. As a consequence of aliasing, a subprogram call may produce unexpected and incorrect results. Aliasing also impairs the possibility of generating optimized code. For example, in the case

$a:= (x-y*z)+w;$
$b:= (x-y*z)+u;$

the subexpression $x-y*z$ cannot be evaluated just once and then used in the two assignments, if a is an alias for x, y, or z.

6.2.2 Disciplined Language Features

The goal of producing correct programs has influenced the design of several modern programming languages, which restrict or altogether eliminate the use of harmful features. Section 5.1.4 analyzed the case of the **goto** statement. Some modern languages do not support the **goto** statement (e.g., Bliss, Euclid, Gypsy). Other languages have retained it as a mechanism to synthesize legitimate control structures that were not provided by the language. Similarly, several modern programming languages constrain or altogether eliminate the sources of side effects.

Euclid and Gypsy are two examples of languages designed with the express goal of supporting the writing of correct programs. Many harmful features mentioned in Section 6.2.1 are simply banished—most prominently **goto**s, aliasing, and side effects in functions. Gypsy does not provide global variables, either. Euclid allows global variables, but provides mechanisms for controlling their access. Euclid and Gypsy thus provide good cases for studying the effects of eliminating harmful features.

Like many languages of the late 1970s, Euclid and Gypsy are based on Pascal. The major goal of these two languages is to enable the writing of verifiable systems programs. The harmful features mentioned above were seen as features particularly troublesome for program verification and, as we have seen, for reasoning about programs; they were therefore not included in either language. Euclid and Gypsy are the best-known languages to try such a whole-hearted approach. To simplify matters, we will restrict our discussion to Euclid.

Aliasing was defined above as the ability to access the same data object with more than one name within the same unit activation. There are basically two ways to eliminate aliasing. One is to do away completely with features that make aliasing possible—for example, pointers, reference parameters, globals, and arrays. This would leave us with a very lean language indeed. The other approach, taken in Euclid, is to place restrictions on the use of such features in order to rule out the possibility of aliasing.

In the case of reference parameters, the problems only arise if actual parameters are overlapping. If the actual parameters are simple variables, it is necessary to ensure that they all be distinct. Thus the procedure call

p (a,a)

is considered illegal by Euclid. Passing an array and one of its components is also prohibited. For example, the call

p (b [1], b)

to a procedure whose heading is

procedure *p (***var** *x: integer;* **var** *y:* **array** *[1:10]* **of** *integer)*

is illegal because *y* [1] and *x* would be aliases. The above forms of illegal aliasing can be caught at translation time. However, the call

swap (b [i], b [j])

to the procedure swap described in Section 6.2.1.2 generates aliasing only if *i* is equal to *j*. One could simply forbid such calls, but the result would be an awkward and difficult-to-use language. Euclid specifies that in such a case the condition

$i \neq j$

be generated by the translator as a *legality assertion*. In the testing phase, legality assertions can be compiled automatically into run-time checks by using a certain compiler option. If at run-time an assertion evaluates to false, execution is aborted and a suitable message produced. The main use of legality assertions, however, is in program verification. The Euclid system, in fact, includes a program verifier, and a Euclid program is considered correct only if the truth of all legality assertions has been proven by the verifier.

Handling aliasing in the presence of pointers is more complex. Consider again the Pascal program fragment discussed in Section 6.2.1.2.

var p,q : $\uparrow T$;

.

.

.

new (p);
$q := p$

The problem of aliasing between $p \uparrow$ and $q \uparrow$ is handled in the same way that arrays and array elements are handled: that is, $p \uparrow$ and $q \uparrow$ are viewed as selectors that reference a component of the collection of data objects of type T, the same way that $b[i]$ and $b[j]$ reference a component of array b. An assignment to $b[i]$ or $b[j]$ is viewed as an assignment to the entire data object b, which happens to change the value stored in a portion thereof. Thus, $b[i]$ and $b[j]$ are not viewed as aliases, because they explicitly name the same data object b. Similarly, an assignment to $p \uparrow$ or to $q \uparrow$ can be viewed as a modification of the collection of components of type T; thus, $p \uparrow$ and $q \uparrow$ are not aliases, because they explicitly name the same collection.

This might appear to be an ingenious but tricky way of looking at the problem of aliasing for pointers. In fact, different data structures might be composed of dynamically generated components of the same type T. Viewing an assignment to $p \uparrow$ as an assignment to the collection—that is, as a modification of any of such data structures—is not really helpful.

In order to allow an extra level of checking for nonoverlapping pointers, however, a further mechanism is introduced—the *collection* (see Section 4.5.3). The programmer is required to divide all dynamic objects into separate collections and indicate which pointers can point into which collections. Each pointer can only be bound to one collection. An assignment between two pointers is legal only if the two pointers point into the same collection.

Detecting illegal aliasing between pointers caused by procedure calls is now similar to the case of arrays. In fact, a collection C and a pointer bound to C are similar to an array and a variable used as an index. Dereferencing is exactly like indexing within an array. For example, if p and q point into the same collection, and $p \uparrow$ and $q \uparrow$ are both passed, the nonoverlapping requirement requires the test

$p \neq q$

to be produced as a legality assertion.

As we saw in the previous section, aliasing can also occur between global variables and formal parameters of a procedure. In Euclid, detection of aliasing in such cases does not require any additional burden. In fact, global variables must be explicitly *imported* by a subprogram if they are needed, and they must be accessible in every scope from which the subprogram is called. For each imported variable, it is also necessary to indicate whether it can be read, or written, or both. Thus, modifiable global variables can be treated by the aliasing detection algorithm as implicit additional parameters passed by reference.

The explicit importation of global variables allows the programmer to restrict the set of variables visible within a procedure to any subset of the (nonmasked) variables declared in the outer scopes. The translator can thus ensure that only visible variables are accessed in a unit and that any access is legal: for example, that a read-only variable cannot be modified. This is an advantage over the pure ALGOL-like scope rules—especially for large programs, in which inner procedures automatically inherit all the (nonmasked) variables declared in the enclosing scopes and can modify them in an uncontrolled way. This point will be discussed further in the following chapter.

Finally, Euclid functions are not allowed to have by-reference parameters and can only import read variables. Thus, their execution cannot cause side effects, and they behave like mathematical functions.

An important consequence of disallowing aliasing in procedures is that passing parameters by reference is equivalent to passing them by copy (see Section 5.2.1). Therefore, the choice of how to implement parameter passing can be made by the translator based exclusively on efficiency reasons. The reader will remember that Ada does not specify whether parameter passing should be implemented by reference or by copy. Unlike Euclid, however, Ada does not require that programs with illegal aliasing be caught before execution time by a program verifier. Some illegal Ada programs might thus remain uncaught, and, as a consequence, a different implementation of parameter passing for the same program might produce different results.

The Euclid (and Gypsy) approach is certainly interesting, and the adopted solutions are clean. Some restrictions imposed by Euclid cannot be enforced by a traditional compiler and require a program development system that includes a program verifier. In particular, all legality assertions need to be proven by the verifier. The success of the approach taken by Euclid and Gypsy is largely dependent on the level of success that program verification will encounter among practitioners. At present, this is a controversial issue, partly because of the paucity of experience with verification in real-life applications.

6.3   PROGRAM CHECKING

In trying to reason about programs, one of the tools at our disposal is the computer. The activity of using a computer to help detect program errors is referred to as *program checking*. Program testing is one form of program checking. The syntax checks and type checks that a compiler performs are other forms of program checking. In fact, there is a spectrum of checks that can be performed on a program, ranging from the purely static, done by a simple compiler, to the completely dynamic, done by a program tester. This section examines these types of checks and their ramifications in language design.

6.3.1 Static Checks

Static checks are checks that can be done without running the program. We have seen (in Chapter 4) that strongly typed languages allow type correctness to be checked at translation time. In the last section, we saw that the specification of global variables imported by a procedure allows yet another level of static checking. At a further level, we could check for such things as the possible use of a variable before assignment, or two consecutive assignments to a variable, or assignment to a variable that is never used. Although these may not be errors in any particular execution of the program, they are symptomatic of possible problems. Such errors can be detected statically based on a control flow model of the program. Since such a model is not necessary for the translation of the program into machine code, traditional compilers do not construct one and therefore are unable to detect the above anomalous conditions. The control flow model—usually a graph—is necessary because the questions we are asking are of the form, ''Is there a possible control flow path along which such a condition is true?'' Such checking is referred to as *data flow analysis*.

6.3.2 Run-time Checks

There are conditions that can be constructed statically but cannot be evaluated statically. Such checks must necessarily be postponed until run-time or must be evaluated by a program verifier. Thus, in Euclid, the requirement that two actual reference parameters to a procedure must be nonoverlapping requires that for the call p (a [i], a [j]), the condition $i \neq j$ holds. Although the condition can be constructed by the compiler, it is passed to the verifier, or, in the testing phase, it can be transformed into a condition to be checked at run-time. Another example is the run-time check to ensure that array indices are within the specified bounds.

6.3.3 Testing

Testing, as we have already said, is another form of program checking. It requires the running of a program on sample input and is aimed at uncovering errors. Often, a printout (*trace*) showing the values of selected variables at some points of the program is also produced, in order to help discover the source of an error. Anyone who has tried to test a program recognizes the difficulty of this activity and the lack of any quantitative criteria for measuring success. Nevertheless, there are a number of criteria for selecting a set of test data that can guarantee a certain degree of thoroughness of testing. For example, test data should be such that (1) each and every statement is executed at least once, or (2) each and every branch of the control flow is executed at least once, or (3) each and every control path is executed at least once (a finite set of paths is selected for consideration if the number of paths in the program is infinite—for example, in the presence of loops).

A detailed discussion of program testing is beyond the scope of this book; the interested reader is referred to the specialized literature referenced in the Further Reading section at the end of the chapter. We would like to stress here, however, that no practical test criteria can guarantee the absence of errors. In particular, it is easy to show that the three criteria mentioned above are inadequate even for a very restricted class of programs.

Suppose that our programs require only a sequence of linear assignment statements—that is, statements of the form

$$y := a1*x1 + a2*x2 + \ldots + am*xm + b$$

where y, $x1$, $x2$, . . . xm are program variables, and $a1$, $a2$, . . . am, b are constants. A program P with input variables $x1,x2,$ . . . xm and output variables $y1,y2,$ . . . yn (these variables are assumed to be disjoint) can be viewed as a function mapping points from a m-dimensional space into points of a n-dimensional space. The function that maps each m-tuple $(x1,x2,$ . . . $xm)$ into a value of yi, $1 \leq i \leq n$, can be viewed as a hyperplane in a $(m+1)$-dimensional space. Any of such planes, for $1 \leq i \leq n$, can be uniquely determined by giving $m+1$ (linearly independent) points. Thus we can conclude that testing the program can guarantee correctness if the hyperplanes identified by our test data are coincident with the desired hyperplanes. It would take at least $m+1$ linearly independent sets of test data to test the program exhaustively. However, each of the three test criteria mentioned above would only require one test run.

6.3.4 Symbolic Execution

Still another form of program checking is symbolic execution, which tries to overcome the problem of too few test cases by running the program on symbolic data and deriving the values of output data as functions of input data. During the course of symbolically executing a program, it is also possible to catch certain program anomalies, such as nontraversable paths (which imply useless code). Symbolic execution has not met with particular success in practice, and the subject is beyond the scope of this text. The interested reader is referred to the material referenced in the Further Reading section.

6.4 PROGRAM PROVING

In verifying a program, we try to prove mathematically that the program is correct— that is, that it meets its specifications. Whereas after testing a program we may only be sure that the program ran correctly on the particular data we happened to choose, with verification we try to guarantee that the program runs correctly on *any* legal input data. This is, of course, a more ambitious and thus more difficult goal.

6.4.1 Formal Semantics

The primary importance of the verification area has been in motivating precise definitions of programming language semantics. For if we hope to prove that a particular program accomplishes a given task, we first need to know precisely what each program statement does. Chapter 3 showed the operational approach to semantic definition, which describes the semantics of a programming language by means of an abstract model of execution of the programs written in the language. The model describes the creation and manipulation of the basic data structures needed by the processor for executing programs. The method is valuable from a pedagogical point of view, because it suggests an abstract model for the implementation. However, the level of the operational description given in Chapter 3 is too informal to be of much use in mathematical proofs.

Several formal methods have been proposed. For example, the *axiomatic method*, which will be briefly illustrated here, is based on mathematical logic. In this approach a state of computation is described not by the contents of the processor's data structures, but rather by a logical expression on program variables (called a *predicate*, or *assertion*) that must be true in that state.

A predicate P that is required to hold after a statement S is called a *postcondition* for S. A predicate Q such that the execution of S terminates and postcondition P holds upon termination is called a *precondition* for S and P. For example, $y = 3$ is a precondition for statement $x := y + 1$ (x and y are integer variables), and postcondition $x > 0$. The predicate $y \geq 0$ is also a precondition for statement $x := y + 1$ and postcondition $x > 0$. Actually, $y \geq 0$ is the *weakest precondition*: that is, the necessary and sufficient precondition for statement $x := y + 1$ that leads to postcondition $x > 0$. A predicate W is called the weakest precondition for a statement S and a postcondition P if any precondition Q for S and P implies W: that is, W holds for any precondition Q. Implication is written as "$\Rightarrow$". In the example, we have

$$y = 3 \Rightarrow y \geq 0$$

In general, given an assignment statement $x := E$ and a postcondition P, the weakest precondition is obtained by replacing each occurrence of x in P with expression E. The weakest precondition is written as $P_{x \to E}$. In the example, $P_{x \to y+1}$ is $y + 1 > 0$—that is, $y \geq 0$. .

The semantics of a programming language can be formally described by a function *wp* (called a *predicate transformer*) that for any statement S and any postcondition P, has as its value the weakest precondition W. This is written as

$$wp\ (S,P) = W$$

In the case of an assignment statement $x := E$ we have

$$wp\ (x := E, P) = P_{x \to E}$$

This characterization of assignments is correct under the assumption that the evaluation of the right-hand side of the statement does not have a side effect. Moreover, the variable being assigned cannot be an alias of other program variables. In such cases the execution of the assignment may also affect variables not appearing at the left-hand side of the statement, and the given predicate transformer would be incorrect. This is an example of how side effects and aliasing can complicate formal as well as informal reasoning about programs.

Simple statements, such as assignment statements, can be combined into more complex actions by means of statement-level control structures. Therefore, *composition rules* are needed to characterize the semantic effect of combining individual statements into a program segment.

For example, in the case of sequencing, if we know that

$$wp\ (S1, P) = Q$$

and

$$wp\ (S2, Q) = R$$

then

$$wp\ (S2;\ S1, P) = R$$

The cases of selection and iteration are more complex. The discussion that follows will use selection and iteration schemes based on guarded commands discussed in Chapter 5.

If P is the postcondition that must be established by the **if** statement

if $B1 \to S1$
▯ $B2 \to S2$
  .
  .
  .
▯ $Bn \to Sn$
fi

the weakest precondition is a predicate that must express the following facts.

a. At least one guard must be true, otherwise the program aborts and cannot satisfy P.

b. For all the branches that have a **true** guard,* the corresponding statement list must establish the truth of *P*.

Formally, this can be written as

wp (**if**-*stat, P*) = (*B1* **or** *B2* **or** . . . **or** *Bn*) **and**
    (*B1* ⇒ wp (*S1, P*) **and** *B2* ⇒ wp (*S2, P*) **and** . . . .
    and *Bn* ⇒ wp (*Sn, P*))

For example, given the program fragment (*x,y,* and *max* are integers)

if $x \geqslant y \rightarrow max:=x$
⫿ $x \leqslant y \rightarrow max:=y$
fi

and the postcondition

(max=x **and** $x \geqslant y$*)* **or** *(max=y* **and** $y \geqslant x$*)*

the weakest precondition is easily proven to be **true**: that is, no constraints on variables
need be imposed to ensure the desired postcondition.
    Suppose now that *P* is the postcondition that must be established by the following
loop.

do   *B1* → *S1*
⫿   *B2* → *S2*
      .
      .
      .
⫿   *Bn* → *Sn*
od

The problem here is that we do not know how many times the body of the loop is
iterated. Indeed, if we knew, for example, that the number of iterations were *n*, the
above construct would be equivalent to the sequential composition of *n* **if** statements,
with the same guarded-command set; and thus its semantics would be straightforward
(based on the semantics of sequencing and **if** statements).
    To overcome this difficulty, we will abandon the goal of providing the weakest
precondition and will characterize the semantics of the **do** statement by showing how
a *sufficient* precondition *Q* can be derived from a given postcondition *P*. Since our
goal is to write correct programs, the truth of *Q* ensures the truth of the (unknown)
weakest precondition and hence the truth of *P* (the desired postcondition).

---

*Recall that there can be more than one, any of which can be chosen nondeterministically.

The condition Q must be such that

a. The loop terminates.

b. At loop exit, P holds.

Thus predicate Q can be written as $Q = T$ **and** R, where T implies termination of the loop and R implies the truth of P at loop exit.

Inventing two predicates T and R that satisfy these properties is not straightforward. For simplicity's sake, we ignore here the problem of termination and focus our attention on inventing R. Suppose we are able to identify a predicate I that holds both before and after each loop iteration and, at loop exit (i.e., when no Bi's are true) I implies P. I is called an *invariant predicate* for the loop. Formally, I satisfies the following conditions.

> **i.** I **and** $(B1$ **or** $B2$ **or** $\ldots$ **or** $Bn) \Rightarrow$ wp (IF,R)
> where IF is the statement obtained by replacing the keywords **do, od** of the loop with **if, fi**;
>
> **ii.** I **and not** $(B1$ **or** $B2$ **or** $\ldots$ **or** $Bn) \Rightarrow P$

If we are able to identify a predicate I that satisfies both (**i**) and (**ii**), then we can take I as the desired predicate R, because P holds upon termination if $R=I$ holds before executing the loop.

An example of the use of invariants is given in the next section.

6.4.2 Program Verification

An in-depth study of the theory of program verification and of the software tools needed for automatic program verification lies beyond the scope of this book. However, we are now in a position to state precisely how programs can be proven correct, and to give a glimpse of the issues involved. First of all, the correctness requirements of the program must be specified formally, by giving two predicates: a precondition IN (or *input assertion*) on input variables and a postcondition OUT (or *output assertion*) on input and output variables. The job of verification is to show that if IN holds before executing the program, execution terminates in a state where OUT holds. This proof requires the use of the semantic characterization of statements such as the one described in the previous section.

Program verification is illustrated here with the aid of a simple example. Consider the following program fragment, in which all variables are assumed to be integers.

```
i:= k; sum:= k;
do i > 1 → i:= i−1;
          sum:= sum+i
od
```

Let the input assertion be

IN: $k > 0$

and let the output assertion be

OUT: sum $= \sum_{j=1}^{k} j$ and $k > 0$

We want to prove the above fragment correct with respect to IN and OUT.

The termination of the loop obviously is assured, because variable i is only altered by instruction $i := i - 1$ and thus can only assume a decreasing sequence of values, which would eventually make $i > 1$ **false**.

For the invariant, the predicate

I: sum $= \sum_{j=1}^{k} j$ and $0 < i \leq k$

easily can be proven to satisfy conditions (**i**) and (**ii**) of the previous section. Thus, starting the execution of the loop with variables satisfying I assures termination in a state satisfying P.

Finally, it is easy to prove that I holds after the instructions

$i := k; sum := k;$

if the precondition $k > 0$ holds before the two instructions.

In conclusion, if IN holds before executing the above fragment, execution terminates in a state where OUT holds: that is, the program is correct with respect to IN and OUT.

Given the input and output assertions, program verification proceeds by deriving *intermediate assertions* that must be proven to hold at various points in the program. In particular, as we have seen, intermediate assertions must be supplied by the verifier (human or machine) in the form of loop invariants. Other examples of intermediate assertions are the legality assertions generated by the Euclid compiler and the assertions that can be explicitly specified by the programmer in Euclid via **assert** statement. The purpose of the Euclid **assert** statement is to supply intermediate assertions to be proven by the verifier as an integral part of the program. In this way, assertions become part of the documentation of the program. Moreover, there are options that allow the programmer to transform **assert** statements into run-time checks automatically during the testing phase or, alternatively, to suppress their evaluation. Finally, if a verifier is part of the set of tools provided by the programming system, assertions can be proven by the verifier and the program is fully certified statically.

The influence of programming language features on the process of reasoning is felt by both human readers and machine verifiers. Many features that make reasoning about programs difficult for humans are also hard to deal with for a program verifier.

For example, side effects in functions complicate the evaluation of the weakest precondition for assignments, as the following example shows. Let $y := f(x) + z$ be an assignment statement and let $P(z)$ be a predicate on variable z that must hold as a postcondition for the assignment. The absence of side effects guarantees that $P(z)$ is also the weakest precondition. The possibility of side effects, however, requires examining the function f, because z might be modified as a side effect. Moreover, the verifier—be it human or automatic—must be careful if aliasing is permitted by the language. In the example, $P(z)$ would not be the weakest precondition if z and y were aliases.

Program verification is still in its infancy, and it is controversial whether it will ever become a computing practice. Nevertheless, program verification issues have a deep influence on programming and programming languages. They stimulate a rigorous approach to programming and provide a formal definition of programming languages. Even in the absence of a program verifier, reasoning rigorously about program correctness can help the programmer in discovering possible errors. Intermediate assertions that should be proven by the verifier (e.g., loop invariants) can be expressed as run-time checks and provide a useful tool for certifying programs via systematic testing.

Before ending this chapter, we want to emphasize why we have chosen to discuss testing and verification even though our primary topic is programming languages. There are basically two reasons for this choice. One is that these areas are increasingly influencing the design of languages. The second and more important reason is that since the motivation for programming languages is software development, the study of techniques for building reliable software is an integral part of the study of languages. Although a comprehensive study of these issues is outside the scope of this book, this chapter provides familiarity with the basic issues and forms a starting point for further study.

SUGGESTIONS FOR FURTHER READING AND BIBLIOGRAPHIC NOTES

Program correctness and reliability, two important aspects of software engineering, have emerged as popular themes since the early 1970s. The paper by Parnas in (Yeh 1977**a**) discusses reliability versus correctness and shows how software structure can have impact on reliability. (Boehm 1976) shows how early error detection and correction in programs can reduce production costs. Practical techniques, such as walk-throughs and code inspections, are described by (Yourdon 1975) and (Baker 1972).

Programming language constructs that make reasoning about programs hard are analyzed in several papers. Dijkstra's famous letter on the **goto** statement (Dijkstra 1968**a**) was followed by several papers on other aspects of languages. (Hoare 1975**a** and **b**) and (Kieburtz 1976) analyze the role of pointers. (Wulf and Shaw 1973) discusses the role of global variables. (Popek et al. 1977) discusses side effects and aliasing. (Reynolds 1979) categorizes most of such harmful features. These findings have strongly influenced the design of several recent languages, such as CLU, Alphard, Gypsy, Euclid, and Russell.

Static program checking is partly discussed elsewhere in this book (e.g., Chapter 4 discusses type checking at length). The role of data flow analysis in detecting program anomalies is discussed in (Fosdick and Osterweil 1976) and (Hecht 1977). Other arguments are given in (Williams 1979).

(Myers 1979) provides a comprehensive view of the activities involved in software testing. Formal approaches to program testing are discussed by several papers collected in (Yeh 1977**b**) and surveyed by Goodenough in (Wegner 1979). The discussion of the inadequacy of the testing criteria reported in Section 6.3.3 is taken from (Tai 1980).

Symbolic execution is presented in (King 1976). Software development systems that incorporate a symbolic executor are described by (Cheatham et al. 1979) and (Asirelli et al. 1979).

The mathematical foundations of program verification were laid by (Floyd 1967) and (Hoare 1969). A detailed presentation of the Floyd-Hoare theory is given in (Manna 1973). The state-of-the-art in the field can be found in (Yeh 1977**b**) and in London's paper in (Wegner 1979). (DeMillo et al. 1979) argues that program verification cannot be used in practice to guarantee software reliability, because of the nature of proofs. They cite examples from mathematics in which proofs of theorems are shown to contain errors years after their truth had been accepted. Our presentation of the axiomatic method is based on (Dijkstra 1976). It is important to observe, however, that Dijkstra's emphasis is not on program verification, but rather on a methodology for developing correct programs. First, he develops a simple language that supports the writing of elegant programs and gives a formal definition for each language construct in terms of predicate transformers. Second, he illustrates a calculus that, given the input and output predicates, allows one to derive a program that is correct with respect to the predicates. Dijkstra's approach is thus *constructive*; programs are not proven correct after being written, but rather are derived correct by the calculus. The approach is presented by developing several examples of low to moderate complexity, and it is not clear whether (and how) it can be used in more complex and larger applications. Nevertheless, the book represents a fundamental contribution to the development of a discipline of programming and is highly recommended reading.

Exercises

6.1   Suppose you are given the following program specification.

The program evaluates and prints the factorial of a positive integer whose value is read.

Is the following Pascal program correct? Is it reliable?

```
program factorial (input,output);
var i,n,fact: integer;
begin read (n);
```

```
        fact: = n; i: = n;
        while i ≠ 1 do
        begin i: = i − 1;
              fact: = fact * i
        end;
        write (fact)
   end.
```

6.2   Consider the following Pascal function.

```
function f (x,y: integer) : integer;
        function g(z: integer) : integer;
        begin

            . . .

        end;
   begin
        f: = g (x) + g (y)
   end.
```

1. Give convincing (but informal) arguments that prove (or disprove) the statement "For any body of function g, the function calls $f(a,b)$ and $f(b,a)$ produce the same results for any pair of integer variables a and b.

2. Let us change the parameter passing mode of the two functions f and g to call by reference, and suppose that f is always called as $f(a,a)$, a being an integer variable. Discuss whether we can safely modify the statement $f: = g(x) + g(y)$ into $f: = 2 * g(x)$.

6.3   Give simple examples that show the difference in number of runs between the testing criteria numbers 1 and 2 mentioned in Section 6.3.3.

6.4   Give simple examples of programs without loops that show the difference in number of runs between the testing criteria numbers 2 and 3 mentioned in Section 6.3.3.

6.5   Suppose you are (manually) trying to identify test data that satisfy one of the criteria mentioned in Section 6.3.3. Briefly comment on the effect of **goto** statements.

6.6   Suppose we modify Dijkstra's guarded **if** statements as shown below:

```
if B1 → S1
▯ B2 → S2

    . . .

▯ BN → SN
else SE
fi
```

The **else** branch can be selected only if no guarded branch has a **true** guard. Give the predicate transformer for this statement.

6.7   Describe the semantics of the following Pascal statements in terms of predicate transformers:

— **if** statement (without an **else** part).
— **if then else**.
— **for** loop.

6.8   Given the input assertion

IN: $n > 0$

and the output assertion

OUT: $fact = n * (n-1) * (n-2) * \ldots * 1$

formally prove the correctness of the program of exercise 6.1 with respect to IN and OUT.

CHAPTER SEVEN

PROGRAMMING IN THE LARGE

"Human fallibility—from grand to grandiose"

(Mills 1979)

The production of large programs—those consisting of more than several thousand lines—presents many challenging problems that do not arise when developing smaller programs. The same methods and techniques that work well with small programs do not necessarily apply to larger programs. As the lack of applicability of this "scaling up" has been recognized, approaches to the production of large programs have been pursued along three paths.

1. Management techniques to provide control over personnel assigned to a software project and monitor their progress.

2. Software design methodologies to attack the particular problems found in large programs. These methodologies have in turn led to the development of supporting language facilities.

3. Software development tools to assist in the creative part and to automate as much as possible the noncreative parts of software development.

To stress the differences between small and large systems production, DeRemer and Kron invented the terms "programming in the small" and "programming in the large." Point 1 above reflects the most striking difference between programming in the small and programming in the large. If only one person can produce the needed software, all problems boil down to the professional skill of that one programmer and the availability of a suitable programming environment. The development of large software systems which requires several programmers, on the other hand, is not merely a matter of "programming," but mainly a management problem. Successful management must be capable of estimating the resources necessary to accomplish a given

201

task, assigning resources to the project at the appropriate times, breaking down the development effort into well-defined and clearly separated phases, monitoring each phase through periodic design reviews, and imposing a set of standards for each activity. Aron notes that the "emphasis on management rather than technology represents a major change in the nature of programming since the 1950s" (Aron 1974). Most of these issues, however, are beyond the scope of this book; the interested reader is referred to the literature referenced in the Further Reading section.

This chapter focuses on points 2 and 3 given above. The two points are strongly related. For example, a program library can be viewed either as simply a tool or as a necessary component of a methodology based on the incremental development and production of reusable software.

The chapter is organized as follows. Section 7.1 further motivates the distinction between programming in the small and programming in the large, with the aid of an example. Section 7.2 reviews software design methodologies and stresses the differences between design methodologies for small and large programs. Section 7.3 evaluates the features provided by current languages in support of programming in the large. Section 7.4 discusses the need for program development systems in which the language and a rich set of tools are integrated to provide a friendly programming environment.

7.1 WHAT IS A LARGE PROGRAM?

The concept of a large program is difficult to define. We certainly do not want to equate the size of a program (e.g., the number of source statements) with its complexity. Largeness relates more to the "size" and complexity of the problem being solved than to the final size of a program. Usually, however, the size of a program is a good indication of the complexity of the problem being solved.

Consider the task of building a reservation system for a particular airline. The system is expected to keep a data base of flight information. Airline agents working at remote sites may access the data base at arbitrary times and in any order. They may inquire about flight information, such as time and price; make or cancel a reservation on a particular flight; update existing information, such as local telephone number for a passenger. Certain authorized personnel can access the data base to do special operations, such as adding or canceling a flight, or changing a plane type. Others may access the system to obtain statistical data about a particular flight or all flights.

A problem of this magnitude imposes severe restrictions on the solution strategy to be followed. The characteristics of such problems include the following.

- The system has to function correctly. A seemingly small error, such as losing a reservation list or interchanging two different lists, could be extremely costly. To guarantee correctness of the system virtually any cost can be tolerated.

- The system is long-lived. The cost associated with producing such a system is so high that it is not practical to replace it with a totally new system. It is expected that the cost will be recouped only over a long period of time.

- During its lifetime, the system undergoes considerable modification. For our example, because of completely unforeseen new Federal regulations, changes might be required in price structure, a new type of airplane might be added, and so on. Other changes might be desirable because experience with the system has uncovered some weaknesses. We might find it desirable to have the system find the best route automatically by trying different connections.

- Because of the magnitude of the problem, many people—tens or hundreds—are involved in the development of the system.

These characteristics impose severe requirements both on the system development process and on the tools used, namely

- The work must be divided among different people. The work assigned to each person must be stated clearly and unambiguously. One person should not have to know the details of other persons' work, just how theirs interacts with his or hers.

- The system is built up from pieces developed independently by several people. We will call such pieces *modules*. These modules must be designed and certified independently. It would be beneficial if some of these pieces could be taken from already-existing systems. Similarly, it would be beneficial if these pieces could be reused in future projects. Indeed, the application itself is so general that the entire system might be reused, with minor modifications, for different airlines.

- The system must be modifiable easily: that is, it should be possible to change the internals of one module without requiring changes to the entire system.

- It must be possible to show the correctness of the system based on the correctness of the constituent modules.

These characteristics illustrate the concept of a large program. These problems are less important with a one-person programming task: For example, there would be less need for dividing the work and thus less emphasis on clear interface specifications. The possibility exists, at least in theory, of redoing the system from scratch, and so modifiability is less important. Correctness is involved only with one module and therefore is easier to assess. On the other hand, a large system is composed of a collection of interacting modules. If no systematic design methodologies are adopted, each module can interact with any other module in some subtle manner. Consequently, each module cannot be designed, understood, and proven correct apart from all the other modules. The complexity of such systems becomes unmanageable.

The boundaries between programming in the large and programming in the small can hardly be stated rigorously. However, we can assume that programming in the large addresses the problem of modular system decomposition, whereas programming in the small refers to the production of individual modules. The methodologies useful for the two activities are discussed in Section 7.2. Section 7.3 evaluates programming languages in light of programming in the large.

7.2 PROGRAMMING IN THE SMALL VERSUS PROGRAMMING IN THE LARGE: DESIGN METHODOLOGIES

Research in software design methodologies has focused on top-down design as an effective way of mastering the difficulties of software production. In top-down design, a problem is iteratively decomposed into subproblems that can be solved independently.

When applied to small programs, the method is named *stepwise refinement*. Stepwise refinement has been illustrated in the literature as a process of writing and rewriting a program. At each step of development, the program consists of declarations and statements, some of them legal in the programming language, others abstract and to be refined at the next step. At each step of refinement, abstract declarations and statements can be left in the code as comments for the purpose of documentation. The process continues until eventually the entire text is a legal program.

Although stepwise refinement is an effective methodology for programming in the small, it fails when applied to large programs. One reason is that it does not favor the recognition of commonalities between parts. Programmers are not encouraged to represent common parts by a unique abstraction, to be refined just once and invoked wherever necessary. Rather, each part is separately refined. Another reason is that the final program does not mirror the design process adequately, even if abstract statements are left as comments in the text. Moreover, abstract statements usually are written in informal English prose, and it may be necessary to read their refinement to understand precisely what they do.* Consequently, readability and modifiability of programs can be hampered for programs of substantial size.

Top-down design of large applications must support system decomposition into small-sized programs (modules). Following the principle of information hiding, the designer must distinguish clearly between what a module does—what the module exports for use by other modules—from how it does it—its internal details. A *module interface* should specify exactly the internally defined entities exported for use by other modules and the externally defined entities imported from other modules. Designing a module consists of designing its interface and, iteratively, any new subsidiary modules that will be used by the module.

---

*This last problem can be solved by stating the abstract statements in a formal notation.

As an example, consider the airline reservation problem of Section 7.1. We might have a *flight module,* which provides information about flights as they are scheduled. Given a flight number, the module provides the total number of seats, the time of departure, possible connecting flights, etc. The module also provides update operations—for example, to modify departure times. We might have a *reservation module* to handle reservation lists for all flights; given a flight number and a date, it allows one to make or cancel reservations on a particular flight. A *statistics module* might provide operations that collect statistics on some or all flights. The reservation module must have a restricted access to the flight module. It can obtain information about flights (e.g., number of seats) but cannot perform any updates. For example, the design of the reservation module can be recorded as sketched below.

module *reservation*
   import function *number_of_seats (flight number)* **return** *integer*
         from *flight;*
   export procedure *make_reservation (flight_number, customer);*
         procedure*cancel_reservation (flight_number, customer);*

Function *number_of_seats* is imported from module *flight;* it receives a formal parameter of type *flight_number* and returns an *integer.* Procedures *make_reservation* and *cancel_reservation* have parameters of type *flight_number* and *customer;* they update the list of passengers for a certain flight.

Design is complete when all module interfaces have been specified. Only at this stage can we turn to the implementation of module bodies. The separation between the two phases of design and implementation distinguishes this approach from stepwise refinement. In stepwise refinement, design and coding are developed hand in hand. Here we first decompose the system into modules, then later address the problem of implementing the module bodies (e.g., using stepwise refinements).

It can be argued that modular system decomposition can be driven by the recognition of two particular classes of abstractions: procedural abstractions and data abstractions. Procedural abstractions are operations that perform a mapping between input and output data objects. Data abstractions are a set of operations that manipulate a particular class of data objects. A module corresponds either to a procedural abstraction or to a data abstraction. At each stage of top-down design, the problem to be solved is how to design an abstraction. Each abstraction is iteratively decomposed into subsidiary abstractions until the program is broken into pieces of moderate complexity.

7.3   LANGUAGE FEATURES FOR PROGRAMMING IN THE LARGE

This section discusses how programming languages support the needs of programming in the large and, in particular, the design methodology presented in Section 7.2. All programming languages provide features for decomposing programs into smaller and largely autonomous units. Such units will be called *physical modules* in the sequel; we will use the term *logical module* to denote a module identified at the design stage. A logical module may be implemented by one or more physical modules.

Our discussion will be organized according to the following three criteria.

1. What is the notion of physical module supported by the language, and how well does it capture the logical properties specified at the design stage?

2. How can a program be built by combining physical modules? How does the program structure imposed by the language mirror the hierarchical modular decomposition found during design?

3. How independently can physical modules be implemented? In particular, how long-lived and reusable are physical modules?

The discussion will be centered around Pascal, SIMULA 67, and Ada. Pascal can be viewed here as a representative of the class of ALGOL-like languages. Our conclusions about Pascal hold, with minor changes, for other members of the class, such as ALGOL 60 and ALGOL 68. A few comments on CLU will be given in the section devoted to Ada.

7.3.1 Pascal

7.3.1.1 Modules

The only features provided by Pascal for physical modular decomposition are procedures and functions. Procedures and functions, however, can only implement procedural abstraction. To implement data abstractions, we must separately describe type and procedure (function) declarations. In fact, the language does not provide any mechanisms for data encapsulation. As a result, there is no immediate one-to-one correspondence between the logical modules identified during design and the physical modules of the program.

7.3.1.2 Program Structure

Every program in Pascal has the following structure.

program *programname (files);*
    declarations of constants, types, variables,
        procedures and functions;
begin
    statements (no declarations)
end.

A program consists of declarations and operations. The operations are either the built-in ones provided by the language or those declared as functions and procedures. A procedure or function itself may contain the declaration of other procedures and/or functions. The organization of a Pascal program is thus a tree structure of modules (static nesting tree—Section 3.6). The tree structure represents the textual nesting of lower-level modules. Nesting is used to control the scope of items declared within modules, according to the static binding rule presented in Section 3.6.

In order to evaluate the structure of Pascal programs, consider the following example. Suppose that the top-down modular design of a module A identifies two modules B and C providing subsidiary procedural abstractions. Similarly, module B invokes two private procedural abstractions provided by modules D and E. Module C invokes a private procedural abstraction provided by F. Figure 7.1 shows a nesting structure for a program that satisfies the design constraints.

A basic problem with the solution of Figure 7.1 is that the structure does not enforce the restrictions on procedure invocations found at the design stage. Actually, the structure allows for the possibility of several other invocations. For example, E can invoke D, B, and A; C can invoke B and A, and so on. On the other hand, the structure of Figure 7.1 imposes some restrictions that might become undesirable. For example, if we discover that module F needs the procedural abstraction provided by module E, the structure of Figure 7.1 is no longer adequate. Figure 7.2 shows a rearrangment of the program structure that is compatible with this new requirement.

The problem with the organization of Figure 7.2 is that the structure no longer displays the hierarchical decomposition of abstractions. Module E appears to be a subsidiary abstraction used by A, although the only reason for its placement at that level in the tree is that both modules B and F need to refer to it.

Similar problems occur for variables (constants and types). The tree structure does not forbid undesired access to variables declared in enclosing modules. In addition, if any two modules M_i and M_j must share a variable, this variable must be declared in a module M that statically encloses both M_i and M_j.

Further problems are caused by the textual layout of Pascal programs. The entire program is a single monolithic text. If the program is large, module boundaries are not immediately visible, even if the programmer uses careful conventions for identation. A module heading can appear well before its body, because of intervening

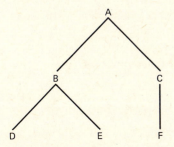

Figure 7.1   Static nesting tree.

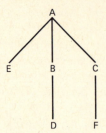

Figure 7.2 A rearrangement of the program structure of Figure 7.1.

inner module declarations. As a consequence, programs can be difficult to read and modify.

The problems with Pascal discussed in this section stem from block structure, and therefore hold for other ALGOL-like languages as well. Block structure is adequate for programming in the small because it supports stepwise refinement quite naturally. It is not so valuable for structuring large programs. The program structure resulting from nesting interferes with the logical structure found during design. This impairs the writability, readability, and modifiability of programs.

7.3.1.3 Module Independence

The question addressed here is how modules can be developed independently, and how long-lived and reusable they are. These requisites are partly attained at the design stage by a clean definition of module interfaces and a systematic application of the principle of information hiding. In addition, it is desirable to support the separate implementation of modules. It should be possible to compile and certify modules separately. Separately compiled and certified modules should be kept in a library, ready for later reuse.

The official description of Pascal does not define a standard facility for separate compilation. Several implementations, however, do support it. In such a case, one might use Pascal to program each module as a separate compilation unit. Separately compiled modules would be combined to form a unique system in a logically distinct phase. This strategy for the implementation of large programs would overcome most of the problems discussed in Sections 7.3.1.1 and 7.3.1.2.

However, the lack of a Pascal standard for separate compilation leaves some important points unanswered:

1. What program entities can a separate compilation unit export?

2. How is a unit interface specified?

3. What amount of type checking across unit interfaces is prescribed to occur?

Different implementations can adopt different solutions to these points. As a result, Pascal programs developed at different installations may be incompatible.

In most current implementations, only outer-level procedures or functions can be compiled separately. Separately compiled units later are assembled via a standard linker provided by the operating system. The linkage editor resolves the bindings between the entities imported by each module and the corresponding entities exported by other modules. Unfortunately, however, the linkage editor does not check module interfaces for type correctness. For example, a call to an external procedure can be inconsistent with the corresponding procedure declaration, and yet this error might remain uncaught. A safer separate-compilation facility could be designed, for example, along the lines of the Ada scheme discussed below, in Section 7.3.3.

7.3.2 SIMULA 67

7.3.2.1 Modules

Logical modules can be represented in SIMULA 67 as procedures, functions, or classes. Although a class can collect a set of related data and subprogram declarations, it provides no means for hiding internal details from other modules. Information hiding can be achieved only by adoption of disciplined programming standards.

7.3.2.2 Program Structure

SIMULA 67 adopts a conventional ALGOL-like block structure. The unusual feature of the language is that blocks and classes may be prefixed by a class name. Prefixing a class defines a subclass (as discussed in Chapter 4). Prefixing a block can be illustrated by the following example. The following class—*list_processing*—defines a set of procedures that may be used in manipulating linked lists.

```
class list_processing;
    ref (element) first;
    boolean procedure empty;
            begin . . . check if list is empty . . . end;
    procedure insert (e);
            begin . . . insert element e in list . . . end;
    procedure remove (e);
            begin . . . remove element e from list . . . end;
begin
    first: = none
end
```

Prefixing a block with a class name makes the attributes of the class visible to the block. For example, a block that starts with

list_processing **begin** . . .

has access to procedures *empty, remove, insert* and reference *first*. This idea has been used in an interesting way to supply a set of commonly used facilities to SIMULA 67 programmers. The two classes, SIMSET and SIMULATION, have been defined to contain, respectively, list-processing and simulation primitives. Any SIMULA 67 program may use these classes simply by using either name as a prefix. These classes may be viewed as providing two fixed libraries of reusable modules.

Prefixing supports top-down modular design. A top-level class may be written to contain only the most global design decisions. Successive subclasses of this class contain further design decisions based on earlier ones—that is, those at lower levels of abstractions. At the lowest level, the program is written prefixed by the most detailed class.

Most large programs—for example, operating systems—exist in many versions. We must be able to control the development of all the versions by exploiting their similarities and considering them all to be members of a *family of programs*. At each design level, certain decisions are made that exclude some family members. At the lowest level, one particular member remains. Since a change in a design decision at a certain level affects all design decisions at lower levels, a change in an earlier design decision affects the program more substantially than a change in a later design decision. The early design decisions should thus be the most general and the least likely to change. SIMULA 67's subclass mechanism can support this methodology. Different subclasses of a class represent different family members with the same ancestor. A class embodies all the design decisions common to all its subclasses. A change in a subclass requires no modifications to the parent class, only to the lower-level subclasses.

The basic problem with SIMULA 67 is that prefixing is embedded within block structure. Consequently, the same criticisms raised for Pascal in Section 7.3.1.2 hold for SIMULA 67 as well.

7.3.2.3 Module Independence

With disciplined use of classes, one can design programs through the composition of highly independent modules. As in the case of Pascal, however, the official definition of SIMULA 67 does not specify a standard for separate development of modules.

A separate compilation facility has been introduced in the DEC System-10 SIMULA 67 implementation. In this implementation, procedure and class declarations can be compiled as separate modules. Each separate module can declare a class or procedure as EXTERNAL, indicating the use of a separately compiled module. Each separately compiled class or procedure must be compiled before any module that references it. This allows modules to be type-checked during compilation. This scheme forces a bottom-up system development: modules implementing subsidiary abstractions must be compiled before the module(s) using such abstractions.

7.3.3 Ada

7.3.3.1 Modules

An Ada module can be a (generic) subprogram, a (generic) package, or a task. Logical modules identified at the design stage can be mapped into Ada modules quite naturally.

Moreover, the language-supported distinction between module specification and module body allows one to separate what is exported by the module from what is hidden within the module.

7.3.3.2 Program Structure

An Ada program is a linear collection of modules that can be either (generic) subprograms or (generic) packages. These modules are called units. One particular unit that implements a subprogram is the main program in the usual sense. Modules can enclose declarations of inner modules. Consequently, a unit can be organized as a tree structure of modules. Any abuse of nesting within a unit causes the same problems discussed for Pascal.

These problems can be mitigated by the use of the *subunit* facility offered by the language. This facility permits the body of a module embedded in the declarative part of a unit (or subunit) to be written separately from the enclosing unit (or subunit). Instead of the entire module, only a fictitious body (stub) need appear in the declarative part of the enclosing unit. The following example illustrates the concept of the subunit.

```
procedure X (. . .) is          --unit specification
    W: INTEGER;
    package Y is                --inner unit specification
        A: INTEGER;
        function B (C: INTEGER) return INTEGER;
    end Y;
    package body Y is separate; --this is a stub
begin --use package Y and variable W
    .
    .
    .
end X;
```

```
separate (X)
package body Y is
    procedure Z (. . .) is separate; --this is a stub
    function B (C: INTEGER) return INTEGER is
    begin --use procedure Z
        .
        .
        .
    end B;
end Y;
```

```
separate (X.Y)
procedure Z (. . .) is
begin .
    .
    .
end Z;
```

The prefix **separate** (*X*) specifies package body *Y* as a subunit of unit *X*. Similarly, **separate** (*X.Y*) specifies procedure *Z* as a subunit of package *Y* nested within *X*.

The subunit facility not only can improve the readability of programs, but also supports a useful technique in top-down programming. When one is writing a program at a certain level of abstraction, it is best to leave some details to be decided at a lower level. Suppose you realize that a certain procedure is required to accomplish a given task. Although calls to that procedure can be immediately useful when you want to test the execution flow, the body of the procedure can be written at a later time.

The subunit facility, however, does not overcome all the problems caused by the tree nesting structure. The textually separate subunit body is still considered to be logically located at the point at which the corresponding stub appears in the enclosing (sub)unit. It is exactly this point that determines the entities visible to the subunit. In the above example, both subunits *Y* and *Z* can access variable *W* declared in unit *X*.

The remaining problem to be addressed is how the interfaces (i.e., import/export relationships) among units are specified in Ada. A unit exports all the entities specified in its specification part. It can import entities from other units if and only if the names of such units are listed in a suitable statement (**with** statement) that prefixes the unit.

For example, the following unit lists *X* in its **with** statement. Consequently, it is legal to call procedure *X* within *T*'s body.

```
with X;
package T is
        C: INTEGER;
        procedure D (. . .);
end T;
package body T is

        .

        .

        .

end T;
```

Similarly, the following procedure *U* can legally call procedure *T.D* and access variable *T.C*. On the other hand, unit *X* is not visible by *U*.

```
with T;
procedure U (. . .) is

        .

        .

        .

end U;
```

The interface of an Ada unit consists of the **with** statement, which lists the names of units from which entities are imported; and the unit specification, which lists the entities exported by the unit. Each logical module discovered at the design stage can be implemented as a unit. If top-down design was done carefully, logical modules should be relatively simple. Consequently, the depth of nesting within units should be very small, or even null. Note, however, that Ada does not forbid an abuse of nesting within units. Actually, the entire program could be designed as a single unit with a deeply nested tree structure. More desirable program structures can be achieved only by adherence to certain program development standards, since the language does not provide any means to enforce them.

7.3.3.3 Module Independence

The set of units and subunits comprising a program can be compiled in one or more separate compilations. Each compilation translates one or more units and/or subunits. The order of compilation must satisfy the following constraints.

- A unit can be compiled only if all units mentioned in its **with** statement have been compiled previously.

- A subunit can be compiled only if the enclosing unit has been compiled previously.

In addition, unit specifications can be compiled separately from their bodies. A unit body must be compiled after its specification. The specification of a unit U mentioned in the **with** statement of a unit W must be compiled before W. On the other hand, U's body can be compiled either before or after W.

These constraints assure that a unit is submitted for compilation only after the compilation of unit specifications from which it can import entities. The compiler saves in a library file the descriptors of all entities exported by units. When a unit is submitted for compilation, the compiler has access to the library file. Consequently, it is able to perform the same amount of type checking on the unit whether the program is compiled in parts or as a whole. If a package unit exports an encapsulated (private) data type, the type's representation is hidden to the programmer but known to the compiler, thanks to the **private** clause appearing in the package specification. Consequently, the compiler can generate code to allocate variables for such types declared in other units submitted for compilation prior to the package body (but after its specification).

When a unit is modified, it may be necessary to recompile several units. The change may potentially affect its subunits as well as all the units that name it in their **with** statements. In principle, all potentially affected units must be recompiled.

The separate compilation facility of Ada supports an incremental rather than a parallel development of programs, since units must be developed according to a partial ordering. This is not an arbitrary restriction, but a conscious design decision in support of methodical program development. A unit can be submitted for compilation only after the interfaces of all used units are frozen. Consequently, the programmer is forced to postpone the design of a unit body after designing such interfaces.

One of the goals of separate compilation is to support production of reusable software. Certified modules can be kept in a library and later combined to form different programs. The Ada solution is deficient on this point in the case of package units exporting encapsulated (private) data types. The visible part (the specification) of such packages must include the type's operations and a **private** clause that specifies the type's internal representation. This representation is not usable outside the package body; it is there only for the purpose of supporting separate compilation. Logically, this information belongs in the package body, together with the procedure bodies implementing the type's operations. Besides being aesthetically unpleasant, this feature has some unfortunate consequences:

- It violates the principle of top-down design. The representation must be determined at the same time as the specification of the data type.

- It limits the power of the language in supporting libraries of reusable modules. For example, a module using FIFO queues is compiled and validated with respect to a FIFO queue package providing a specific representation for FIFO queues (e.g., as arrays). The module must be recompiled if one wants to reuse it in a different program in which FIFO queues are implemented by a different data structure, even though the primitives for manipulating FIFO queues are the same in both cases.

On this particular point we can contrast the Ada approach with the scheme implemented by CLU. CLU's separate compilation facility is similar to Ada's. However, CLU allocates objects of an abstract type in the heap. Objects are created by a create procedure encapsulated within the cluster defining the abstract type. Created objects are accessed by other modules via pointers. Consequently, there is no need for such modules to know the representation of the abstract type. These modules need to know only the headings of the procedures that create and manipulate abstract objects. This is the only information that need appear in the specification part of a module implementing an abstract data type. A change of representation for abstract objects does not require recompilation of modules that use such abstract objects. In conclusion, CLU is more supportive of independent development than Ada.

7.3.4 An Ideal Scenario

The previous sections have stressed the conceptual differences between programming in the small and programming in the large. In particular, Sections 7.3.1 through 7.3.3 presented an evaluation of the features provided by existing programming languages in support of programming in the large. This section outlines an ideal scheme for the support of programming in the large. This scheme is somewhat similar to that found in Mesa.

The programming language should be composed of two sublanguages: the language for programming in the small (LPS) and the language for programming in the large (LPL). The more clearly distinguishable the two levels, the more readable the programs and the more suitable the language for programming large systems. Most current languages do not recognize LPS and LPL as two separate levels of system description and therefore merge them into the same notation. Mesa does, and provides a special LPL called Mesa Configuration Language (C/Mesa).

As an example of the distinction between LPL and LPS, consider a module that imports some external resources and exports some internal resources (data or procedures). The specification of imported and exported resources is indicated in the module interface written in LPS. For abstract data types, only the allowed operations are specified—no representation details. The interface specification allows each LPS module to be compiled independently from other modules. In particular, each module can be type-checked completely with respect to its interface. LPS specifies imported resources without naming the module(s) that provides them. The LPL commands map resources imported by each module to resources exported by other modules.

For example, a module P importing two procedures $P1$ and $P2$ and exporting a procedure $P3$, may have the following LPS interface specifications.

import *P1 (integer, boolean);*
      P2 (integer, character);
export *P3 (real, real);*

A module Q with the interface specification

import *. . . ;*
export *Q1 (integer, character);*

and a module R with the interface specification

import *. . . ;*
export *R1 (integer, boolean);*

may be structured in a system by the following LPL commands.

bind *P1* **of** *P* **to** *R1* **of** *R;*
      P2 **of** *P* **to** *Q1* **of** *Q;*

LPL is responsible for type checking the interface of each module with respect to the resources provided by other modules and specified in their own interfaces. It is also responsible for linking a set of validated LPS modules into a unique executable unit. LPL can be viewed as a glorified job control language that allows the programmer to specify the interconnections among the modules that constitute a software system. Besides facilities for specifying system configuration, an LPL should provide facilities for controlling versions and maintaining libraries of module descriptions. Such descriptions evolve as systems are developed, and LPL should support this evolution. This section basically concentrates on LPL as a language for system configuration.

LPL commands are executed by a processor that is somewhat similar to a linkage editor. This processor operates on object modules. To know whether an imported resource is provided by one module or another requires no recompilation of any module, but simply LPL processing. This approach favors the use of libraries of validated and reusable object modules.

This ideal scenario presents a problem in the case of modules importing abstract data types. When these modules are compiled, the compiler ignores the representation of local variables of abstract type.

In a heap-based language such as CLU, this lack of information is not a problem, because objects of an abstract type are allocated by the module implementing the abstract type, and other modules access them only via pointers (see also Section 7.3.3.4). In other languges, such as Ada, objects of an abstract type must be allocated at the activation of the modules where they are declared. But the run-time actions necessary to allocate variables of an imported abstract type become known only after LPL is processed. Consequently, the LPL processor must be capable of inserting such run-time actions into the object version of LPS modules.

The above discussion shows that the LPL processor is considerably more complex than the standard linkage editor. Besides binding imported resource names to the corresponding exported resources, it must perform intermodule type checking and, for some kinds of LPSs, generate code for storage allocation of abstract type variables.

The fact that this ideal scenario requires an entire extra piece of system software—the LPL processor—would traditionally be a reason to abandon the scheme. But as we have been stressing throughout, the ultimate goal is the attainment of an environment for reliable software development consisting of a language and other tools. The LPL processor should not be viewed as a tool that is necessitated by a language feature, but as one that supports a modular design methodology. Separating the linking function from the compiler corresponds to separating system structuring from module implementation.

The separation between the compiler and the linker that results from this scheme is somewhat reminiscent of the philosophy of older languages such as FORTRAN and PL/I. These languages, in fact, do have a separate compilation facility and separately compiled units are assembled by the linkage editor. However, the linkage editor is a low-level tool that does not type-check module interfaces. Using such a linkage editor as a LPL processor in the ideal scenario would mean abandoning the safety of strong typing at the system structuring level when errors are likely to be more costly.

7.4   SYSTEM DEVELOPMENT TOOLS

This chapter has emphasized the differences between programming in the large and programming in the small. We noted in Section 7.3 that most programming languages do not have specific facilities for supporting programming in the large. In Section 7.3.4, we noted that a type-checking linker is required in order for the language to help us distinguish between the two levels of activity. In theory, of course, such a facility is not necessary. Its utility lies in the help it can provide us in producing reliable software. This section reviews the kinds of tools used along with programming languages for software production. Although these tools also are employed for programming in the small, their use becomes essential in a programming-in-the-large environment.

The need for support tools was recognized very early in the programming era. In fact, assemblers were once viewed as helpful tools in programming the computer (in machine language). At present, a variety of development tools are often provided to establish friendly programming environments even on very small machines, such as personal computers. When confronted with the task of programming large systems, however, one comes to appreciate the fact that the programming language by itself is not sufficient. In this framework, the computer is viewed by the individual programmer not as a personal computational resource, but rather as a warehouse of public and private tools. Some of the tools are provided by the system; others—the modules designed by other programmers—are developed for the purpose of the particular project. The computer is also the medium through which all relevant information flows; it can be used for recording documentation, sending messages, and general management functions.

Basic Tools

Listed and described briefly below are the basic tools required for system development. These tools are basic in the sense that they are needed for any method of software development. Later, we will discuss some tools that support specific design methodologies.

1. **Text Editor**   That system component used to enter programs (as well as other types of documents) into the computer. The common method of program entry is by interactive text editing, which makes it easier to make corrections to the program text.

2. **Macroprocessor**   A simple translator that in a source document can replace specified strings with indicated target strings. More sophisticated macroprocessors allow the parameterization of the source string. This adds considerably to the tool's utility. A macroprocessor can be used

   (a) To overcome some language deficiencies, such as the absence of symbolic constants. For example, one can use MAXSIZE in the program and just before compilation let the macroprocessor replace it with the specific value.

      More generally, one can supplement a language with certain desired constructs. For example, RATFOR is a "structured" FORTRAN language based on this scheme. A number of control structures (e.g., **if**, **for**, **while**) have been defined as macros. A RATFOR program may contain these control structures. First, the RATFOR system replaces these macros by their definition in terms of FORTRAN, and then the program is compiled by a standard FORTRAN compiler.

   (b) To increase the readability and writability of programs. The use of a macroprocessor can lead to a reduction of clerical errors by giving a name to pieces of code that are repeated several times. One can then use this name instead of repeating the code. As the length of the named code segment increases, the advantages of this technique also increase. These writability advantages can be translated to readability advantages if one considers the input to the macroprocessor as the source program. The sequence of code that is repeated several times in the target program (i.e., the output of the macroprocessor) need only be read and understood once in the source program.

(c) To replace subprogram calls with the body of the subprogram. In this way, one can design the program such that every unit is regarded as a subprogram. The efficiency-related decision of whether to implement something as a subprogram or in-line code can be postponed and be based later on sample system runs. Ada allows this procedure by providing a directive to the compiler (**pragma** INLINE *subprogram_name*) that can appear in the same declarative part as the named subprogram.

3. **Interpreter/Compiler**   An interpreter is used to run a source program. It can usually produce better error diagnostics than a compiler and is therefore better suited for program debugging. On the other hand, an interpreter is less efficient in the use of time. It would be desirable to have a compiler and an interpreter that accept the same language so that once the program is validated, the interpreter can be used for debugging and the compiler for production. The INTERLISP system includes such a combination for LISP.

4. **File System**   A file system can be used to store data and/or programs either in source or in object format. The programmer can thus keep libraries of program components on mass storage. The system may provide help in administering such components by updating version numbers, creation dates, and so on. It is also possible to restrict access to the components to a specified set of users. Programmers working in a team can thus share their components, and the system prevents unauthorized users from accessing such components.

5. **Linkage Editor,** *or* **Linker**   A linker takes several independently compiled modules and merges them into one. The availability of a linker has many advantages: it allows different programmers to work on different modules concurrently, and it allows one module to be compiled once and then used in building different systems. To carry the latter advantage further, one can create a library of reusable modules that at different times are combined in different ways. Finally, if a bug is found in one module, only that module need be recompiled. As we have seen, these are the advantages that *could* be attained in principle, depending on the rules of the language and on the sophistication of the linker.

These are the basic tools required to make efficient use of a programming language. Even with these basic tools, however, the strong interdependence of language, methodology, and tools is apparent. A good example of this interdependence is the concept of separate compilation in a programming language, which requires the use of a linker and a library as tools and can support a methodology based on modular design and reusable software.

Other Tools

The abovementioned tools are used to aid the productivity of the coding phase of software development. Tools have also been developed for other phases and for the express purpose of supporting a specific design methodology.

There are a number of tools that support the requirements phase by helping in recording the various requirements and keeping them consistent. The other major use of these systems is in producing system documentation. PSL/PSA (Teichrow 1975) and SREM (Alford 1977) are two prominent examples of such systems. PSL/PSA provides a "language" (PSL) in which the requirements can be expressed and an analyzer (PSA) that examines the requirements for consistency and completeness. Because there is great variation in the requirements of systems in different application areas, these so-called *requirements systems* are suitable only for certain applications. For example, PSL/PSA is suited for business systems, whereas SREM is appropriate for real-time systems.

To support the certification phase there are *program verifiers,* which try automatically, or with the help of the user, to prove the correctness of a program with respect to a specification. Less ambitious than a program verifier is a *data flow analyzer,* which examines a program statically and tries to pinpoint potential sources of error, such as successive assignments to a variable without an intervening use of the variable, potential use of a variable before initialization, a boolean condition that is always false, etc. *Test data generators* help in producing data on which to test the program; test data should be saved for retesting the program after later enhancements. *Symbolic executors* can run the program on symbolic data and produce symbolic formulas that characterize the values of output variables and conditions for traversal of program paths. These formulas are then used by the programmer to reason about the program.

The certification tools must have a knowledge of the semantics and the syntax of the programming language built into them. They are heavily dependent on the semantics of the language. Those features that make reasoning about programs hard (see Chapter 6) also make it hard for these tools to do their job.

A requirement shared by all program processing tools is that they need to operate on an internal representation of the program. If the tools are to be integrated and to work well together, all must use the same representation. Although this requirement restricts some tools to using a representation that may not be ideal, the benefits of the compatibility of the tools outweighs this disadvantage. Such a uniform representation would also encourage the development of compatible programs—as evidenced in the UNIX system (Section 7.4.1), in which viewing files uniformly as sequences of characters allows the routing of output from one program to different destinations quite easily.

Another motivation for program development tools is to support certain program construction methodologies. One such methodology insists on developing a provably correct version of the program first, without particular concern for program efficiency. After a correct program has been achieved, the next task is to modify the program to make its efficiency acceptable. Necessary for that methodology are the following.

- **Dynamic frequency analyzer**, which can run a program with typical data and determine which portions of the program are executed most often and therefore most in need of time optimization. It has been shown that programmers' intuition in pinpointing such areas of the code is not reliable.

- **Source program optimizer**, which can detect and transform inefficient code into a more efficient one.

- **Source program control**, which can maintain the different versions of a program and their relationships. These different versions are especially important during the maintenance phase, because the original version of the program, which was easier to program, is the one that is easier to modify as well.

7.4.1 An Example of a Program Development System

There are several example systems that combine the programming language with a set of tools to provide a friendly program development environment. APL and LISP are both supported by such environments. This section considers the programming environment supported by UNIX. The reason for this choice is that UNIX is more widely available and the reader is likely to have access to such a system for experimentation.

UNIX is an operating system for the DEC PDP-11 computer family. It is one of the few operating systems to provide the user with a friendly environment in which to develop programs (among other things). The system is written almost entirely in the programming language C, which also serves as a sort of official language on the system. Although C is not in any sense a superior language, there are many tools in the system that combine with C to make for an excellent program development environment. This fact partially accounts for the popularity and growth of the UNIX system. It is no exaggeration to say that the best thing about the language C is that it comes with the UNIX system.

Reviewed below are some of the tools provided by UNIX in order to show the integration of a programming language with a set of support tools.

C compiler The compiler has a number of interesting and useful options. One is object code optimization, which usually is used only after the program has been debugged. Another option provides for the object code to be augmented with counters, to keep track of how many times each routine is called. This, as we have seen, can guide the programmer to those parts of the program that are candidates for further optimization. It can also help the programmer to assess the thoroughness of testing by pinpointing which control paths have been traversed during execution. Finally, one can produce an object code that later may be combined with other object modules (possibly written in other languages).

C debugger   This tool allows a program to be run and debugged interactively. Under this system, the user can trace the execution of the program, stop the execution at different points, and examine the values of the program variables. After the program has terminated, a trace and an indication of the cause of failure can be produced.

Lint   The C compiler is not strong in detecting errors or producing good diagnostic messages. The task of program checking is left to *lint*, which searches a C program for suspicious-looking sequences of coding. *Lint* can be used for different purposes. One is to enforce the type rules of C. The compiler does not do much type checking and applies many type conversions liberally; *lint*, on the other hand, is more strict and flags those code sequences that require automatic conversion. So *lint* can be used to make C appear to be almost a strongly typed language.

Lint can also do type-checking for intermodule references in a set of routines on different files. This way, large C programs can be divided into modules, and each module can be separately developed in any order. While compiling a module, the C compiler assumes the external references in each module are correct. Once some or all modules have been developed, *lint* can be used to check their type consistency. The division of labor between the compiler and *lint* simplifies the compiler, because it can concentrate on producing efficient object code quickly and not be sidetracked by error checking and producing diagnostic messages.

Another purpose of *lint* is to help in producing portable programs. Under one of its options, *lint* flags those statements in the program that contain nonportable features, such as comparisons that depend on the machine's character representation.

The last class of properties checked for by *lint* is that of error-prone constructions, which include unused variables and functions, variables used before they have been assigned, unreachable program segments, and boolean expressions whose values are compile-time constants (always true or always false). These conditions might originally exist in the program, or they might develop after the program has gone through a number of modifications. In either case, the programmer should be notified of their existence. It is particularly easy during maintenance to create these conditions. Their existence will reduce the readability of the program—and, as a result, its maintainability, if not its reliability. *Lint* should, therefore, be systematically applied after any system modification.

Make   This tool is not designed for the exclusive use of C programmers, but instead can be used in any nontrivial system development in which (possibly) several languages are used. The motivation for this tool is that in building a large system consisting of several modules, the modules commonly are modified individually and therefore exist in several versions. The task of assembling the system into a running unit after one or more modules are changed, although in principle trivial, is rather time-consuming and error-prone. One has to remember which modules to recompile, relink, run through *lint*; which libraries to include and in what order; and so on. The purpose of *make* is to ease this task. The user specifies in a file all the modules making up the system, their dependencies on one another, and what needs to be done to each module (e.g., compiled with C or FORTRAN). After the user makes some modifications to the system, *make* can be requested to reassemble the system by using the latest version of each module and running the user-specified sequence. It only recompiles, relinks, and so on the minimum number of required modules.

This tool is especially useful when several programmers are involved in the development of a system and update their modules independently.

Linkage editor   The standard linker, *ld*, is used to combine several object modules into one.

cref   Cross-reference listings can be produced with *cref*. Both C programs and assembly language programs may be used as input to *cref*.

yacc and **lex**   These are, respectively, a parser generator and a lexical scanner generator. Their use has traditionally been confined to compiler development, although they are being used increasingly in other applications. Any program that reads input and checks its validity requires at least a lexical scanner, which may be produced by *lex*. If, in addition, the program needs to read and interpret complicated input, it requires a parser, which may be generated with *yacc*. Finally, if the program takes different actions based on what input it has received—as is commonly the case with interactive programs—the full generality of *yacc* may be used by organizing the program as a syntax-directed translator: the semantic actions correspond to the actions the program needs to take for each input. In this case, *yacc* completely dictates the overall structure of the program and generates the parser and the scanner automatically. The programmer needs to define the input language—the lexical and syntactic structure of input—and the actions for each input.

These compiler generation tools may be viewed as a special case of *automatic software generators*. An automatic software generator is a system that generates a program from the program specification. The use of such a tool helps in the initial creation, validation, and maintenance of programs (since it is only necessary to modify the specification).

More important than the availability of the above-listed tools is their compatibility with one another and with the operating system. For example, all files have a uniform format, and the different tools preserve this format. Therefore, the different text editors can be used on the same file. This is in sharp contrast to other systems in which each text editor requires a different file format; therefore, if a file is created with one editor, it is impossible to use another editor on it. Under UNIX, a different text editor may be used based on the requirements of the moment, regardless of the previous history of the file.

Another strong suit of UNIX is the ease with which these tools—and in general, any set of programs—may be combined. The operating system provides the ability to direct the output of one program to another through a *pipe* mechanism. For example, if A and B are two programs,

$A \mid B$

says to run A, use its output as input to B, and run B (A and B are actually run concurrently in a true producer/consumer relationship, but this implementation issue need not concern us here). This facility is useful in the common case in which one program is needed to act on the output of another. For example, *opr* is a printer program that copies its input to the line printer. If we write a program, P, whose output we want to be printed, all we need say is

$P \mid opr$.

In particular, we do not need to worry, when writing P, about the device on which the output is to be printed (as in FORTRAN); and we do not need to invoke a complicated job-control procedure to create an intermediate file for P to put its output on and then, in a separate step, print the results of this file (as in OS/360). In fact, all programs are written assuming that the input is from the standard input device (the terminal) and that the output goes to the standard output device (the terminal). It is, however, quite easy to redirect the input and output.

For example,

$P < fi$

says that the input to P comes from the file fi; and

$P > fo$

says that the output of P goes to the file fo (which will be created automatically if it does not exist already).

These facilities combine to encourage the development of small, reusable programs, because every program being written is viewed as a potential component of a future system.

One creates complex programs not by writing them from scratch, but by inter-connecting relatively small components. These components concentrate on single functions and therefore are easy to build, understand, describe, and maintain. It has been shown experimentally that the average length of a UNIX program written in C is rather small (about 240 lines long).

UNIX, however, is not the final answer in program development systems. The most obvious deficiency in UNIX is that the tools are still very closely geared to the coding and testing phase. What we need now are tools for the requirements, main-tenance, and validation phases. Such tools exist in isolated cases but are not integrated in a hospitable environment such as UNIX.

The importance of the environment on programmer productivity is now recog-nized, and we can expect to see strides in this direction. For example, the requirements for the DOD's common language have specified the desiderata not only of the language (Ada), but also of the entire programming environment. We are, however, years away from seeing a complete, coherent, and integrated system that supports the facilities of the idealized scenario outlined in the first chapter of this book (Section 1.2).

SUGGESTIONS FOR FURTHER READING AND BIBLIOGRAPHIC NOTES

The distinction between programming in the small and programming in the large has been pointed out in (DeRemer and Kron 1976). The difficult and challenging problems arising in the production of large software systems are discussed in several books, such as (Metzger 1973), (Brooks 1975), (Horowitz 1975). The papers by H. D. Mills, L. A. Belady and M. M. Lehman, C. L. McGowan and R. C. McHenry in (Wegner 1979) address several aspects of programming in the large.

The methodology of stepwise refinement is described in (Wirth 1971**b**), (Wirth 1976**a**), and (Dijkstra 1972). Another methodology mentioned in Chapter 6 tries to develop a program and its correctness proof hand-in-hand. The methodology is based on the use of predicate transformers and invariants, and is illustrated in (Dijkstra 1976). Both methodologies are adequate for designing small programs but are of little use in the case of large programs. An interesting debate on this point is reported in (Wegner 1979). (See paper by D. Gries and the discussion by B. Liskov and D. Parnas.)

Methodologies supporting top-down modular design are described in (Parnas 1972**a**), (Parnas 1972**b**), (Myers 1975), and (Myers 1978). The concept of ''program families'' is used in (Parnas 1975).

A critical evaluation of tree structure in structuring large systems has been raised in (Wulf and Shaw 1973). (Clarke et al. 1980) contains further criticisms and advo-cates a nest-free structure for Ada.

(Lauer and Satterthwaite 1979) describes the Mesa system and, in particular, how it supports the design of large systems. Smalltalk (Ingalls 1978) is another language with interesting structuring facilities; it is based on SIMULA 67. PROTEL (Foxall et al. 1979) allows more than one interface to be associated with the same module. This technique allows different users of a module to be given different access rights. Experience with the use of PROTEL, which is a strongly-typed language, is reported in (Lasker 1979) and (Cashin et al. 1981).

Separate compilation facilities for Pascal are described in (Jensen and Wirth 1975), (Kieburtz et al. 1978), (LeBlanc and Fisher 1979), and (Celentano et al. 1980). Separate compilation facilities for SIMULA 67 are described in (Birtwistle et al. 1976) and (Schwartz 1978**a**). The use of SIMULA 67's prefix mechanism in top-down design is illustrated by several examples in (Birtwistle et al. 1973).

The need for sophisticated computer-assigned software development systems is advocated by (Winograd 1979). (Cheatham 1977) analyzes program development tools and the need for integrating them in a coherent system. (Cheatham et al. 1979) presents a program development system developed at Harvard University. (Tichy 1979) and (Habermann 1979) present another system developed at Carnegie Mellon University. (DOD 1980**a**) states the requirements for the Ada programming environment. (Buxton 1980) gives an annotated bibliography of works in the area of program development systems. For references on LISP and APL, see Chapter 8.

The UNIX system is described in (Ritchie and Thompson 1974). (Kernighan and Mashey 1979) describes UNIX from the user's viewpoint, as derived from the experience of a large community of users. The language C is described in (Kernighan and Ritchie 1978). (Kernighan and Plauger 1976) describes a number of tools available under UNIX.

Exercises

7.1 Discuss the effect of global variables on the writability and readability of large programs.

7.2 Present the main features of FORTRAN's separate compilation.

7.3 Why is the ALGOL-like program structure inadequate for programming in the large?

7.4 Design the interface of an Ada module that provides a symbol table for a translator (e.g., an assembler), and show how a separately compiled procedure can access the symbol table. The data structure representing the symbol table should be hidden to the procedure, and all accesses to the symbol table should be routed through abstract operations provided by the symbol table module. Can you compile the procedure before implementing a representation for the symbol table? Why? What is wrong if you cannot?

7.5 Suppose two Ada units $U1$ and $U2$ must use the same procedure P. Can P be embedded in a single subunit? Can P be embedded in a single unit? In the latter case, what are the constraints on the order of compilation?

7.6   Describe the tools that an ideal program-development system should provide to support independent development of modules, system structuring from independently developed modules, and complete intermodule type checking.

7.7   The following two sets of UNIX commands accomplish almost the same tasks. What is the difference between them?

i. $x >$ *file*1
      $y <$ *file*1 $>$ *file*2
      $z <$ *file*2

ii. $x \mid y \mid z$

The letters x, y, and z represent programs; *file*1 and *file*2 are files.

CHAPTER EIGHT

FUNCTIONAL PROGRAMMING

". . . the next revolution in programming will take place only when both *of the following requirements have been met: (a) a new kind of programming language, far more powerful than those of today, has been developed, and (b) a technique has been found for executing its programs at not much greater cost than that of today's programs." (Backus 1978b)*

The majority of programming languages in existence today, including almost all the languages we have discussed so far, can be considered to form a progression along the same lines of ideas. What characterizes this line of development, and dictates its essential characteristics, is the Von Neumann machine architecture. All the languages we have studied so far are abstractions built upon this architecture.

In providing these abstractions, a language must strike a balance between usefulness of features and efficiency of execution. This concern for efficiency is evident in nearly all programming languages today. And efficiency of execution is measured by performance on a Von Neumann computer. Thus the Von Neumann computer architecture has formed the basis for the design of programming languages.

The purpose of this chapter is to examine another basis for language design— that of mathematical functions. The contrast between these two bases for language design helps us appreciate the influence of the underlying model on a language. Some of the subtlest language features can only be explained in terms of this influence.

8.1 CHARACTERISTICS OF IMPERATIVE LANGUAGES

In the first seven chapters, we have been primarily concerned with *imperative* or *statement-oriented* languages. This class of languages, which contains such different members as FORTRAN, COBOL, Pascal, CLU, and Ada, draws its name from the

227

dominant role played by imperative statements. The unit of work in a program written in these languages is a ''statement.'' The effects of individual statements combine to achieve the desired results in a program. This section examines the close relationship between languages and the architecture of conventional computers. We shall see that computer architecture has played a profound role in shaping imperative languages.

This influence can be seen in three pervasive characteristics of our languages:

1. **Variables** A major component of the architecture is the memory, which is comprised of a large number of *cells*. The memory is where the data are stored. The cells must be named, so that one can keep track of the location of the information.

   The need to name every cell is most apparent when programming in assembly languages. Values are stored in cells and can be accessed by naming such cells. In higher-level languages, the underlying notions of memory cell and name are represented by the concept of a variable— perhaps the most important concept in programming languages. A programming language variable is essentially a named memory cell in which values are stored. Thus, even though our purpose in programming is to produce values, we do not merely talk of values, but also of the cells in which the values of interest reside. The problems of side effects and aliasing arise from the existence of variables.

2. **Assignment Operation** Closely tied to the memory architecture is the notion that every value computed must be ''stored''—that is, assigned to a cell. This accounts for the eminence of the assignment statement in programming languages. The low-level notions of memory cell and assignment pervade all programming languages. They force on the programmer a style of thinking that is shaped by the details of the Von Neumann architecture.

3. **Repetition** A program in an imperative language usually accomplishes its task by executing a sequence of elementary steps repeatedly. This is a consequence of the Von Neumann architecture, in which the instructions are stored in the memory. The only way to accomplish anything complicated is to repeat a sequence of instructions.

8.1.1 An Imperative Program

To illustrate the interaction of these characteristics and their effects, consider the following Pascal program for producing prime numbers:

```
{print prime numbers in the range 2 . . n}
program primes (input,output);
    const n = 50;
    var i: 2 . .n;
        j: 2 . . 25;
        i_is_prime: boolean;
```

```
begin
    for i: = 2 to n do
    begin {is i prime?}
        j: = 2; i_is_prime: = true;
        while i_is_prime and (j ≤ i div 2) do
            if ((i mod j) <> 0) then j: = j + 1
                                else i_is_prime: = false;
        {if so, print its value}
        if i_is_prime then write (i)
    end
end
```

The program is based on two loops, one nested within the other. The outer loop (**for** i: = 2 **to** n . . .) sequences through the values in the range of interest (2 to n), whereas the inner loop checks each one of these numbers for "primeness." To understand each loop, we must mentally execute it for at least a few iterations, we must check its termination conditions, and we must check the conditions under which it is executed correctly. In this case, the inner loop depends—in some not-so-simple ways—on the "index" of the outer loop (i). The outer loop also depends—in the **if** statement—on the assignment made in the inner loop.

In other words, the program is not hierarchical in the sense of each component being composed of several other (lower-level) components. Instead, each component uses the effect(s) of other ones. In our case, the inner loop builds upon the outer loop's modifications to i, and the outer loop builds upon the inner loop's modifications to i_is_prime. These components are intimately related. A component is used not to compute a value but to produce an effect—specifically, the effect of assigning values to variables. Control structures are used to order the statements such that the combined effects meet the desired end.

8.1.2   Problems with Imperative Languages

To summarize the preceding section, the essence of programming in imperative languages is the repeated and step-by-step computation of low-level values and the assignment of these values to memory locations. This is, of course, not the level of detail we want to deal with when programming a complicated application. Indeed, programming languages have been attempting more and more to hide this low-level nature of the machine.

A good example of this attempt is provided by expressions, which are a step removed from the cell-based memory because they allow the programmer to keep intermediate values anonymous. They hide the fact that all cells must be named. In the absence of side effects, component expressions of a complex expression are independent from one another. FORTRAN provided this advantage over assembly language—that was indeed one of FORTRAN's greatest achievements. ALGOL 60 extended FORTRAN's expressions further by providing conditional expressions. For example, instead of

if $x > y$ **then** *max:= x*
       else *max:= y*

we can use a conditional expression and write

max:= **if** $x > y$ **then** *x* **else** *y.*

    The term *expression-oriented* (as opposed to statement-oriented) refers to languages in which expressions play a greater role than statements. Both are relative terms, and no language relies entirely on expressions or entirely on statements. We can say only that ALGOL 60 is more *expression-oriented* than FORTRAN.

    ALGOL 68 is even more expression-oriented. It requires every construct to be an expression—that is, to have a value that can be used in other expressions. A block, for instance, can be used in expressions. Example:

max:= **begin int** *x,y;*
             read ((x,y));
             if $x > y$ **then** *x* **else** *y* **fi**
   end

    The value of the right-hand side is the value of x if $x > y$; otherwise, it is the value of y.

    The usefulness of this generalization of ALGOL 68 is questionable. Expressions have been found useful mainly because they are simple and hierarchical. They can be combined uniformly to build more complex expressions. The component expressions of a complex expression are independent of one another. Expressions thus do not suffer from the influence of the Von Neumann architecture. An entire block in an expression, however, is quite different: it is capable of making the expressions as complicated as any other language construct, because an expression may be composed of any of these constructs. As a result, additional rules are needed to explain the semantics of expressions. In ALGOL 68 we must know that the last value computed in the block is the value of the block. If the value of the block is not used (e.g., assigned), coercion to **void** is applied automatically. Building upon a good idea—the expression—can go only so far. The generalization of ALGOL 68 makes the expressions also subject to the problems of naming, repetition, and assignment.

    Actually, there are two somewhat disjoint domains in an imperative language: that of expressions, which is simple, regular, and hierarchical; and that of statements. It is the world of statements that is most influenced by machine characteristics. The world of expressions also loses its mathematical properties in the presence of such things as side effects or the construct given above.

    Another example of the interference of the machine-level details with otherwise sound language constructs is offered by the procedure mechanism. Procedures localize much of the reasoning that must be done about the behavior of variables. They allow the building of independent components. But call by reference and global variables interfere with this high-level concept by enabling all memory locations to become addressable, thus revealing the cell-based memory.

Perhaps the most serious problem with imperative languages arises from the difficulty in reasoning about the correctness of programs. This difficulty is caused by the fact that the correctness of a program in general depends on the contents of each and every memory cell. The state of the computation is determined by the contents of memory cells. To understand loops, we must mentally execute them. To observe the progress of the computation through time, we must take "snapshots" of the memory at each step after every instruction. This is a tedious task when the program deals with large amounts of memory. We have seen that scope rules in languages limit this problem somewhat by reducing the number of accessible cells. We have also seen (in Chapters 6 and 7) that the use of global variables can make programs hard to analyze.

But we must remember that mechanisms such as global variables, call-by-reference parameters, and (in general) side effects, which appear to defeat the purposes of higher-level constructs, are introduced into languages for the purpose of achieving execution efficiency. It is this efficiency that is based on the characteristics of the Von Neumann architecture. And this explains the reasons behind Backus's belief quoted at the beginning of this chapter.

The next section will examine a style of programming based on functions and mathematics, rather than on the Von Neumann memory, elementary actions, and repetition. The purpose is to see what alternatives exist if we disregard our reliance on the Von Neumann architecture.

8.2 THE ESSENCE OF FUNCTIONAL PROGRAMMING

Whereas the style of programming in a statement-oriented language consists of arranging for the execution and repetition of certain sequences of individual statements using appropriate control structures, the essence of functional programming is to combine functions to produce more powerful functions.

8.2.1 Functions

A *function* is a rule for mapping (or associating) members of one set (the *domain set*) to those of another (the *range set*). For example, the function "square" might map members from the set of integer numbers to the set of integer number. A *function definition* specifies the domain, the range, and the mapping rule for the function. Once a function has been defined, it can be *applied* to a particular element of the domain set; the application *yields* (or results in, or returns) the associated element in the range set.

For example, the function definition

square(x) $\equiv$ x∗x , x is an integer number

defines the function named "square" as the mapping from integer numbers to integer numbers. We use the symbol "$\equiv$" for "is equivalent to." In this definition, *x* is a *parameter*. It stands for any member of the domain set.

At application time, a particular member of the domain set is specified. This member, called the *argument*, replaces the parameter in the definition. The replacement is purely textual. If the definition contains any applications, they are applied in the same way until we are left with an expression that can be evaluated to yield the result of the original application.

The application

square (2)

results in the value 4 according to the above definition.

The parameter x is a mathematical variable, which is not the same as a programming variable. In the function definition, x stands for any member of the domain set. In the application, it is given a value—*one value*. Its value never changes thereafter. This is in contrast to a programming variable which takes on different values during the course of program execution.

In the above function definition, we bound the definition of the function $(x*x)$ to the name "square." It is sometimes convenient simply to use a function without giving it a name. We can do this by using *lambda expressions*. A lambda expression specifies the parameters and the mapping rule together. The symbol "." separates the specification of parameters from that of the mapping rule. For example,

$\lambda x.x*x$

is a function exactly the same as *square* above, except that we have not assigned a name to it. It can be applied

$(\lambda x.x*x)2$

just like "square."

The result of the application can be derived by replacing the parameter and evaluating the resulting expression.

$(\lambda x.x*x)2 \equiv$
  $2*2 \equiv$
   4

We could in fact define *square* as

square $\equiv \lambda x.x*x$

In other words, a lambda expression allows us to construct an expression whose value is a function. This is a useful property, as we will see shortly.

Lambda expressions can be used to define functions with more than one parameter, as in

sum$\equiv \lambda x,y.x+y$

The parameters following the "λ" and before the "." are called *bound variables*. When the lambda expression is applied, the occurrences of these variables in the expression following the "." are replaced by the arguments.

New functions may be created by combining other functions. The most common form of combining functions in mathematics is function composition. If a function F is defined as the composition of two functions G and H, written as

F≡ G∘H,

applying F is defined to be equivalent to applying H, and then applying G to the result. For example, if we define

to_the_fourth≡square∘square

then the value of *to_the_fourth (2)* is 16.

Function composition is an example of a *functional form*, also called a *combining form* or a *higher order function*. A functional form provides a method of combining functions; it is a function that takes other functions as parameters and yields a function as its result. Function composition is a functional form that takes two functions as parameters and yields the function that is equivalent to applying one and then the other as explained above.

8.2.2 Mathematical Functions Versus Programming Language Functions

Let us consider the differences between mathematical functions and those provided by conventional programming languages. The most important difference stems from the notion of a modifiable variable. The parameter of a mathematical function simply represents some value that is fixed at function application time; the function application results in another value. Data parameters in a programming language function, on the other hand, are names for memory cells; the function may use a name to change the contents in the cell. The function may also interact with the invoker of the function by changing other cells known to both of them. Because of these side effects, programming language functions, unlike mathematical functions, cannot always be combined hierarchically (like expressions).

Another significant difference is in the way functions are defined. In programming languages, a function is defined procedurally—the rule for mapping a value of the domain set to the range set is stated in terms of a number of steps that need to be "executed" in certain order specified by the control structure. Mathematical functions, on the other hand, are defined functionally—the mapping rule is defined in terms of applications of other functions. Mathematical functions are in this sense more hierarchical.

Many mathematical functions are defined *recursively*: that is, the definition of the function contains an application of the function iteslf. For example, the standard mathematical definition of factorial is

$n! \equiv$ **if** $n=0$ **then** 1 **else** $n*(n-1)!$

The Fibonacci number sequence is defined as

$F(n) \equiv$ **if** $n=0$ **or** $n=1$ **then** 1 **else** $F(n-1)+F(n-2)$.

As another example, we can readily formulate a (recursive) solution for the prime numbers problem of Section 8.1.1. The following predicate function determines whether a number is a prime:

$prime(n) \equiv$ **if** $n=2$ **then** true **else** $p(n,n$ **div** $2)$

where function p is:

$p(n,i) \equiv$ **if** $(n$ **mod** $i) = 0$ **then** false
$\qquad\qquad\qquad$ **else if** $i=2$ **then** true
$\qquad\qquad\qquad\qquad$ **else** $p(n,i-1)$

Recursion is a powerful problem-solving technique. It is a natural and heavily used strategy, when programming with functions. However, as we have seen in Chapter 3, not all programming languages support recursive subprogram activations. When recursion is not permitted, the implementation of functions can become complicated and unnatural.

8.2.3 Functional (or Applicative) Languages

A functional programming language makes use of the mathematical properties of functions. In fact, the name "functional" (or "applicative") language is derived from the prominent role played by functions and function applications. A *functional* (or *applicative*) *language* has four components.

- A set of primitive functions.
- A set of functional forms.
- The *application* operation.
- A set of data objects.

The primitive functions are predefined by the language and may be applied. The functional forms are the mechanisms by which functions may be combined to create new functions. The application operation is the built-in mechanism for applying a function to its arguments and producing a value. The data objects are the allowed members of the domain and range sets. It is characteristic of functional languages to provide a very limited set of data objects with simple and regular structure (e.g., arrays in APL and lists in LISP). The essence of functional programming lies in the combining of functions by using the functional forms.

In addition to the above-listed four components, a functional language also provides a mechanism for binding a name to the new functions being defined. This is a convenience feature that affects the way we use the language. It avoids the repetition of the function definition each time the function is to be applied. For example, in Section 8.2.1 we defined a function and gave it the name *"to_the_fourth."* Had we not named the function, we would have had to use the definition

square∘square

whenever we needed to apply it.

The next section examines a purely functional language and illustrates its use.

8.3   A SIMPLE AND PURELY FUNCTIONAL LANGUAGE

John Backus, the originator of FORTRAN, has been working on a purely functional programming language since the early 1970s. This section presents a simplified view of Backus's work. In particular, we will define, FP, a very simple language for functional programming.

The objects of the language are quite simple: an object may be an *atom* or a *sequence* (of objects); the empty sequence is known as **nil**. Atoms are sequences of characters such as *A, ABC*, 26.

There is a set of functions and a set of functional forms. There are no variables; all data must be used literally.

FP is actually a family of languages. Each member provides a choice of functions and functional forms. Backus maintains that the language should provide "widely useful and powerful primitive functions rather than weak ones that could then be used to define useful ones." The more functional forms a language has, the more "expressive" it is, since functional forms are the mechanisms for writing programs.

Following Backus's notation, we will show a sequence of n objects $x_1, x_2, \ldots x_n$ as

$$< x_1, x_2, \ldots x_n >$$

and application of function f to parameter x as

f:x.

We will use the conditional expression **if_then_else** in the definitions. This is part of our defining language, *not* part of the language being defined. Remember that this language is not fully defined; we are just interested in the flavor of the language.

8.3.1 Primitive Functions

The language provides a number of primitive functions that roughly correspond to the built-in operations of imperative languages. Since sequences are the manipulable objects, the functions provide mechanisms for sequence manipulation. These functions can be broken into a number of different classes. Given below is a classification, along with some sample primitive functions. Of course, a particular language might include a different set of functions.

a. *Selection operations*

Useful examples include functions FIRST, to extract the first element of a sequence; LAST, to extract the last element; and TAIL, to extract everything but the first element. Thus,

$$\text{FIRST: } < x_1, x_2, \ldots \ldots x_n > \equiv x_1$$
$$\text{LAST: } < x_1, x_2, \ldots \ldots x_n > \equiv x_n$$
$$\text{TAIL: } < x_1, x_2, \ldots \ldots x_n > \equiv < x_2, \ldots \ldots x_n >$$

It would also be useful to be able to select an arbitrary element in a sequence simply by giving its position: that is,

$$i: < x_1, \ldots \ldots x_n > \equiv x_i, \qquad 1 \leq i \leq n$$

b. *Structuring operations*

These operations allow us to combine, dissect or rearrange sequences.

(rotate right)	ROTR:	$< x_1, \ldots \ldots x_n > \equiv$ $< x_n, x_1, \ldots \ldots x_{n-1} >$
(rotate left)	ROTL:	$< x_1, x_2, \ldots \ldots x_n > \equiv$ $< x_2, x_3, \ldots \ldots x_n, x_1 >$
(length)	LENGTH:	$< x_1, \ldots \ldots x_n > \equiv n$
(construct sequence)	CONS:	$< x, < x_1, x_2, \ldots \ldots x_n >> \equiv$ $< x, x_1 \ldots \ldots x_n >$

c. *Arithmetic operations*

Arithmetic operations apply to sequences of two atoms and produce an atom as a result. We consider the usual operations "+," "−," "*," "/," "**div**" and also the residue operation ("*mod*" in Pascal) "|". That is,

$$|: < x, y >$$

yields the remainder of the division "*x* **div** *y*." The unary minus will be denoted by NEGATE. Keeping the functional notation, we use the

prefix form for all arithmetic operations (e.g., $+:< x, y >$) instead of
the usual infix (e.g., $x+y$).

d. *Predicate functions*

Predicate functions are functions whose results are truth values. We will
represent true by the atom T and false by the atom F. A predicate
function thus yields either T or F. In addition to the familiar predicates
for comparing numbers (e.g., $<$, $>$, $=$), we also need predicates to
inquire about sequences and atoms.

ATOM: x ≡ **if** x is an atom **then** T **else** F
NULL: x ≡ **if** x = **nil then** T **else** F

e. *Logical operations*

Logical operations allow us to combine truth values. The usual operations are AND, OR, NOT.

f. *Identity*

Function ID is the identity function: that is,

ID: x ≡ x

8.3.2 Functional Forms

By far the most unusual feature of FP languages is the functionl form. Since we are
not used to functional forms in conventional languages, it is difficult to decide which
functional forms are useful to include in an FP language. It is also difficult to get used
to functional forms as programming constructs. Just as with conventional languages,
it takes practice.

We examine below a few functional forms that Backus suggests as being useful,
for the purpose of introducing the reader to the power of functional form programming.

a. *Composition*

(f∘g): x ≡ f: (g:x)

The functional form "∘" is defined to take two functions as parameters;
it results in a function that is equivalent to the application of the first
parameter to the result of the application of the second parameter. In
other words, this is the mathematical function composition. We have
already seen an example of its use in the definition of the
"to_the_fourth" function in Section 8.2.1.

To find the value of a function application that is a composition
of other functions, we keep repeating the application steps as before,
until no applications remain in the expression. In general, inner applications are performed first, then the next level out, and so on.

Example

$$\text{ROTL} \circ \text{CONS:} \ < x_1, < x_2, x_3 >> \ \equiv$$
$$\text{ROTL:} \ \text{CONS:} \ < x_1, < x_2, x_3 >> \ \equiv$$
$$\text{ROTL:} \ < x_1, x_2, x_3 > \ \equiv$$
$$< x_2, x_3, x_1 >$$

It is truly surprising that in spite of the prevalence and importance of function composition in mathematics, no programming language allows it as a primitive construct, explicitly or so succinctly.

b. *Construction*

$$[f_1, f_2, \ldots f_n] :x \equiv < f_1 :x, \ldots, f_n :x >$$

The functional form "[]" is defined to take as parameters n functions and to yield a function that is equivalent to applying each of the functions to the same parameter and forming a sequence of the results.

As an example of the use of construction, consider the task of producing the minimum, maximum, average, and median of a sequence of values. Having defined individual functions for each of the subtasks, the final task of combining them can be done with construction—for example,

[MIN,MAX,AVG,MED]

is a function and can be applied or combined with other functions.

Example

$$[\text{MIN,MAX,AVG,MED}] : \ < 0,1,2,3 > \ \equiv$$
$$< \text{MIN:} \ < 0,1,2,3 >, \text{MAX:} \ < 0,1,2,3 >, \text{AVG:} \ < 0,1,2,3 >, \text{MED:}$$
$$< 0,1,2,3 >> \ \equiv$$
$$<0,3,1.5,2>$$

Notice the second step. We have a sequence consisting of four applications. Because of the absence of side effects, these applications can be evaluated in any order, or even simultaneously.

c. *Insert*

$$/f:x \equiv \textbf{if } x \text{ is } < x_1 > \textbf{ then } x_1$$
$$\textbf{else if } x \text{ is the sequence } < x_1, \ldots, x_n >$$
$$\textbf{and } n \geq 2 \textbf{ then } f: \ < x_1, /f: \ < x_2, \ldots, x_n >>$$

The functional form "/" takes one function as parameter and yields as a result a function that is applicable only to sequences (i.e., not to atoms) and equivalent to applying the parameter function to successive elements of the sequence. The most obvious use of "/" is in distributing a function defined for two parameters over a sequence of any number of elements. For example, assuming that the primitive function of addition ("+") has been defined to apply to two parameters, we can find the sum of a sequence of any length by the function "/+."

$$
\begin{aligned}
/+:<1,2,3,4> &\equiv +:<1,/+:<2,3,4>> \\
&\equiv +:<1,+:<2,/+:<3,4>>> \\
&\equiv +:<1,+:<2,+:<3,/+:<4>>>> \\
&\equiv +:<1,+:<2,+:<3,4>>> \\
&\equiv +:<1,+:<2,7>> \\
&\equiv +:<1,9> \\
&\equiv 10
\end{aligned}
$$

This example shows the power of programming with functional forms. Consider the simple and succinct way in which we define the sum function "/+" and contrast it with how this function would have to be written in an imperative language.

d. *Constant*

This functional form takes an object (x) as a parameter and produces a function.

$$\bar{x}:y \equiv x$$

For example,

$$
\begin{aligned}
\bar{0}:y &\equiv 0 \\
\bar{T}:y &\equiv T \\
\bar{1}:y &\equiv 1
\end{aligned}
$$

A sample use of this functional form is given in **(g)** below.

e. *Apply to all*

$$
\begin{aligned}
\alpha\ f:x \equiv\ &\textbf{if } x \text{ is } \textbf{nil then nil} \\
&\textbf{else if } x \text{ is the sequence } <x_1,x_2, \ldots .x_n> \\
&\qquad \textbf{then } <f:x_1, \ldots .f:x_n>
\end{aligned}
$$

The functional form "α" takes a function as parameter and yields a function, applicable only to sequences, that is equivalent to applying the parameter function to each element of the sequence and forming a sequence of the results.

As an example of the use of "α," consider the following problem. We have a sequence of sequences. Each of the inner sequences contains two atoms. We want to produce a sequence each of whose elements is the sum of the corresponding two-element sequence in the argument. For example, applied to the argument <<1,2>, <3,4>, <5,6>>, our function should yield <3,7,11>.

The task can be simply done by the function

α+

(See Exercise 1 for a generalization of this function, and Exercise 3 for an example of its use.)

Like the *insert* functional form, *apply to all* points to the contrast between imperative and functional programming. If the same operation is to be performed on each of the elements of a sequence, a programmer using an imperative language must design the operation, then design a "loop" to apply the operation to each element. Designing the loop entails dealing with such matters as the accessing of each element and detecting and handling end-of-sequence, empty sequence, and so on. In a functional programming language, however, designing the operation itself is all that is needed; *apply to all* takes care of the "loop."

f. *Condition*

(IF p f g):x ≡ **if** p:x = T **then** f:x **else** g:x

The functional form IF takes three functions as parameters and yields either the second or the third function, depending on whether or not the result of the first function is the atom T.

This functional form can be used in tasks for which conditional statements are used in imperative languages; but because p, f, and g are all applied to the same parameter, its use requires a different approach. For example, the function

(IF ATOM NEGATE ROTR)

negates its argument, if it is an atom; or rotates it, if it is a sequence.

g. *While*

(WHILE p f):x ≡ **if** p:x = T **then** (WHILE p f):(f:x) **else** x

The WHILE functional form arranges for the repeated application of its second parameter as long as the application of its first parameter yields the atom T.

For example, let us write a function that produces the image of the argument sequence, except for leading zeroes. First we define the following function ISZERO, which determines whether or not an atom is zero.

$$= \circ [\text{ID}, \overline{0}]$$

Then we define the following function FIRSTZERO, which determines whether or not the first element of a sequence is zero:

(ISZERO∘FIRST)

Finally, we define the desired function as

(WHILE FIRSTZERO TAIL)

Following the first few steps of an application of this function helps us understand how much ''execution'' is involved in the application of such a simple-looking function.

(WHILE FIRSTZERO TAIL): <0,0,2> ≡
    if FIRSTZERO:<0,0,2> = T **then** (WHILE FIRSTZERO
    TAIL):(TAIL: <0,0,2>) **else** <0,0,2> ≡
(WHILE FIRSTZERO TAIL): <0,2> ≡
if FIRSTZERO: <0,2> = T **then** (WHILE FIRSTZERO TAIL):
(TAIL: <0,2>) **else** <0,2> ≡
(WHILE FIRSTZERO TAIL): <2> ≡
. . .   ≡
<2>

8.4   APPLICATIVE FEATURE IN EXISTING LANGUAGES

The previous section provided a glimpse of FP languages. These purely functional languages are being investigated as bases for a new generation of programming languages. They are not everyday programming languages, yet they provide us with a model for studying the potential benefits and drawbacks of functional programming. They can also help us evaluate the functional features of existing languages. We have already discussed at length the applicative and nonapplicative features of expressions. The purpose of this section is to examine other important functional features in current languages.

8.4.1   LISP

Of all existing programming languages, LISP (for List Processing) comes closest to being a functional language. In fact, the original LISP introduced by John McCarthy in 1960, known as pure LISP, is completely functional. In order to improve execution efficiency, however, current versions of LISP have introduced nonapplicative features into the language.

This section will show how close LISP comes to being a functional language. We do not intend to provide a complete discussion, or even an introduction, to LISP— simply to its functional characteristics. LISP is a good example of how a few simple primitives together with a few simple but powerful data-structuring facilities can yield an elegant and powerful language.

8.4.1.1 Objects

LISP objects are symbolic expressions that are either *atoms* or *lists*. An atom is a string of characters (letters, digits, and others). The following are atoms:

A
SYNAPSE
M68000

A list is a series of atoms or lists, separated by space and bracketed by parentheses. The following are lists:

(FOOD VEGETABLES DRINKS)
((MEAT CHICKEN) (BROCCOLI POTATOES TOMATOES) (WATER))
(UNC TRW SYNAPSE)

The empty list "( )" also called NIL, has special significance. Like the FP *sequence*, a *list* is the only data structuring mechanism for encoding information in LISP.

A LISP program is itself a list. It is functional in that it is composed of applications of functions that produce results that may be used by other functions. Even the notation is functional—that is, prefix, as opposed to infix of other languages [e.g., (PLUS A B) instead of $A + B$].

8.4.1.2 Functions

There are very few primitive functions provided in pure LISP. Existing LISP systems have added to this list considerably. These new functions, however, can all be expressed in terms of the original primitive functions.

QUOTE is the identity function. It returns its (single) argument as its value. This function is needed because, in contrast to FP, the atom A does not represent itself but is the name of a value stored somewhere. The distinction between the name and value of objects, as we have seen, is a direct consequence of the memory architecture. The QUOTE function allows its argument to be treated as a constant. Thus, (QUOTE A) in LISP is analogous to "A" in conventional languages.

Examples

(QUOTE *A*) ≡ *A*
(QUOTE (*A B C*)) ≡ (*A B C*)

The most common functions are those that manipulate lists—what we have called structuring operations.

CAR returns the first element of a list; CDR returns all elements of a list except the first; CONS appends an element to a list. Example:

(CAR (QUOTE (A B C))) ≡ A

The argument needs to be "quoted," because the rule in LISP is that a function is applied to the *values* of its arguments. In our case the evaluation of the argument yields the list (*A B C*), which is operated on by CAR. If QUOTE were missing, an attempt would be made to evaluate (*A B C*), which would result in using *A* as a function operating on arguments *B* and *C*. If *A* is not a previously defined function, this would result in an error.

Other examples

(CDR (QUOTE (A B C))) ≡ (B C)
(CDR (QUOTE (A))) ≡ ( ) ≡ NIL
(CONS (QUOTE A) (QUOTE (B C))) ≡ (A B C)
(CONS (QUOTE (A B C)) (QUOTE (A B C))) ≡ ((A B C) A B C)

A few predicates are also available. A true value is denoted by the atom *T* and a false value by NIL.

ATOM tests its argument to see if it is an atom.

NULL tests its argument to see if it is NIL.

EQ compares its two arguments, which must be atoms, for equality.

Examples

(ATOM (QUOTE A)) ≡ T
(ATOM (QUOTE (A))) ≡ NIL
(EQ (QUOTE A) (QUOTE A)) ≡ T
(EQ (QUOTE A)) (QUOTE B)) ≡ NIL

The function COND takes as arguments a number of (predicate, expression) pairs. The expression in the first pair (in left to right order) whose predicate is true is the value of COND.

Example

(COND ((ATOM (QUOTE (A))) (QUOTE B)) (T (QUOTE A))) ≡ A

The first condition is false because (A) is not an atom. The second condition is identically true. This function, known as the McCarthy conditional, is the major building block for user-defined functions.

Function definition is based on lambda expressions. The function

$$\lambda x,y.x + y$$

is written in LISP as

(LAMBDA (X Y) (PLUS X Y))

Function application also follows lambda expressions.

((LAMBDA (X Y) (PLUS X Y)) 2 3)

binds *X* and *Y* to 2 and 3, respectively, and applies PLUS, yielding 5.

The binding of a name to a function is done by the function DEFINE.

(DEFINE (ADD (LAMBDA (X Y) (PLUS X Y))))

Now, the atom ADD can be used in place of the function above: that is, the atom ADD has a value that is a function. The use of DEFINE is one of two ways in pure LISP that an atom can be bound to a value. The other is through function application, at which time the parameters are bound to the arguments. The conventional assignment is not present.

The variables in pure LISP are more like the variables in mathematics than those in other languages. In particular, variables may not be modified: they can be bound to a value and they retain that value throughout a given scope (i.e., function application); and at any moment, there is only at most one access path to each variable.

8.4.1.3 Functional Forms

Function composition was the only technique for combining functions provided by original LISP. For example, the *"to_the_fourth"* function of Section 8.2.1 can be defined in LISP as

(LAMBDA(X) (SQUARE (SQUARE X)))

(We assume SQUARE has been defined.) Most current LISP systems, however, offer a functional form, called MAPCAR, which is equivalent to "α" of FP. It allows the application of a function to every element of a list. For example,

(MAPCAR TOTHEFOURTH L)

raises every element of the list L to the fourth power. Like α, this functional form reduces the need for repetition.

Using the above-cited functional features of LISP, we can write the prime-numbers program directly from the functions in Section 8.2.2. This is left as Exercise 10.

As a functional language, LISP is quite limited by the lack of a rich set of functional forms.

8.4.1.4 Nonapplicative Features in LISP

Above, we have considered the applicative features of LISP. But even though it is possible to use LISP as a functional language, very few applications written in LISP are purely applicative. Efficiency considerations have forced the introduction of many nonapplicative features in LISP, and any realistic program makes heavy use of these features to achieve a reasonable level of efficiency.

The principal nonapplicative features added to LISP are SET and PROG. The SET function is simply the assignment statement. PROG is a function that takes a list of expressions as its argument. These expressions are executed in sequence, one after another. In other words, PROG allows expressions to be regarded as statements. Furthermore, within PROG one can use labels and **goto** statements for explicit control of the execution sequence.

Yet another way that LISP has been made less applicative is with the introduction of operations for modification of variables. For example, the operation RPLACA (for "Replace CAR") can be used to replace the first element of a list with another: that is, for efficiency reasons, operations are introduced that work by side effects rather than by producing values.

Even pure LISP shows the effects of machine architecture in its design. The most important of these occurs, as we have seen, in the distinction between names and values. Another occurs in the set of functions provided. The reason that the two selectors CAR and CDR are provided and, for example, selectors to get an arbitrary element of a list, or the last element, are not, is because of the way lists are implemented. Because of the implementation, CAR and CDR can be performed with one memory reference, whereas the other ones cannot.

We have examined LISP only within a limited scope. LISP is a powerful and interesting language with a wide following. It is the language of choice for developing experimental systems and a standard language in artificial intelligence. The references can be consulted for more information.

8.4.2 APL

APL was designed by Kenneth Iverson at Harvard University during the late 1950s and early 1960s. It is based on mathematics, with a few concessions to machine efficiency. The assignment operation is an integral part of the language. Yet APL can be viewed as an applicative language because of its heavy reliance on expressions.

Just as with LISP in the last section, here we will examine the functional features of APL. Our purpose is not to cover APL fully.

8.4.2.1 Objects

The objects supported by APL are scalars, which can be numeric or character, and arrays of any dimension. Numeric 0 and 1 may be interpreted as boolean values. APL provides a rich set of functions and a few functional forms.

8.4.2.2 Functions

In contrast to LISP, APL provides a large number of functions (called *operations* in APL terminology). An operation is either monadic (taking one parameter) or dyadic (taking two parameters).

All operations that are applicable to scalars also distribute over arrays. Thus, $A \times B$ results in multiplying A and B. If A and B are both scalars, then the result is a scalar. If they are both arrays and of the same size, it is element-by-element multiplication. If one is a scalar and the other an array, the result is the multiplication of every element of the array by the scalar. Anything else is undefined.

The usual arithmetic operations, $+$, $-$, $\times$, $\div$, $|$ (residue), and the usual boolean and relational operation, $\vee$, $\wedge$, $\not\vee$, $\not\wedge$, $\sim$, $<$, $\leq$, $=$, $\geq$, $>$, $\neq$, are provided. But there are also a number of unusual operations.

The operation "ι" is a "generator" and can be used to produce a vector of integers. For example, $\iota 5$ produces

1 2 3 4 5

The operation "$;$" concatenates two arrays. So $\iota 4; \iota 5$ results in

1 2 3 4 1 2 3 4 5

The operation "ρ" forms its right operand into an array of the desired dimensions (left operands). Example:

$$2\ 2\ \rho\ 1\ 2\ 3\ 4 \equiv \begin{matrix} 1 & 2 \\ 3 & 4 \end{matrix}$$
$$2\ 3\ \rho\ 1\ 2\ 3\ 4\ 5\ 6 \equiv \begin{matrix} 1 & 2 & 3 \\ 4 & 5 & 6 \end{matrix}$$

The compress operation "$/$" takes two arguments of the same dimensions and selects elements of its right-hand argument, depending on whether the corresponding left-hand argument is a (boolean) 1 or 0. Example:

$$1\ 0\ 0\ 1\ /\ \iota 4 \equiv 1\ 4$$

The left argument may consist of boolean expressions. For example

$$A{<}B\ \ B{<}C\ \ C{<}D\ /\ X$$

will pick certain values from X, depending on the comparisons on the left. X must be a three-element vector in this case.

The lines in a user-defined function are numbered consecutively starting with 1. A line may be labeled, in which case the label is equated to the line number. The only control structure in APL is the branch, shown as ''→''; it transfers control to the line whose number is specified as the argument. For example, → 3 transfers control to line 3 of the function. If the operand is 0 or larger than the number of lines in the function, the branch is defined to be a function return; if the operand is a vector, the first element is used as the target; and if the operand is null, no branch takes place at all.

The branch operation can be combined with the compress operation to build conditional and multiway branches. For example, → ($A<B$ $A=B$ $A<B$/*case1 case2 case3*) transfers to the appropriate label, depending on the relative values of A and B.

$$\rightarrow (A<B/case1)$$

transfers to case1 if $A<B$; otherwise, the next statement is executed.

By now it must be clear to the reader that the branch is not an appropriate operation for a functional language. It does not allow the hierarchical building of expressions. This is one of the reasons that APL is a nonfunctional language. Another nonapplicative, or imperative, feature is the assignment ''(←),'' which assigns the value of the right operand to the left-hand variable. The assignment operation does produce a value, and therefore it can be used in building expressions: for example,

$$D \leftarrow C+B \times (A\leftarrow2)$$

However, the introduction of assignment in an expression introduces the possibility of side effects.

There are many other primitive operations in APL. They can be regarded as mathematical functions since they operate on operands and produce values. User-defined functions are similar to the primitive functions in that they also are either monadic or dyadic (niladic functions correspond to subroutines). They are used in infix notation and thus can be used in expressions, just as built-in functions can.

8.4.2.3 Functional Forms

There are three functional forms (*operators* in the APL terminology) supplied by APL. They operate on APL's primitive operations to produce other operations. They are

a. The **reduction** operator ''/'' (same symbol as compress), which is the same as the ''insert'' of FP (with the same symbol). For example, the sum of the elements of the vector A is given by

$$+/A$$

Again, compare this with summing the elements of a vector in an imperative programming language. The repetition and step-by-step computation are handled by the functional form.

If the right operand is a matrix, the reduction operation applies to successive rows, that is, if *A* is the matrix

1   2
3   4

then $+/A$ is

3
7

which is represented as

3   7

In general, a reduction applied to an *n*-dimensional array results in an $(n-1)$ dimensional array.

b. The **inner product** operator ``.'' takes two primitive dyadic operations as arguments and produces a dyadic operation as result. The operands of an operation formed this way must be arrays that ``conform'' in size. For example, if they are matrices, the number of rows of the left operand must be the same as the number of columns of the right operand; the result will be a matrix with as many rows as the left operand and as many columns as the right operand. If *f* and *g* are two primitive dyadic functions, the effect of

A f.g B

is to apply *g*, element by element, to the corresponding rows of *A* and columns of *B* (i.e., first row of *A* with first column of *B*, and so on). This is followed by an *f* reduction (*f/*) on the resulting vector.

As an example of the power of inner product in building operations, matrix multiplication can be accomplished by

$+.\times$

Again, we can see the power of functional forms by comparing this solution with a matrix multiplication procedure in an ALGOL-like language.

c. The **outer product** ``°.'' takes one primitive operation as operand and has a dyadic operation as result. The operation °.*f* applied to arrays *A* and B (i.e., $A°.f\,B$) has the effect of applying f between each element of A and *every* element of B. For example, if A has the value $(1\ 2\ 3)$ and B has the value $(5\ 6\ 7\ 8)$, the result of $A°.\times B$ is the matrix

$$
\begin{array}{cccc}
5 & 6 & 7 & 8 \\
10 & 12 & 14 & 16 \\
15 & 18 & 21 & 24
\end{array}
$$

The effect can be seen as forming a matrix with the rows labeled with elements of A and columns labeled with elements of B. The entries of the matrix are the result of applying the operation to the row and column labels. So the above matrix was derived from

×	5	6	7	8
1	5	6	7	8
2	10	12	14	16
3	15	18	21	24

The outer product finds many applications in data processing when producing tables of interest rates, taxes, etc. It has other uses as well. As an example, to find which elements of A occur in B,

$$A°.=B$$

provides a map of boolean values, with a 1 in the position where an element of A equals an element of B.

In addition to these three functional forms, there are two operations in APL that can be used to modify the behavior of (certain) other operations. These are the *axis-specifier* and the *scan* operator. The axis specifier "[ ]" allows us to specify along which dimension of the operand the operation is to be applied (i.e., which index varies most rapidly). For example, if the matrix A has the value

$$
\begin{array}{ccc}
1 & 2 & 3 \\
4 & 5 & 6
\end{array}
$$

then the plus reduction operation, $+/A$, will have the result

$$
\begin{array}{c}
6 \\
15
\end{array}
$$

That is, the elements added have indices $(1,1)$, $(1,2)$, $(1,3)$ and $(2,1)$, $(2,2)$, $(2,3)$. The index varying most rapidly is the second one. Therefore, $+/A$ is equivalent to

$$+/[2]A$$

If, instead, we wanted to add the columns of *A*, we would write

$+/[1]A$

which would result in

5 7 9

The scan operator "$\backslash$" applies its argument operation to successively longer sequences of its other argument. It is useful for producing running totals and similar operations. For example,

$+\backslash 1 \quad 2 \quad 3 \quad 4$

produces

1 3 6 10

Despite its many applicative features, APL does not go far enough in divorcing itself from the machine. The assignment operation is still quite present and side effects are a common means of accomplishing results. There are too few functional forms and they can only be applied to primitive functions. This is a serious weakness for an applicative language, because it means that the power of functional forms cannot be exploited fully.

8.4.2.4 An APL Program

Now let us return to the problem of producing the prime numbers in the range of 1 to *N*. The limited information about APL given in this section is nevertheless sufficient to write this program. The purpose of this section is to illustrate the APL style of programming contrasted to that of, say, Pascal.

We cannot use a solution directly based on the strategy derived in Section 8.2.2, because APL does not have the "apply to all" functional form. Even if it did, functional forms are not allowed to apply to user-defined functions.

Our emphasis should be on exploiting arrays and expressions rather than scalars, assignments, and repetition. Thinking in APL, we must produce a vector of prime numbers. We can start with a vector of numbers in the range 1 to *N* and compress it, using the compress operator, to be left with primes only. In other words, our task is to find the vector of boolean expressions in the following APL program:

vector of boolean expressions/ιN

We can start with the definition of a prime number: a number that is divisible only by 1 and by itself. So, for each number in the range of interest, 1 to *N*, we can (*a*) divide it by all the numbers in the range and (*b*) identify those which are divisible only by two numbers.

Step (*a*) can be done with the residue operation and an outer product

$$(\iota N)^\circ . | (\iota N)$$

The result of this operation will be a vector of remainders. We are interested in whether the remainder is equal to 0.

$$0 = (\iota N)^\circ . | (\iota N)$$

Now the result is a boolean matrix indicating whether the numbers were divisible (1) or not (0).

In step (*b*), we want to see how many times the number was divisible—that is, the number of 1's in each row.

$$+/[2] \; 0 = (\iota N)^\circ . | (\iota N)$$

But we are only interested in those rows which have exactly two 1's.

$$2 = (+/[2]0 = (\iota N)^\circ . | (\iota N))$$

The result is a boolean vector indicating whether the index is a prime (1) or not (0). This is the desired vector of boolean expressions. To get the actual prime numbers, we apply compression.

$$(2 = (+/[2]0 = (\iota N)^\circ . | (\iota N)))/\iota N$$

The essence of this solution is that it builds successively more complicated expressions from simpler ones, and this is the only mechanism used for combining actions. This combining mechanism is simple and uniform regardless of the constituents being combined. It is mathematical in nature in that all operations and expressions are used in the way that they are used in mathematics.

Our program is a typical APL one-liner. It has been said that APL is flawed because its one-liners are not readable. But, to be fair, the readability of the above one-liner must be compared with the readability of the entire Pascal program that accomplishes the same task, rather than with one Pascal statement. It is likely that an APL programmer can understand the APL program with no more effort than is required by a Pascal programmer to understand the Pascal program. The important point is that the programmers must be fluent in the language *and* its style.

8.5 COMPARING APPLICATIVE AND IMPERATIVE LANGUAGES

Let us review the differences between applicative and imperative programming languages. Imperative languages are based on conventional computers, whereas applicative langues are based on mathematical functions. The characteristics of the two classes of languages are dictated by their two different foundations.

Imperative languages are more efficient in terms of execution time because they reflect the structure and operations of the machine. As a result, however, they require that the programmer pay attention to machine-level details. This influence can be seen in the style of programming promoted by these languages, which is based on naming of elementary cells, assignments to these cells, and repetition of elementary actions.

The functional programming style does not depend on these three actions. The simple and uniform data objects (e.g., sequences, lists, arrays) allow the design of data structures without concern for memory cells; rather than being assigned, values are produced by function application and passed on to other functions; and functional forms and operations that distribute over the data objects (as in APL) reduce the reliance on repetition. On the whole, functional programming appears to be at a higher level than imperative programming. It could thus make programming easier.

The cost of this ease of programming shows up in terms of execution efficiency. The inefficiency stems not only from all the function calls, but also from the fact that many objects are created and discarded dynamically. The dynamic creation of objects such as lists and arrays cannot be efficiently supported (for LISP, garbage collection—see Section 4.7.4—was invented to deal with this problem).

We have seen that efficiency is so important that APL and LISP have opted for nonapplicative features in order to achieve it. But we must realize that efficiency considerations could be different with a different machine model.

For example, consider the prime-number program of Section 8.1.1. One technique for increasing the speed of our Pascal prime-number program is to use the history of what numbers have already been computed in the generation of future prime numbers. In particular, we only need to test if a number is divisible by prime numbers. In APL and LISP, however, the tendency is to repeat exactly the same operation for the entire set. If the program were executed on a multiprocessor, however, in which each prime number is computed on a separate processor, then the APL or LISP programs might indeed be more efficient.

An applicative programming language provides a natural way of exploiting a parallel machine architecture, because the inner applications can be applied in parallel.

These examples show the danger of designing our programming languages on the grounds of efficiency. Efficiency is dictated by the machine, and the machine should be there to support the language. We get trapped in a circle. Ideally, we should design a languge based on what we know to be good problem-solving strategies. Then we can design a machine to support the language. Finding the right problem-solving strategy is the primary challenge. However, designing an architecture to support the language is also of decisive importance. If we must stay with our traditional machines, efficiency considerations will rule out functional languages. Different architectures supporting functional languages are presently being investigated, but it is premature to state whether they will become practically relevant.

Apart from efficiency problems, it is difficult to determine whether a purely functional language such as FP will be successful. The success of a language is not based on the mathematical elegance of its underlying principles as much as on a complex combination of its surface properties, the systems supporting it, and other tools available with it.

There is a long way to go before FPs yield a usable language. Do we need types?

Input/output? What particular primitive functions and functional forms? The way these practical issues are decided will determine to a great extent whether the language will be accepted by the programming community.

Another reason for the difficulty of assessing FPs is that we really have no experience with them yet. We can criticize conventional languages much more easily because there are so many programmers using and misusing them every day, and thus providing us with data on the weaknesses of these languages. Even though it is a reasonable hypothesis, there is no empirical evidence that applicative problem decomposition will make programming easier.

The final test for any language will be when it is being used by great numbers of ordinary programmers on everyday programming tasks.

SUGGESTIONS FOR FURTHER READING AND BIBLIOGRAPHIC NOTES

The FP languages appear in (Backus 1978), which, together with (Backus 1973), is the major source for this chapter. These papers have sparked a great deal of interest in functional programming and its implications.

(Pozefsky 1977) discusses programming in Backus's language. (Berkling 1976) and (Magó 1980) present machine architectures supporting efficient execution of functional programming languages.

(Henderson 1980) is an excellent introduction to functional programming that also covers the implementation of a functional language on a conventional computer.

Both APL and LISP are widely used and popular with their users. Both languages are supported by complete environments. The discussion of these languages in this chapter has only scratched the surface. The foundations of LISP are developed in (McCarthy 1960). (McCarthy et al. 1965), (Siklóssy 1976), and (Allen 1978) provide good descriptions of LISP. (Sandewall 1978) and (Teitelman and Masinter 1981) are accounts of friendly and productive LISP systems. (Steele and Sussman 1980) describes a microprocessor designed to execute LISP. APL was defined in the book *A Programming Language* (Iverson 1952), from which the name of the language derives. (Polivka and Pakin 1975) provides a comprehensive view of APL. (Iverson 1979) discusses the usefulness of functional forms in APL.

Other bases for language designs not mentioned in this chapter have been and are being tried: SETL (Schwartz 1973), (Kennedy and Schwartz 1975) is based on set theory; LUCID (Ashcroft and Wadge 1977) is based on logic; SNOBOL4 (Griswold et al. 1971) is based on Markov algorithms.

Exercises

8.1   The function $\alpha+$ of Section 8.3.2.**e** requires that each inner sequence of its argument sequence be of length 2. Modify this function to be able to work on inner sequences of any length.

8.2   Using FP, write the function "COMBINE," defined as

$$\text{COMBINE: } <<x_1,x_2, \ldots x_n>, <y_1,y_2, \ldots y_n>> \equiv \\ <<x_1,y_1>,<x_2,y_2>, \ldots <x_n,y_n>>$$

That is, "COMBINE" applies to two sequences of equal length and yields a sequence consisting of sequences of length 2. The ith inner sequence of the result is the ith element from the first argument and the ith element from the second argument.

   Use any primitive functions from this chapter if needed.

8.3   Write a function to add two vectors represented as sequences:

$$\text{ADDV: } <<x_1,x_2, \ldots x_n>, <y_1, \ldots y_n>> \equiv <x_1+y_1, \ldots x_n+y_n>$$

8.4   Write a function to add any number of vectors:

$$\text{ADDVS: } <<x_{11},x_{12}, \ldots x_{1n}>, <x_{21},x_{22}, \ldots x_{2n}>, \ldots <x_{m1}, \\ x_{m2} \ldots x_{mn}>> \equiv <x_{11}+x_{21}+ \ldots x_{n1}, \ldots, x_{1m}+x_{2m}+x_{nm}>$$

8.5   Write the prime number program of Section 8.2.2 in FP.

8.6   Define a "REPEAT" functional form.

8.7   Explain why LISP's COND is a function and not a functional form.

8.8   Design an FP language suitable for matrix operations such as addition and multiplication. What primitive functions and what functional forms are necessary and/or useful?

8.9   FPs, as defined by Backus, have an important attribute that was not discussed in the chapter. There is a special value "$\perp$" called "bottom" or "undefined," which is returned by functions in case of abnormal conditions. For example, if a function is applied to arguments it does not expect, or if one of the arguments is "$\perp$," it returns "$\perp$." Why is this a useful property? How should the definitions of the primitive functions in Section 8.3.1 be modified to account for this feature?

8.10   Write the prime-number program using only functional features of LISP.

CHAPTER NINE

LANGUAGE DESIGN

". . . consolidation, not innovation . . ."   *(Hoare 1973)*

The leitmotiv of this book is that programming languages are tools for software production. The previous chapters have expounded this viewpoint in depth by discussing programming language concepts and comparing and evaluating the many solutions adopted by existing programming languages. In particular, we have suggested a number of criteria for evaluating programming languages, centered around the concepts of data types, control structures, program correctness, and programming in the large. Viewed slightly differently, however, these criteria also suggest a number of guidelines for programming language design. This is the reason why many of the considerations that follow have been mentioned in the previous chapters. The purpose of this chapter is mainly recapitulatory; we will try to put together the many facets of the problem and, in several cases, show how different language features, each desirable in itself, can often interfere with one another when combined.

According to C. A. R. Hoare (Hoare 1973), "The language designer should be familiar with many alternative features designed by others, and should have excellent judgment in choosing the best and rejecting any that are mutually inconsistent. He must be capable of reconciling, by good engineering design, any remaining minor inconsistencies or overlaps between separately designed features. He must have a clear idea of the scope and purpose and range of application of his new language, and how far it should go in size and complexity. . . . One thing he should not do is to include untried ideas of his own. His task is consolidation, not innovation."

Having designed a language, it is also necessary to design an implementation for it. According to Wirth (Wirth 1975a), "In practice, a programming language is as good as its compiler(s)." In fact, much of the popularity of older languages such as FORTRAN probably stems from the availability of efficient, reliable compilers—that is, compilers that produce efficient code and have good diagnostic systems. Wirth further states that "a successful language must grow out of clear ideas of design goals and *simultaneous* attempts to define it on a computer, or preferably even on several computers." These issues will be discussed below, especially in Section 9.2.

Finally, one should not forget that the user of a language often interacts with other tools provided by the programming system. In most existing solutions, as we have seen, such interactions are not carried out within a unified programming system. Instead, they use independent support tools such as text editors, linkers, and compilers. This often allows the programmer to circumvent the features of the language designed to enhance program reliability. For example, job-control language commands can be used to combine several separately compiled units into a unique executable program. However, the invoked linkage editor provided by the system does not (usually) type-check the interfaces of the components. Similarly, the standard text editor provided by the system does not guarantee that a correct program is left in a correct state after modification. Integrating the language with the tools into a unique coherent programming system should be a prominent design goal; in fact, there is a definite trend in this direction.

9.1 DESIGN CRITERIA

Programming languages must assist the programmer in designing, documenting, and validating programs. As such, language design criteria can be classified according to the following principles: program writability, readability, and reliability. Each of these principles will be discussed separately, in Sections 9.1.1, 9.1.2, and 9.1.3.

We should also remember that programming languages ultimately are executed by computers. *Efficient translation* and *efficient execution* are thus two additional goals of language design. In most practical cases, efficient execution of compiled code is more important than efficient translation, because programs, once delivered, are executed many times or even continuously (in the case of monitoring programs) without being recompiled. However, in certain environments (e.g., educational or research), programs are translated almost every time before being run.

The requirements of the translator have sometimes influenced language design, but only in minor aspects. The usual rule (e.g., in Pascal) that each name be declared before being used, which allows programs to be translated in a single pass, is one such example. (The rule, however, has also a justification from the viewpoint of readability.)

Efficient execution is a hard-to-state requirement if no reference is made to a particular machine architecture. It will be assumed as a design goal in the following section, but rather informally. It is worth mentioning that in some instances, efficient execution becomes such a prominent design goal that the programming language directly reflects aspects of the underlying architecture. This is especially true of languages for systems programming applications. Discussed below are language design criteria for machine-independent languages—that is, languages intended to run on any machine. References to machine-dependent high-level languages are given in the Further Reading section.

Machine independence itself is a language design goal whose attainment requires special attention. Many supposedly machine-independent languages turn out to contain machine-dependent features. One example is the restriction on the cardinality of sets imposed by implementations in order to make sets representable by a single word.

9.1.1 Writability

Programming languages assist in program design by providing constructs that make the adopted design methodology easily expressible. This means that a programmer can concentrate on understanding and solving the problem rather than on the tools used for expressing solutions. The basic properties that contribute to writability can be classified as simplicity, expressiveness, orthogonality, and definiteness. These properties can hardly be defined formally, and they often complement one another.

9.1.1.1 Simplicity

A language should be easy to master. All different features should be easy to learn and remember, and the effect of any combination thereof should be predictable and easily understood. A typical example of a language that does not satisfy this requirement is PL/I. The number of different features that are present in the language make it difficult to master in its entirety; even a look at the size of the reference manual can be discouraging and frustrating.

It is often claimed, however, that the programmer who cannot (and does not need to) understand the entire language can live happily with a subset. As Hoare (Hoare 1973) points out, this claim is not justified. Knowledge of a subset may be sufficient for programs that work as the programmer intended; but if the program does not work properly, and accidentally invokes some unknown feature of the language, then serious troubles arise for the programmer.

Simplicity is impaired if the language provides several alternative ways of specifying the same concept. Providing more than one form to denote a concept increases the size of a language and favors the development of ''dialects'' that use only subsets of such forms. A user expert in one dialect can have difficulties in understanding programs written in a different dialect. An example of this problem can be found in COBOL, in which both a concise, mathematical notation and an English-like notation are supported. For example, one can write either

MULTIPLY WORK_HOURS BY HOURLY_PAY GIVING DAILY_PAY

or

DAILY_PAY = WORK_HOURS * DAILY_PAY

PL/I provides many features that cause the same problem. For example, access to record components can be done either by full qualification (i.e., specifying all field selectors) or by partial qualification (when no ambiguity arises). Declarations have default values for unspecified attributes.

C offers many examples of this problem. Adding 1 to the integer variable *a* can be done by any one of the following four statements.

1) a + +;
2) a = a + 1;
3) a + = 1;
4) + + a;

Element *i* of array *a* may be accessed as *a* [*i*], or as

*(a + i)

A component *x* of a structure *S* pointed at by pointer *p* can be retrieved by either *p*→*x* or (*p).*x*.

Ada suffers from similar problems. For example, parameters can be transmitted to subprograms with the keyword method, or with the positional method, or with a mixture of the two (Section 5.2.1). Record values can be specified in a similar way. For example, a variable *X* of following type *T*

type T **is**
    record
         A : CHARACTER;
         B : INTEGER,
    end record;

can be assigned a value by

X: = (B ⇒ 3,A ⇒ 'F');

or by

X: = ('F',3);

Simplicity is also impaired if the language allows different concepts to be expressed by the same notation. Overloading is an example. We have stated that a judicious use of overloading can be useful (Section 4.1). Arithmetic operators are usually overloaded; this reduces the proliferation of operators and makes the language simpler.

Some languages (e.g., ALGOL 68 and Ada), however, generalize the concept of overloading to user-defined operators and subprograms. A call to an overloaded subprogram is ambiguous (and illegal) if the types and the order of actual parameters (or the names of formal parameters in the Ada keyword method) are not sufficient to identify exactly one subprogram declaration. Overloading and the scope rules of the language can easily make programs difficult to read.

Finally, there are cases in which different, seemingly simple, language features interact in a way that is critical or produces programs whose behavior is hard to predict. For example, consider the interaction between subprogram parameter passing and exception handling in Ada. A subprogram raising an exception can produce different results if parameter passing is implemented by sharing or by copy. An example of combination of features that generate a behavior that is difficult to predict is illustrated by multitasking and exception handling in Ada. (We urge the reader to refer to the language manual on this point.)

Simplicity alone, however, can be a deceptive goal. For example, machine languages are usually simple, in the sense that the number of machine instructions is often rather small and each machine instruction has a definite, easily understood effect. The difficulty with machine language programming, however, arises not strictly from the use of the language, but rather from its low level. Complexity is not in the language, but mostly in the difficult process of mapping a solution into elementary actions performed by the machine on unstructured data.

9.1.1.2 Expressiveness

The above discussion criticizes machine languages on the grounds of their low expressive power. Expressiveness of a language is a measure of how naturally a problem-solving strategy can be mapped into a program structure. One central point expounded in this book is that abstraction on data and control, along with modularization mechanisms, are the basic structuring tools to be used in program design. They can be used by the programmer at various levels, from the overall strategy—in the decomposition of a complex task into simpler subtasks and the design of the subtask interfaces—to the details of coding and data representation.

Pascal is perhaps the best-known example of a simple language with a high expressive power, even though it fails to provide adequate modularization mechanisms. Its rich set of control and type structures is responsible for much of its success.

9.1.1.3 Orthogonality

The appealing simplicity and expressiveness of Pascal is often impaired by its lack of orthogonality. Orthogonality means that any composition of the basic primitives should be allowed. This would achieve the greatest degree of generality, without any restrictions or special cases. A typical example of Pascal's lack of orthogonality is given by procedures (functions) and procedure (function) calls, which are subject to the following restrictions.

- Files cannot be passed by value.

- Components of a packed data structure cannot be passed by reference.

- Procedures and functions passed as parameters can only have by-value parameters.

- The type of formal parameters must be stated in the procedure (or function) heading, except for procedure (or function) parameters.

- Functions can only return values of a restricted set of types; they cannot return arrays, records, sets, and files.

- The type of formal parameters can only be specified by a type identifier, and not by its representation.

For example,

procedure *nonorthogonal (***var** *x:* **array** *[1..10]* **of** *real; y: char)*

is not legal, whereas

procedure *nonorthogonal (***var** *x: T; y: char)*

where *T* is declared in an outer scope as

type *T* = **array** *[1..10]* **of** *real*

is legal.

Another example is given by Pascal's constant declarations, such as **const** *null* = 0, which allows constants to be given a symbolic name. Pascal does not allow pointers or structured objects (such as arrays and records) to be given a constant value. Finally, variables of an enumerated type can be initialized only by assignments and not by input values. In fact, such variables cannot be read (nor written). This often makes Pascal programs awkward. The programmer is forced to code input values of an enumerated type variable into, say, integers, and then to convert the values read via program statements.

The lack of orthogonality can be disturbing. The programmer cannot apply uniform generalizations, which might be illegal, and must often refer to the language manual to confirm the legality and correctness of what is being written.

ALGOL 68 is perhaps the best-known example of an orthogonal programming language. For example, objects of any type are permitted as parameters and results of subprograms. Identity declarations—the ALGOL 68 mechanisms for defining constants—have the form

m *id* = *e*

where **m** is a mode, *id* is an identifier, and *e* is an expression. Here **m** can be *any* (nonvoid) mode and *e* can be *any* expression whose value is assigned nonmodifiably to *id*. Even more generally, identity declarations are used to declare procedures and functions in the conventional way, as in

proc *sum* = (**real** *a, b*) **real:** *a* + *b;*

As a design goal, orthogonality should not be considered a replacement for simplicity. However, the tradeoff between the two goals is hard to quantify and appears to be a central decision in language design. It is not always clear whether it is better to have a few simple concepts with general, restriction-free composability or a larger collection of less simple concepts with several minor, annoying restrictions. In fact, the composition of orthogonal features in ALGOL 68 can lead to exceedingly hard-to-understand programs (and hard-to-implement compilers). For example, almost every ALGOL 68 construct, including those that look like conventional statements, can in principle yield a value, as the following fragment illustrates:

$$(\textbf{real } x, y; \textbf{ read } ((x, y)); \textbf{ if } x{<}y \textbf{ then } a \textbf{ else } b \textbf{ fi}) :=$$
$$b + \textbf{ if } a{:=} a + 1; a > b \textbf{ then } c{:=} c + 1; + b$$
$$\qquad\qquad\qquad\qquad \textbf{else } c{:=} c - 1; a$$
$$\quad\textbf{fi}$$

The left-hand side of this assignment statement is a unit that declares local variables x and y and yields variable a or b as its value, depending on the values read for x and y (a, b, and c are assumed to be **real** global variables). The second operand of the right-hand side expression is expressed as a conditional. The value of

$$a{:=} a + 1; a > b$$

is the value of the final component—that is, a boolean. Similarly, the value of

$$c{:=} c + 1; +b$$

is the real value $+b$, which can be used as a component of an expression.

According to Wirth (Wirth 1975**a**), ''If we try to achieve simplicity through generality of language we may end up with programs that through their very conciseness and lack of redundancy elude our limited intellectual grasp. . . . The key, then, lies not so much in minimizing the number of basic features of a language, but rather in keeping the included facilities easy to understand in all their consequences of usage and free from unexpected interactions when they are combined.'' The balance between orthogonality and simplicity that we need to achieve can perhaps be called ''predictability.'' The combination of language features should not provide unexpected results; and, based on the knowledge of the language primitives, it should be possible to predict the effect of their various combinations.

We may say—in rather simplistic terms—that Pascal is simple and rather expressive, but not orthogonal. ALGOL 68 is orthogonal and rather expressive, but not simple. Ada is expressive, but neither simple nor orthogonal (the analysis of the lack of orthogonality in Ada is left to the reader as an exercise).

Functional languages have the potential of achieving both simplicity and orthogonality, because of the restricted amount of interaction among language elements and the simplicity of the combining forms.

9.1.1.4 Definiteness

An important issue in the usability of a programming language is the accuracy of the description of its syntax and semantics. Vagueness is an enemy to the programmer in two important aspects. First, the programmer cannot rely completely on the language, and any attempt to find a definite response by referring to the standard definition results in mere frustration. Second, different implementations can choose to resolve ambiguously stated features differently, with unfortunate consequences for program portability.

Pascal is defined by a rather informal report that is attractively simple and easily readable, but leaves a considerable number of subtle questions unresolved. The syntax of the language is defined by a simple context-free BNF grammar, which does not rule out an infinite number of incorrect programs. For example, the grammar does not specify that an arithmetic expression, such as $x + 3.75$, cannot be assigned to a boolean variable. Thus, syntactically correct programs are legal Pascal programs only if they satisfy an additional set of conditions described by the Report in English prose, with all the ambiguities (and omissions) that entails. A formal axiomatic definition of Pascal has also been given. This definition, however, does not deal with procedures in their full generality and fails to answer questions about type compatibility that are also left unanswered by the Report.

ALGOL 68 is defined by an extremely precise document: the Revised Report. The syntax of the language is described by a W grammar, which takes all context-sensitive aspects of the language into account. The semantic description is given in a stylized version of English that is seldom ambiguous. The ALGOL 68 definition is complete. The Report explicitly defines all checking and processing that is to be done at compile-time (including mode compatibility), as well as all actions to be executed at run-time (including signaling run-time errors).

The ALGOL 68 Report is generally considered to be very hard to read; in fact, the need for a more palatable language description was soon recognized and led to an official informal introduction to the language (Lindsey and Van der Meulen 1977). Unreadability, however, is perhaps more a property of formal definitions in general than of the language itself. In fact, the question of how to provide clear and simple formal descriptions of programming languages is still a matter for investigation.

9.1.2 Readability

Readability is the main factor influencing program modifiability and maintainability. Consequently, it has a considerable impact on the overall cost of software production. Readability is strictly related to writability: language features that favor program writability usually favor readability also. This is not surprising, since when writing a program, the programmer must often reread parts of it. Simplicity and expressiveness greatly encourage and assist the programmer to write self-documenting code, and even to develop a clear writing style. In particular, abstractions on data and control and program modularization give the greatest assistance in understanding the program gradually, through levels of increasing detail. Thus, the distinction between readability and writability is often somewhat arbitrary.

An important aspect of readability is program documentation. The purpose of documentation is to explain to a human reader how a program works, so that subsequent modifications to meet changing requirements, or to maintain the program, can be done successfully. There is widespread consensus that "the view that documentation is something that is added to the program after it has been commissioned seems to be wrong in principle and counter-productive in practice. Instead, documentation must be regarded as an integral part of the process of design and coding" (Hoare 1973).

Comment conventions of the programming language play an important role in program documentation. In line-oriented languages (i.e., languages in which each statement occupies a line) a comment starts either in a fixed-line position or with a special marker reserved for this purpose. On the other hand, stream-oriented languages (i.e., languages in which the text is viewed as a continuous stream of characters) introduce special delimiters, such as "{" and "}" in Pascal, to enclose comments, which can appear anywhere in the program.

This has an unfortunate and frequently occurring consequence. When the closing delimiter is forgotten by the programmer, entire pieces of program are taken as further comments and thus ignored by the translator. Even worse is the case of ALGOL 68, which uses the same symbol (**comment**, **co**, ¢, or **#**) as both opening and closing delimiters. Forgetting one of them can cause a comment to be treated as program text, and vice versa. Line-oriented languages do not suffer from this problem because the end of the line is interpreted as an implicit closing delimiter. The Ada convention that a comment is implicitly terminated at the end of the line is a good solution.

The lexical conventions of the language have an influence on program readability. Strict restrictions on the length of identifiers, as in FORTRAN and C, can force the programmer to give cryptic names to variables and procedures. Readability is further enhanced if the underscore character '_' or a space can be used in identifiers. For example, a record field identifier *spouse_name* or *spouse name* is preferable to *spousename*. Pascal forbids underscore characters and spaces inside identifiers. However, for readability purposes, we have largely ignored this annoying restriction in our examples. A good compromise, if the language allows upper and lower case letters, is to start each part of the name with an upper case letter—for example, *SpouseName*.

Another key factor influencing program readability is the *syntax* of the language. Explicit delimiters (**if** . . . **fi**, **do** . . . **od**, **case** . . . **esac**, etc.) are preferable to the **begin** . . . **end** pairs required by Pascal for grouping statements, because they clearly indicate the purpose of the group of statements. In stream-oriented languages the syntactic structure of the program can be made evident by adopting suitable conventions for indentation. Although this is an effective method of self-documentation, it is difficult to achieve in practice. The programmer often starts writing a program with good intentions, but, as soon as the program undergoes some modifications, the initial careful indentations are lost, and the program assumes a sloppy and confused structure. Reindenting the entire program can be costly and error-prone if done manually. Some programming systems, however, contain a specialized tool (called a *pretty-printer*) that can automatically reshape the program by means of a text processing procedure.

Program readability is also affected by the semantics of the language. In Chapter 6 we discussed at length language features that make programs hard to analyze, and we also discussed language proposals that tend to minimize (or eliminate altogether) some undesirable side effects. For example, procedures with parameters passed by reference and global variables can produce aliasing. Euclid imposes semantic restrictions that make aliasing illegal (and detectable).

As already mentioned, semantic restrictions make programs more readable, at the price of reduced generality. For example, a data base system is intrinsically based on the fact that a recorded set of data is concurrently viewed as a different logical entity by different classes of users. A particular data base might be viewed by a payroll program as a set of data about individual employees, whereas it might be viewed as a set of hierarchically organized working groups for managerial purposes. In other words, data base systems are intrinsically based on side effects and aliasing, and it is hopeless to design such systems with a language that gets rid of these features.

It is important to note that in all of the foregoing discussions of readability, the term means "readability by a person familiar with the language." Thus, the fact that the Pascal statement

$A := B + C$

may be written in COBOL as

ADD B TO C GIVING A

does not make COBOL more readable. The COBOL statement has more of an English-like syntax, which may give a nonprogrammer the false feeling of understanding the program. If we could indeed describe the entire program in pseudo-English, then that language would be more readable by all people familiar with English. This, however, is well beyond the state of the art at present. Thus the COBOL solution merely leads to verbosity and is in fact dangerous, because it might give rise to a false sense of understanding.

Finally, readability is even more important when a team of programmers is involved, rather than one programmer alone. In a team, it is important to be able to institute conventions and reduce the amount of individual variations so that programs written by one team member can be read by another team member. As mentioned in Section 9.1.1.1, a language that allows the expression of the same concept in several ways encourages the development of local "dialects." It is inevitable that some programmers will become comfortable with one form and others with another. The two groups will have difficulty reading one another's programs. The variations, rather than encouraging creativity, hamper readability.

9.1.3 Reliability

Needless to say, program reliability is strictly related both to writability—the easier we can write programs the more confident we are of the correctness of what we are writing—and to readability—the easier we can read programs the better we can reason about programs to assess their correctness. Indeed, Chapter 6 was devoted entirely to a discussion of these concepts.

Reliability can be enhanced if the language makes a rigorous distinction between static and dynamic checks that must be performed on programs. Such a distinction makes programmers fully aware of the degree of validation of the program at each step of its processing. ALGOL 68 and Ada are two examples of languages that do make this distinction. On the other hand, Pascal does not clearly specify how and when checks should be performed.

Because of the intrinsic unreliability, languages should not support features that are either impossible or too hard to check. An example of the former is provided by the parameter passing conventions of Ada, which can give different results in the presence of aliasing (Section 6.2.1.2). An example of the latter is given by Pascal variant records (Section 4.3.2).

An attractive language design goal is to make programs statically checkable as far as possible, since run-time checks alone not only cannot certify program correctness, but also lead to slow execution speed. Some languages allow run-time checks to be turned off on request, to make programs efficiently executable after they have been thoroughly certified. This solution however, has its own risks, as is sharply pointed out by Hoare (Hoare 1973): "It is absurd to make elaborate security checks on debugging runs, when no trust is put in the results, and then remove them in production runs, when an erroneous result could be expensive or disastrous. What would we think of a sailing enthusiast who wears his life-jacket when training on dry land but takes it off as soon as he goes to the sea?"

Reliability can be enhanced by a language that allows programs to be developed and certified one module at a time. Thoroughly certified program modules can be kept in a library and combined at any time to build new programs. The Ada separate compilation scheme, as we saw in Chapter 8, is a step in this direction.

Modifiability also contributes to reliability, because during maintenance we must be able to modify the program while retaining its reliability. The syntax of the language largely determines the ease of program modifiability. Again, the ALGOL 68 and Ada explicit delimiters have advantages over the **begin** . . . **end** pair required by Pascal for grouping statements. Adding a new statement to a single-statement **else**-branch or loop-body in Pascal requires adding a bracketing pair of keywords **begin** and **end**. These words are easy to forget, and their absence will produce incorrect programs. This is especially troublesome because the program will in all probability be syntactically valid.

There is a strong relationship between program reliability and rigorous definition of the language semantics. Besides affecting program readability, as discussed in Section 9.1.1—and consequently, reliability—formal semantics provide the basis for program verification (Section 6.4.2). A program verifier for the language can become one major component of the programming environment.

Finally, reliability of a language depends on the reliability of its implementation. The larger and more complex the language, the more difficult it is to produce reliable implementations. It is certainly easier to produce a reliable Pascal compiler than an equally reliable PL/I or Ada compiler.

9.2 LANGUAGE IMPLEMENTATION

Implementing a programming language requires more effort than merely designing a processor for the language. The implementer should also have "the resources to write user manuals, introductory texts, advanced texts; he should construct auxiliary programming aids and library procedures; and, finally, he should have the political will and resources to sell and distribute the language to its intended range of customers" (Hoare 1973).

This section briefly discusses the design of language processors based on translation. Translator design is a widely studied area of computer science, and much of the developed theory can be used in practice to construct reliable and efficient translators. We do not cover these aspects in any detail here, but refer the interested reader to the specialized literature.

For our purposes, a language processor can be viewed as a black box, as shown in Figure 9.1. The input to the processor is a text written in a *source language* **Ls**. Its output is the translation of the input program into an *object* (or *target*) *language* **Lo**. The translator itself is a program written in an *implementation language* **Li** and, obviously, can only run on host machines that provide a processor for **Li**.

Object programs can only run on machines (*target machines*) that provide a processor for **Lo**. As mentioned in Section 3.1, there are cases (cross translators) in which the target machine(s) and the host machine(s) are different.

Portability of the translator is a desirable design goal that can result in several benefits. First, only one highly reliable translator need be developed, and then many versions can be obtained at a much lower cost. Second, programs written in the language are automatically movable to any installation that provides the same translator. An important factor in the popularity of Pascal is probably the availability of a portable translator, which makes the language easily implementable on different computers. Portable C is a subset of C that has been designed for portability; the original compiler has been transported to many different target machines, including microcomputers. The ease of producing such a compiler for a new machine has caused a proliferation of these compilers and thus an increase in the use of C. SNOBOL4 is another example of a language for which a portable implementation is available.

Portability issues have a strong influence on the overall design of a translator. Briefly discussed below is how portability has been achieved for Pascal. A Pascal translator (Nori et al. 1976) is available in the two forms shown in Figure 9.2: one

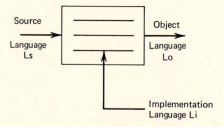

Figure 9.1 A Translator.

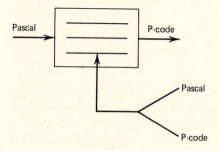

Figure 9.2   A Portable Pascal translator.

implemented in Pascal, the other implemented in P-code. P-code is a language for a virtual machine. This machine has two data areas: a stack and a heap, allocated from the opposite ends of a data segment and growing toward each other. Instructions, stored in a separate area and addressed by a program counter, consist of an operation code and two optional operand fields that specify the operands in the data areas. Most of the instructions (e.g., arithmetic and logical instructions) do not have explicit operands, but they implicitly name the locations on top of the stack. Thus the virtual machine is basically a stack machine.

To implement a Pascal compiler on a machine X, the following procedure— which is known as *bootstrapping*—must be followed.

1. Write an interpreter for P-code in a language available on X.

2. Modify the Pascal version of the translator shown in Figure 9.2 to generate X's assembly language instructions. The change is confined within the code generating routines of the original compiler. The result of this step is shown in Figure 9.3**a**.

3. Using the P-code interpreter developed in step 1, executing the P-code version of the translator of Figure 9.2, the translator of Figure 9.3**a** is translated into P-code. The result of this step is shown in Figure 9.3**b**.

4. The translator of Figure 9.3**a** can now be translated by the translator of Figure 9.3**b** using the P-code interpreter developed in step 1. The resulting translator (Figure 9.4) is the desired product.

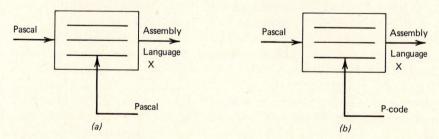

Figure 9.3   Intermediate translators.

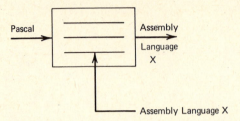

Figure 9.4   A Pascal compiler for machine X.

Many Pascal compilers have been successfully installed on different machines by modifying the original CDC 6600 compiler. The bootstrapping procedure is conceptually simple, mainly because of the clarity of the compiler's structure, which makes the program modification performed in step 2 easy—a notable consequence of the readability of Pascal.

SUGGESTIONS FOR FURTHER READING AND BIBLIOGRAPHIC NOTES

Much of the material presented in this chapter is taken from (Hoare 1973) and (Wirth 1975**a**). Language design is also studied in (Richard and Ledgard 1977). The ALGOL 68 and Pascal designs are compared by (Tanenbaum 1978). (Hoare and Wirth 1973) gives a formal definition of Pascal. The ALGOL 68 Revised Report provides a formal definition of the language. The development of Ada illustrates quite well the relation between programming language requirements and programming language design. The U.S. Department of Defense set down the requirements in a series of documents that were extensively reviewed by the Armed Forces and by industrial organizations, universities, and foreign military departments. The culmination of this process was the Steelman Report (DOD 1978). Ada was chosen among a set of languages designed to meet such requirements. The Ada preliminary design (ACM-SIGPLAN 1979) subsequently was reviewed, and the proposed standard appears in (DOD 1980**b**). (Kahn et al. 1980) is a preliminary report on the formal definition of the language.

Several compiler design textbooks address the topic of programming language implementation: (Gries 1971), (Bauer and Eickel 1976), (Aho and Ullman 1977), and (Barrett and Couch 1979). The paper by P. C. Poole in (Bauer and Eickel 1976) discusses compiler portability. (Amman 1974), (Wirth 1971**c**), and (Nori et al. 1976) discuss the implementation of Pascal. (Griswold 1972) describes a portable implementation of SNOBOL4. (Johnson 1978) describes a portable C implementation.

This chapter has studied the design of machine-independent high-level programming languages. In several system software applications, absolute independence from the machine cannot be achieved with acceptable efficiency. One solution to this problem consists of augmenting assembly languages with a few high-level constructs (e.g., control structures). This solution is well illustrated by PL360 (Wirth 1968) and by several languages described in (van der Poel and Maarsen 1974). More recent solutions provide truly high-level languages for systems software applications. However, such languages provide limited escapes from the high-level language into a machine-dependent domain. Bliss, C, Mesa, Euclid, Modula, and PLZ follow this general philosophy.

A recent language, Edison, is described in (Brinch Hansen 1980**a**). (Brinch Hansen 1980**b**) argues that even Pascal is not simple enough and many features have been either eliminated or greatly simplified in order to design Edison. (Brinch Hansen 1980**c**) gives examples of Edison programs.

Exercises

9.1   Some programming languages permit the use of overloading. Give examples of overloading in Pascal, ALGOL 68, and Ada (Ada is particularly supportive of overloading). Discuss the effects of overloading on both readability and writability.

9.2   Give examples of nonorthogonal Ada features.

9.3   Give examples of automatic type conversions in programming languages. What is the effect of these conversions on readability and writability?

9.4   You are given two translators (see Figure 9.5) for a new programming language

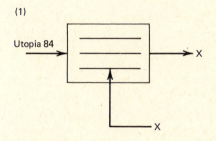

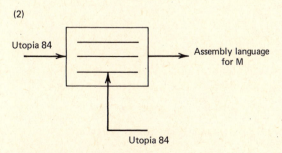

Figure 9.5   Translators for Exercise 9.4.

(UTOPIA 84, say). Suppose that machine M is equipped with an assembler and a translator for the X programming language. Your goal is to obtain an executable form of translator (2) on machine M.

a. Show how you can obtain an executable form of translator (2) on machine M.

b. When (and why) is this implementation strategy for UTOPIA 84 useful?

c. Suppose your goal is to produce a translator for UTOPIA 84 on M that produces optimized code. Of (1) and (2), which should be an optimizing translator?

A GLOSSARY OF SELECTED PROGRAMMING LANGUAGES

Ada

Overview

Ada has been designed to support numerical applications, systems programming, and applications with real-time and concurrent requirements.

Data Types

Ada provides built-in types and constructors. The precision of numeric data can be controlled by the programmer. Ada distinguishes carefully between static and dynamic properties of types. Several insecurities of Pascal types have been eliminated. The package construct (see below under "Programming in the Large") can be used to define (generic) abstract data types.

Control Structures

Ada provides Pascal-like control structures. It provides a specialized **exit** statement to break loops, as well as the **goto** statement. The language also provides a rich set of unit-level control stuctures: namely, procedure and function calls, exceptions, and concurrent activations.

Program Correctness

Ada retains several harmful features (such as **goto** and side effects). Aliasing is termed illegal, but erroneous Ada programs can remain undetected. A formal definition of Ada is described in (Kahn et al. 1980) and can be used as a basis for program verification.

Programming in the Large

Besides subprograms and functions, packages are the major program structuring units in Ada. Packages collect related declarations and provide initialization. Several procedures may also be packaged together. Units can be nested, à la ALGOL. They can also be separately compiled according to a partial ordering rule.

Official Definition

(DOD 1980**b**), which supersedes (ACM-SIGPLAN 1979).

Important Papers

(ACM-SIGPLAN 1979), (ACM-SIGPLAN 1980), (Kahn et al. 1980).

Textbooks

(Wegner 1980), which refers to (ACM-SIGPLAN 1979), not to (DOD 1980**b**), (Ledgard 1981); (Pyle 1981)

ALGOL 60

Overview

ALGOL 60 (**Algo**rithmic **L**anguage 19**60**) is an algebraic language for scientific computations. It has influenced the design of almost every language since 1960.

Data Types

The type of all data must be explicitly declared. Besides built-in types, **integer, real** and **boolean**, the language provides dynamic arrays. User-defined types are not supported. ALGOL 60 provides semistatic and semidynamic variables.

Control Structures

ALGOL 60 provides **if-then-else** and counting- and condition-driven loops. **Goto** and multiway branching are also provided. Procedure calls comprise the only unit-level control structure. Recursive calls are permitted.

Program Correctness

This was not a design goal. The language provides several harmful features. The **goto** is available. Procedure and function calls may generate side effects, thanks to call by name (which is standard) and access to global variables. The syntax of the language has been defined formally, but its semantics is described only in informal English prose.

Programming in the Large

Procedures (and blocks) are the only abstraction mechanisms provided by ALGOL 60. Programs are tree-structured, and inner units automatically inherit outer declarations.

Official Definition

(Naur 1963).

Important Papers

(Knuth 1967), (Perlis 1978), (Naur 1978).

Textbooks

(Dijkstra 1962); see also (Sammet 1969).

Implementation Issues

(Randell and Russell 1964), (Gries 1971), (Wichmann 1973).

ALGOL 68

Overview

ALGOL 68 was designed to communicate algorithms, to execute them efficiently on a variety of computers, and to aid in teaching them to students.

Data Types

ALGOL 68 provides built-in types and constructors to build new types. The language does not provide abstract data types. Type compatibility is defined by structural equivalence. The language provides for extensive automatic type conversions (coercions). The language is strongly typed.

Control Structures

ALGOL 68 provides **if-then-else**, **case**, generalized loop, and **goto**. Procedure calls govern the flow of control among units; procedures may be passed as parameters. The language supports concurrent execution and provides semaphores for synchronization.

Program Correctness

The language provides the **goto** statement and permits (controlled and limited) side effects. In the official language definition, the semantics is defined partly formally, partly in semiformal English. The semantics of ALGOL 68 has also been defined axiomatically in (Schwartz 1978**b**), in an attempt to aid program verification.

Programming in the Large

The only abstraction capabilities are blocks, procedures, and user-defined operators. Programs are tree-structured and inner modules automatically inherit outer declarations. The official language definition does not specify a standard separate compilation facility.

Important Papers

(Branquart et al. 1971), (Lindsay 1972), (Tanenbaum 1976), (Valentine 1974), (Tanenbaum 1978).

Textbooks

(Lindsay and van der Meulen 1977), (Pagan 1976).

Implementation Issues

(Peck 1970), (Hill 1976), (Branquart et al. 1976).

APL

Overview

APL (**A P**rogramming **L**anguage) has been designed as a notation for expressing mathematical algorithms concisely. APL is supported by an interactive programming system that has contributed to its popularity among scientific programmers who use the computer as a powerful desk calculator, and also among other classes of users.

Data Types

APL is a dynamically typed language. Built-in types are numeric, character, and boolean. It provides a rich set of operations on arrays, which eliminate the need for element-by-element manipulation for most array operations. Arrays are the only aggregate-structuring method.

Control Structures

APL provides very powerful composition rules for operations, and APL programs often take the form of one-liners. The language provides only rudimentary control structures, including the jump.

Program Correctness

This was not a goal of APL. Program readability suffers from dynamic binding. Interactive execution provides a flexible testing support, which is particularly valuable for programs that are not too large.

Programming in the Large

APL programs can be decomposed into subprograms. Nonlocal referencing is based on dynamic scope binding, which can hamper readability and modifiability of large programs. APL is supported by a complete programming system.

Official Definition

(Iverson 1962).

Important Papers

(Falkoff and Iverson 1978), (Iverson 1979), (Iverson 1980).

Textbooks

(Polivka and Pakin 1975).

Implementation Issues

(Breed and Lathwell 1968).

Bliss

Overview

Bliss is a high-level, expression-oriented language for writing systems software. It is presently used for this purpose on DEC machines.

Data Types

Data have no types. Data structures are defined not by their storage layout, but rather in terms of the algorithm used to access an element of the structure.

Control Structures

Bliss is a block-structured, **goto**less, expression-oriented language. Every executable construct is an expression and computes a value. Expressions may be concatenated with semicolons to form sequences. Bliss also provides conditional statements, loop statements, **leave** statements (for breaking loops), and subprograms (called **routines**). It also provides features for exception handling.

Program Correctness

Bliss provides advantages over assembly languages, which would otherwise be used for the same applications. Formal program correctness, however, was not a design goal.

Programming in the Large

Bliss has a conventional ALGOL-like structure. It has both blocks and routines. Routines can be external.

Official Definition

(Wulf et al. 1972).

Important Papers

(Wulf et al. 1971).

Implementation Issues

(Wulf et al. 1975).

C

Overview

C was developed for writing systems programs for the PDP-11. It has been generalized and implemented on many computers, large and small. It is supported by a full set of support tools in the UNIX operating system. A portable subset has been defined. C is based on BCPL (Richards 1969), a language for compiler writing.

Data Types

The primitive data types can be aggregated by arrays, structures, and unions (similar to ALGOL 68 **union**). The precision of integers and reals can be specified. Type conversions are applied freely and automatically. Pointers are qualified.

Control Structures

Repeat, while, and for loops are provided, with possibility of exit from loop (break) or skipping the rest of the current loop iteration (continue). A limited form of the case statement and the general goto also are available. Functions and procedure calls are the only unit-level control structures.

Program Correctness

No special attention has been paid to this issue. The goto, pointer, side effects, and automatic type conversion are all present. Readability can be a problem because of the existence of many different ways of stating the same concept and the possibility of producing extremely terse code. The syntax of the type declarations is rather cryptic. The definition is informal and leaves many questions unanswered.

Programming in the Large

Functions and procedures are the only program-structuring mechanisms. They may not be nested but may include nested blocks. Procedures and functions may be compiled separately, but type checking across modules is not done by the compiler.

Official Definition

(Kernighan and Ritchie 1978).

Textbooks

(Kernighan and Ritchie 1978), (Zahn 1979).

Implementation Issues

(Johnson 1978).

CLU

Overview

CLU was designed to support a programming methodology based on the recognition of abstractions.

Data Types

CLU provides built-in types and constructors. The construct **cluster** allows the programmer to define abstract data types. Data objects are uniformly accessed via pointers. An assignment changes the reference bound to a name, rather than changing the value in the cell referenced.

Control Structures

CLU provides conventional predefined statement-level control structures. There is no **goto**, only a **break** statement to exit from loops. In addition, the programmer can define new looping control structures via iterators. CLU provides exception handling facilities.

Program Correctness

Several harmful features, such as **goto** and global variables, are absent from CLU. However, assignment by sharing encourages heavy use of side effects. The semantics of CLU is defined in informal English prose. Verification is not explicitly addressed, although it is claimed that CLU supports it.

Programming in the Large

Iterators, procedures, and clusters provide a suitable basis for modular system decomposition. Procedures and iterators can be declared within clusters, but there is no other nesting. Iterators, procedures, and clusters can be compiled separately, in any order. When a module is compiled, only the interfaces of used modules need to have been compiled already.

Official Definition

(Liskov et al. 1978).

Important Papers

(Liskov and Zilles 1974), (Liskov 1974), (Liskov and Zilles 1975), (Liskov et al. 1977), (Liskov and Snyder 1979).

Implementation Issues

(Atkinson, et al. 1978).

COBOL

Overview

COBOL (**CO**mmon **B**usiness **O**riented **L**anguage) is a language for business applications. COBOL programs usually perform very simple computations on large amounts of data. It is perhaps the most widely used language today, but it did not play a significant influence on later language designs.

Data Types

Data are described in a DATA DIVISION. Most data are grouped as components of records, which are stored in a file. COBOL provides instructions for handling records and files. The types of individual record components and simple variables must be declared. Numbers and character strings of programmer-specified precision are the basic types.

Control Structures

COBOL provides a restricted form of IF-THEN-ELSE, the GOTO statement, and a PERFORM statement that serves both as a loop statement and as a unit call. The PERFORM provides control transfer to the unit and return from the unit without changing environment. The early versions of COBOL did not provide true subprograms. This is also true for many present implementations of COBOL subsets.

Program Correctness

This was not an issue in the design of COBOL. To facilitate the use of the language, COBOL introduces a natural-language-style programming. Programs easily become verbose and errors are difficult to spot. The syntax of COBOL is defined formally; its semantics is not.

Programming in the Large

A COBOL program consists of an IDENTIFICATION DIVISION, which identifies the programmer and the program; an ENVIRONMENT DIVISION, which specifies the hardware configuration and the relation between logical and physical files; a DATA DIVISION, which specifies the structure of data; and a PROCEDURE DIVISION, which specifies the algorithms that operate on data. No real modularity can be achieved within the PROCEDURE DIVISION.

Official Definition

(ANSI 1968), (ANSI 1974).

Important Papers

(Sammet 1978).

Textbooks

The essentials of COBOL can be found in (Rosen 1967) and (Sammet 1969).

Concurrent Pascal

Overview

Concurrent Pascal is a language for writing structured concurrent programs—in particular, operating systems. It is an extension of Pascal.

Data Types

The language provides the types of Pascal and **class** types to define abstract data types. **Process** types and **monitor** types are the basic tools for describing concurrency. **Class** types, **process** types, and **monitor** types are collectively called system types.

Control Structures

The language provides the statement-level control structures of Pascal. In addition, a **process** type can repeat the execution of a set of statements forever by means of a **cycle** statement. Unit-level control structures are procedure and function calls, as well as concurrent activation of processes (by an **init** statement).

Program Correctness

The language supports the writing of well-structured, readable concurrent programs. The language supports extensive static checks. In particular, it guarantees statically that no deadlock (processes blocking each other) ever occurs. The language is amenable to program verification (Hoare 1974), (Howard 1976**a**), (Howard 1976**b**).

Programming in the Large

A program consists of nested definitions of system types. The outermost system type is an anonymous process (initial process). The initial process is instantiated after the program is loaded; in turn, it initializes the other components. The language supports modular system decomposition but relies on an ALGOL-like tree structure.

Official Definition

(Brinch Hansen 1975).

Important Papers

(Hoare 1974), (Howard 1976**a**), (Howard 1976**b**).

Textbooks

(Brinch Hansen 1977).

Implementation Issues

(Hartmann 1977).

Euclid

Overview

Euclid is a language designed for writing verifiable system programs.

Data Types

Euclid's type structure is based on Pascal, but several unsafe features of Pascal are absent. Type compatibility is rigorously defined. The tag field of variant records cannot be assigned by itself. Pointers are bound to collections. The language is strongly typed, but the programmer can explicitly override type checking at compile-time, if need be. Abstract data types can be implemented by modules (see below under "Programming in the Large").

Control Structures

Euclid provides Pascal-like control structures. There is no **goto**, but an **exit** statement is provided to exit from loops. The **module** construct can be used to define new looping control structures (similar to CLU's iterators). Unit-level control structures are procedure and function calls.

Program Correctness

Euclid does not provide **goto**. Functions cannot produce side effects. Syntactically correct programs allow potential aliasing, and the compiler generates legality assertions that must be proven to certify program correctness. The Euclid system includes a verifier. Both user-supplied assertions and compiler-generated legality assertions must be proven to hold by the verifier.

Programming in the Large

Besides procedures and functions, Euclid provides a **module** construct that can be used to define both control and data abstractions. Modules are similar to Ada **packages**. They can be nested, but there is control over imported global entities. External modules can be compiled separately.

Official Language Definition

(Lampson et al. 1977).

Important Papers

(Popek et al. 1977), (Elliott and Barnard 1978), (London et al. 1978), (Wortman 1979).

Implementation Issues

(Holt et al. 1978**b**).

FORTRAN

Overview

FORTRAN (**For**mula **Tran**slator) is a language for scientific and numeric applications. The language has been designed with the primary goal of execution efficiency. Outlined below is the standard FORTRAN described in (ANSI 1966). A new standard is reported in (ANSI 1978).

Data Types

FORTRAN provides booleans, integer, real (both single and double precision), and complex numbers. Fixed-sized array is the only aggregate constructor. Data may be either explicitly or implicitly declared. User-defined types are not supported.

Control Structures

FORTRAN provides logical IF statements (with a single-statement THEN branch), three-way branch, counting loops, and GOTOs. Subprogram calls are the only allowed unit-level control structures. Recursive calls are not allowed.

Program Correctness

This was not a goal of the language. FORTRAN provides several harmful features. The GOTO must be used often, because of the lack of suitable control structures. It can easily be misused. Aliasing is possible (via EQUIVALENCE). Subprograms may generate side effects by manipulating actual parameters (transmitted by reference) or global variables (specified by COMMON). The language is defined in informal English prose.

Programming in the Large

FORTRAN supports nest-free program structures. A program is a collection of external subprograms, which may share COMMON data. Subprograms may be compiled independently and assembled to construct a system. Intermodule type checking is usually not provided.

Official Definition

(ANSI 1966), (ANSI 1971), (ANSI 1978).

Important Papers

(Backus 1957) (Backus 1978**b**), (Brainerd 1978).

Textbooks

The essentials of FORTRAN can be found in (Rosen 1967) and (Sammet 1969).

Implementation Issues

(Gries 1971).

Gypsy

Overview

Gypsy is a language designed for supporting specification, coding, and verification of systems software, with particular emphasis on communications software.

Data Types

Gypsy provides built-in types and constructors. The language does not provide explicit pointer variables. Instead, it has some fully dynamic data types, such as sequences and mappings. A Gypsy unit can contain a type definition, and an access list may specify the legal accesses (see below under ''Programming in the Large''). It is thus possible to implement abstract data types.

Control Structures

Gypsy provides Pascal-like control structures. There is no **goto**, but there is a **leave** statement to exit from loops. Unit-level control structures are procedure and function calls, exceptions, and concurrent invocations.

Program Correctness

The language does not provide a **goto** statement. Functions cannot modify actual parameters. There are no global variables or pointers. Most harmful features have thus been excluded. A program verifier is an integral part of the Gypsy system.

Programming in the Large

Program units are routine (procedure, function, or process), type, and constant definition. Units are not nested, and each is provided with an access list that states the access rights to the unit. There are no global variables. Units are verified and compiled separately.

Official Language Definition

(Ambler et al. 1976).

Important Papers

(Ambler et al. 1977), (Good 1977).

Implementation Issues

(Good et al. 1978).

LISP

Overview

LISP (**LIST** **P**rocessing) is a functional language. It is used in most applications of artificial intelligence. There are several dialects that augment LISP with nonfunctional features.

Data Types

LISP has two types of objects: atoms and lists. It provides functions to operate on lists. LISP programs are uniformly mapped into list structures; the evaluation of a LISP program can be described by an interpreter (function EVAL) that transforms into values a list structure representing a program.

Control Structures

Pure LISP provides neither assignment statements nor GOTO statements. It is a purely functional language, heavily based on recursion. Dialects of LISP provide both assignment and GOTO.

Program Correctness

LISP was the first language to be designed upon a firm mathematical basis: (McCarthy 1963**a**), (McCarthy 1963**b**).

Programming in the Large

This is not an issue in pure LISP. Many existing LISP systems support program development with a variety of tools.

Official Definition

(McCarthy et al. 1965). Two LISP dialects are described by (Moon 1974) and (Teitelman 1975).

Important Papers

(McCarthy 1960), (McCarthy 1963**a**), (McCarthy 1963**b**), (McCarthy 1978), (Sandewall 1978).

Textbooks

(Siklóssy 1976), (Allen 1978).

Implementation Issues

(McCarthy et al. 1965), (Henderson 1980).

Mesa

Overview

Mesa is one component of a programming system aimed at developing and maintaining a wide range of system and application programs.

Data Types

Mesa provides conventional built-in types, enumerations, subranges, and constructors (array, record, record with variant, pointer). Mesa is strongly typed, but the programmer may explicitly disable type checking. The language provides several automatic type conversions. Mesa modules (see below under ''Programming in the Large'') support the definition of abstract data types.

Control Structures

Statement-level control structures include **if** statement, **select** statement (much like a Pascal **case**), loop statements, loop exit, and **goto**. Unit-level control structures include subprogram calls, coroutine activations, exception conditions, and concurrent activation (interprocess communication is provided by monitors).

Program Correctness

The language provides safe features but also allows the use of harmful features, such as **goto** and elimination of type checking. The language is defined in informal English prose and does not address verification issues explicitly.

Programming in the Large

Mesa provides the **module** construct to encapsulate abstractions. Each module has a definition, which specifies the module's interface, and a program, which contains actual data and executable code. Definitions have no existence at run-time, but they allow programs to be compiled separately with full type checking. Programs can be loaded and interconnected to form complete systems, via commands written in the Mesa configuration language.

Official Definition

(Mitchell et al. 1979).

Important Papers

(Geschke and Mitchell 1975), (Lampson et al. 1974), (Geschke et al. 1977).

Modula

Overview

Modula is a language for programming dedicated computer systems, including process control on smaller machines. The language provides limited visibility of the underlying hardware. The language is based strongly on Pascal.

Data Types

Modula adopts most data-type concepts of Pascal. The most notable exception is the absence of pointers. Abstract data types can be defined by the **module** construct (see below under ''Programming in the Large'').

Control Structures

Modula adopts the Pascal control structures with minor variations. A loop with exits in the middle also is provided. Modula provides procedures and functions. Concurrently executable units (processes) can be explicitly initiated. Synchronization is achieved by signals. Signals can be sent, and a process may wait for a signal. (Signals are similar to the queues of Concurrent Pascal). Interface modules (corresponding to monitors) are code sections executed in mutual exclusion.

Program Correctness

The language is intended to cover applications for which assembly language traditionally is used. Modula considerably improves the readability of such programs and supports a variety of static checks. No formal language definition is presently available. (Wirth 1977) discusses the use of Modula in proving correctness of real-time programs.

Programming in the Large

Modula retains Pascal-like block structure. In addition, it provides the construct **module**. A module is a collection of declarations and an initialization part, much like an Ada **package**. A module can explicitly import entities from, and export entities to, the rest of the program.

Official Definition

(Wirth 1976**b**); revised in (Wirth 1978).

Important Papers

(Wirth 1976**c**), (Wirth 1977), (Wirth 1979).

Implementation Issues

(Wirth 1976**d**).

Pascal

Overview

Pascal was originally designed for teaching disciplined programming. The language has met with an enormous success, and there are now implementations on most machines, including microprocessors. Pascal has influenced nearly all recent languages.

Data Types

Pascal provides built-in types, enumeration types, subranges, and constructors (record, record with variants, array, file, pointer, and set) to construct new types. Type compatibility is not defined rigorously. Pascal does not provide abstract data types.

Control Structures

Pascal provides **if-then-else**, **case**, **while-do**, **repeat-until**, **for** loops, and **goto**. Procedure and function calls are the only unit-level control structures.

Program Correctness

Pascal permits side effects and provides the **goto** statement. The semantics of the language has been defined axiomatically (Hoare and Wirth 1973), but axioms for full Pascal have not been developed.

Programming in the Large

Pascal provides only procedures and functions as abstraction capabilities. Programs are tree-structured and inner modules automatically inherit outer declarations. The official language definition does not specify a standard separate compilation facility.

Official Definition

(Jensen and Wirth 1975).

Important Papers

(Wirth 1971**a**), (Hoare and Wirth 1973), (Wirth 1975**b**), (Habermann 1973), (Lecarme and Desjardins 1975), (Welsh et al. 1977), (Tennent 1978), (Tanenbaum 1978).

Textbooks

(Wirth 1973), (Wirth 1976**a**), (Findlay and Watt 1978), (Alagić and Arbib 1978).

Implementation Issues

(Wirth 1971**c**), (Ammann 1974), (Nori et al. 1976).

PL/I

Overview

PL/I (**P**rogramming **L**anguage **I**) represents an attempt to incorporate into a unique multipurpose language the most notable features of earliest languages (FORTRAN, ALGOL 60, and COBOL).

Data Types

PL/I provides built-in types for which a variety of attributes may be specified (e.g., base, precision). Aggregate constructors include structures (record), arrays, and pointers. Data may be allocated statically (à la FORTRAN), automatically (à la ALGOL 60), or explicitly.

Control Structures

PL/I provides IF—THEN—ELSE, WHILE—DO, counting loop, and GOTO. Unit-level control structures include subprogram call, exception handling, and multitasking (for concurrent units).

Program Correctness

This is not an express goal of PL/I. The language provides several harmful features. The GOTO is permitted; pointers are not typed and may be left dangling; subprogram calls may generate side effects; aliasing is permitted. Educational subsets of the language supporting good programming practices have also been defined: PL/C in (Conway and Gries 1979); PLCS in (Conway 1978); and SP/k in (Conway et al. 1977). The language has been defined formally by researchers at the IBM Vienna Laboratory. The method is known as Vienna Definition Language: (Lucas and Walk 1969), (Wegner 1972). PL/C has also been formally defined; a program verifier is described in (Constable and O'Donnell 1978).

Programming in the Large

A program may be structured à la FORTRAN as a set of external subprograms. Each subprogram may be structured à la ALGOL 60 as a set of nested units.

Official Definition

(ANSI 1976).

Important Papers

(Lucas and Walk 1969), (Radin 1978).

Textbooks

(Conway and Gries 1979). The essentials can be found in (Sammet 1969).

Implementation Issues

(Abrahams 1979).

PLZ

Overview

PLZ was designed by Zilog Corporation to facilitate the construction of microcomputer system programs. The language design has been strongly influenced by Pascal. The portions of a program that are time-critical or need explicit access to machine devices may be written in "low-level PLZ" (called PLZ/ASM).

Data Types

PLZ provides built-in types (byte, word, short-integer and integer), and constructors (record, array, and pointer). Type compatibility is defined precisely. Explicit type conversions are provided to allow a controlled breach of type checking.

Control Structures

Statement-level control structures include **if__then__else**, **case**, and **loop** statements. Loops can be terminated by explicit **exit**; it is also possible to terminate the currently active iteration (**repeat** statement).

Program Correctness

The language improves reliability of programs intended for applications that are traditional strongholds of assembly coding. Low-level harmful features (e.g., **goto**) are not provided. Semantics is defined informally. Program verification is not explicitly addressed.

Programming in the Large

A PLZ program is a set of modules; a module is the basic compilation unit. A module consists of data and procedure declarations. Procedures and data made available for use in other modules must be specified explicitly. Modules support program design by information hiding.

Official Definition

(Snook et al. 1978).

Important Papers

(Crespi-Reghizzi et al.) which surveys several other high-level languages for microprocessors.

Textbooks

(Conway et al. 1980).

Implementation Issues

(Snook et al. 1978).

SIMULA 67

Overview

SIMULA 67 is a general-purpose language whose main application area has been simulation.

Data Types

Besides built-in types and arrays, SIMULA 67 provides classes for defining abstract data types. Class instances may exist simultaneously at run-time. They can be assigned by reference (:-), and the dot notation provides access to individual components. Representation details are not hidden by the class.

Control Structures

Besides conventional ALGOL-like statement-level control structures and procedure calls, SIMULA 67 provides coroutines to simulate concurrent execution.

Program Correctness

SIMULA 67 provides the **goto** statement and side effects that hamper program readability. The semantics is described in informal English. Program verification was not an issue in the design of SIMULA 67.

Programming in the Large

Procedural abstractions are supported by SIMULA 67. Data abstraction can be implemented (with self-discipline) by classes. Class prefixing allows the definition of hierarchical program structures. Overall, SIMULA 67 preserves the ALGOL-like tree structure of programs. The language does not define an official, separate compilation scheme.

Official Definition

(Dahl et al. 1970).

Important Papers

(Ichbiah and Morse 1972), (Dahl and Hoare 1972), (Nygaard and Dahl 1978).

Textbooks

(Birtwistle et al. 1973).

Implementation Issues

(Dahl and Myhrhaug 1969).

SNOBOL4

Overview

SNOBOL4 (**Str**ing **O**riented Sym**bo**lic **L**anguage) is a string manipulation language. Its major application lies in areas in which character string data must be processed in complex ways—for example, in processing natural language texts.

Data Types

SNOBOL4 is a dynamically typed language. It provides powerful pattern-matching operations on strings. It also supports the definition of new data types. Through its TABLE data type, it provides for a form of associative retrieval. Strings generated at run-time may be treated as programs and executed.

Control Structures

Statement-level control structures are rather simple. The most complex control structures arise in the control of pattern matching. Subprograms may be called recursively. The language supports the handling of exceptional conditions. Exception handling is basically used for tracing during program debugging.

Program Correctness

This was not a goal of the language. Dynamic binding hampers program readability if programs are large. The trace facility helps in program testing. A formal definition of much of the semantics of SNOBOL4 is described in (Tennent 1973).

Programming in the Large

SNOBOL4 programs can be decomposed into subprograms. Subprogram definition, however, is strictly a run-time operation. This is another example of the highly dynamic bindings established by the language. Dynamic binding makes it difficult to produce large programs.

Official Definition

(Griswold et al. 1971).

Important Papers

(Griswold 1978), (Tennent 1973).

Textbooks

(Griswold et al. 1971), (Griswold and Griswold 1973).

Implementation Issues

(Griswold 1972) describes a portable implementation of SNOBOL4.

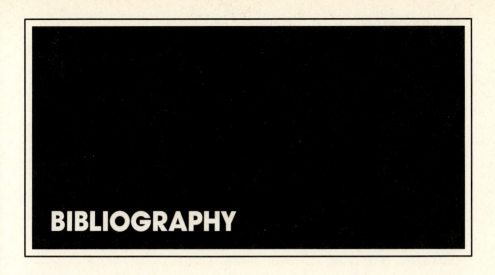

BIBLIOGRAPHY

(Abrahams 1979)
P. Abrahams, "The CIMS PL/I Compiler." **Proceedings SIGPLAN Symp. on Compiler Construction—SIGPLAN Notices 14** 8 (Aug. 1979).

(ACM-CS 1974)
ACM Computing Surveys, special issue: **Programming 6** 4 (Dec. 1974).

(ACM-SIGPLAN 1976)
Proceedings of Conference on Data: Abstraction, Definition and Structure. **SIGPLAN Notices 8** 2 (1976).

(ACM-SIGPLAN 1977)
Proceedings ACM Conference on Language Design for Reliable Software. SIG-PLAN Notices 12 3 (March 1977).

(ACM-SIGPLAN 1978)
ACM-SIGPLAN History of Programming Languages Conference. SIGPLAN Notices 13 8 (Aug. 1978).

(ACM-SIGPLAN 1979)
J. D. Ichbiah, J. C. Heliard, O. Roubine, J. G. P. Barnes, B. Krieg-Bruckner, and B. A. Wichmann. "Preliminary Ada Reference Manual" and "Rationale for the Design of the Ada Programming Language." **SIGPLAN Notices 14** 6, Parts A and B (June 1979).

(ACM-SIGPLAN 1980)
Proceedings ACM-SIGPLAN Symposium on the Ada Programming Language. **SIGPLAN Notices 15** 11 (Nov. 1980).

(Aho and Ullman 1977)
A. V. Aho and J. D. Ullman. **Principles of Compiler Design**. Reading, Mass.: Addison-Wesley, 1977.

(Alagić and Arbib 1978)
S. Alagić and M. A. Arbib. **The Design of Well-Structured and Correct Programs**. New York: Springer Verlag, 1978.

(Alford 1977)
M. W. Alford. "A Requirements Engineering Methodology for Real-Time Processing Requirements." **IEEE Transactions on Software Engineering SE-3** 1 (Jan. 1977): 60–68.

(Allen 1978)
J. Allen. **Anatomy of LISP**. New York: McGraw-Hill, 1978.

(Ambler et al. 1976)
A. Ambler, D. I. Good, and W. F. Burger. "Report on the Language Gypsy." Univ. of Texas at Austin, ICSCA-CMP-1 (Aug. 1976).

(Ambler et al. 1977)
A. L. Ambler, D. I. Good, J. C. Browne, W. F. Burger, R. M. Cohen, C. G. Hoch, and R. E. Wells. "Gypsy: A Language for Specification and Implementation of Verifiable Programs." **Proceedings ACM Conference on Language Design for Reliable Software—SIGPLAN Notices 12** 3 (March 1977): 1–10.

(Ammann 1974)
U. Ammann. "The Method of Structured Programming Applied to the Development of a Compiler." In **Proceedings ACM Int. Comp. Symp.**, eds. A. Gunther et al. Amsterdam: North-Holland, 1974.

(ANSI 1966)
American National Standard FORTRAN (ANS X3.9-1966). New York: American National Standards Institute, 1966.

(ANSI 1968)
USA Standard COBOL (ANS X3.23-1968). New York: American National Standards Institute, 1968.

(ANSI 1971)
"Clarification of FORTRAN Standard—Second Report." **Comm. ACM 14** 10, (Oct. 1971): 628–642.

(ANSI 1974)
American National Standard Programming Language COBOL (ANSI X3.23-1974). New York: American National Standard Institute, 1974.

(ANSI 1976)
American National Standard Programming Language PL/I (ANS X3.53-1976). New York: American National Standards Institute, 1976.

(ANSI 1978)
   American National Standard Programming Language FORTRAN (ANS X3.9-1978). New York: American National Standards Institute, 1978.

(Aron 1974)
   J. D. Aron. **The Program Development Process, Part I: The Individual Programmer**. Reading, Mass.: Addison-Wesley, 1974.

(Ashcroft and Wadge 1977)
   E. A. Ashcroft and W. W. Wadge. "LUCID: A Nonprocedural Language with Iteration." **Comm. ACM 20** 7 (July 1977): 519–526.

(Asirelli et al. 1979)
   P. Asirelli, P. Degano, G. Levi, A. Martelli, U. Montanari, G. Pacini, F. Sirovich, and F. Turini. "A Flexible Environment for Program Development Based on a Symbolic Interpreter." **Proceedings 4th Int. Conference on Software Engineering**. IEEE Cat. No. 79CH1479-5C (Munich, Sept. 1979): 251–263.

(Atkinson et al. 1978)
   R. R. Atkinson, B. H. Liskov, and R. W. Scheifler. "Aspects of Implementing CLU." **Proceedings ACM National Conference** 1 (Dec. 1978): 123–129.

(Backus 1957)
   See (Rosen 1967).

(Backus 1973)
   J. Backus. "Programming Language Semantics and Closed Applicative Languages." **Conf. Record ACM Symp. on Principles of Programming Languages** (Boston, Oct. 1973): 71–86.

(Backus 1978**a**)
   J. Backus. "Can Programming Be Liberated from the von Neumann Style? A Functional Style and Its Algebra of Programs." **Comm. ACM 21** 8 (Aug. 1978): 613–641.

(Backus 1978**b**)
   See (ACM-SIGPLAN 1978).

(Baker 1972)
   F. T. Baker. "Chief Programmer Team Management of Production Programming." **IBM System Journal** Jan. 1972: pp. 56–73.

(Barrett and Couch 1979)
   W. A. Barrett and J. D. Couch. **Compiler Construction: Theory and Practice**. Chicago: SRA, 1979.

(Bauer and Eickel 1976)
F. L. Bauer and J. Eickel, eds. **Compiler Construction: An Advanced Course**, 2nd edition. New York: Springer Verlag, 1976.

(Berkling 1976)
K. J. Berkling. "Reduction Languages for Reduction Machines." ISF-76-8 GMB (Bonn, Sept. 1976).

(Berry 1979)
See (Wegner 1979).

(Birtwistle et al. 1973)
G. M. Birtwistle, O-J. Dahl, B. Myhrhaug, and K. Nygaard. **SIMULA Begin**. New York: Petrocelli/Charter, 1973.

(Birtwistle et al. 1976)
G. Birtwistle, L. Enderin, M. Ohlin, and J. Palme. "DEC System-10 SIMULA Language Handbook—Part 1." In **Report N. C8398**. Stockholm: Swedish National Defense Research Institute, March 1976.

(Bjørner and Jones 1978)
D. Bjørner and C. B. Jones, eds. **The Vienna Development Method: The Meta Language**. Lecture Notes in Computer Science 61. New York: Springer Verlag, 1978.

(Bobrow and Raphael 1974)
D. G. Bobrow and B. Raphael. "New Programming Languages for Artificial Intelligence." **ACM Computing Surveys 6**. (1972): 155–174.

(Boehm 1976)
B. Boehm. "Seven Basic Principles of Software Engineering." In **Infotech State of the Art Report on Software Engineering Techniques**. Maidenhead, U.K.: Infotech International Ltd., 1976.

(Böhm and Jacopini 1966)
C. Böhm and G. Jacopini. "Flow-diagrams, Turing Machines, and Languages with Only Two Formation Rules." **Comm. ACM 9** 5 (May 1966): 366–371.

(Brainerd 1978)
W. Brainerd, ed. "FORTRAN 77." **Comm. ACM 21** 10 (Oct. 1978): 806–820.

(Branquart et al. 1971)
P. Branquart, J. Lewi, M. Sintzoff, and P. Wodon. "The Composition of Semantics in ALGOL 68." **Comm. ACM 14** 11 (Nov. 1971): 697–708.

(Branquart et al. 1976)
P. Branquart, J.-P. Cardinael, J. Lewi, J.-P. Delescaille, and M. Vanbegin. **An Optimized Translation Process and Its Application to ALGOL 68**. Lecture Notes in Computer Science 38. New York: Springer Verlag, 1976.

(Breed and Lathwell 1968)
L. M. Breed and R. H. Lathwell. "The Implementation of APL/360." In **Symposium on Interactive Systems for Experimental and Applied Mathematics**, eds. Klerer and Reinfelds. New York: Academic Press, 1968.

(Brinch Hansen 1973)
P. Brinch Hansen. **Operating Systems Principles**. Englewood Cliffs, N.J.: Prentice-Hall, 1973.

(Brinch Hansen 1975)
P. Brinch Hansen. "The Programming Language Concurrent Pascal." **IEEE Transactions on Software Engineering SE-1** 2 (June 1975): 199–207.

(Brinch Hansen 1977)
P. Brinch Hansen. **The Architecture of Concurrent Programs**. Englewood Cliffs, N.J.: Prentice-Hall, 1977.

(Brinch Hansen 1979)
P. Brinch Hansen. "Distributed Processes: A Concurrent Programming Concept." **Comm. ACM 21** 11 (Nov. 1979): 934–941.

(Brinch Hansen 1980**a**)
P. Brinch Hansen. **Edison—A Multiprocessor Language**. Los Angeles, Cal.: Dept. of Computer Science, Univ. of Southern California, September 1980.

(Brinch Hansen 1980**b**)
P. Brinch Hansen. **The Design of Edison**. Los Angeles, Cal.: Dept. of Computer Science, Univ. of Southern California, September 1980.

(Brinch Hansen 1980**c**)
P. Brinch Hansen. **Edison Programs**. Los Angeles, Cal.: Dept. of Computer Science, Univ. of Southern California, September 1980.

(Brooks 1975)
F. P. Brooks, Jr. **The Mythical Man-Month—Essays on Software Engineering**. Reading, Mass.: Addison-Wesley, 1975.

(Burge 1975)
W. H. Burge. **Recursive Programming Techniques**. Reading, Mass.: Addison-Wesley, 1975.

(Buxton 1980)
J. N. Buxton. "An Informal Bibliography on Programming Support Environments." **ACM SIGPLAN Notices 15** 12 (Dec. 1980): 17–30.

(Cashin et al. 1981)
P. M. Cashin, M. L. Joliat, R. F. Kamel, and D. M. Lasker. "Experience with a Modular Typed Language: PROTEL." **Proceedings 5th International Conf. Software Engineering** (March 1981): 136–143.

(Celentano et al. 1980)
A. Celentano, P. Della Vigna, C. Ghezzi, and D. Mandrioli. "Separate Compilation and Partial Specification in Pascal." **IEEE Transactions on Software Engineering SE-6** 4 (July 1980): 313–319.

(Cheatham 1977)
T. E. Cheatham, Jr. "Some New Directions in Program Development Tools." **AICA Proceedings** (Italian Computer Society) 3 (Pisa, Oct. 1977): 3–29.

(Cheatham et al. 1979)
T. E. Cheatham, Jr.; J. A. Townley; and G. H. Holloway. "A System for Program Refinement." **Proceedings 4th Int. Conf. on Software Engineering**. IEEE cat. no. 79CH1479-5C (Munich, Sept. 1979): 53–62.

(Clarke et al. 1980)
L. A. Clarke, J. C. Wileden, and L. Wolf. "Nesting in Ada Is for the Birds." **Proceedings Symposium on the Ada Programming Language—SIGPLAN Notices 15** 11 (Nov. 1980).

(Constable and O'Donnell)
R. L. Constable and M. J. O'Donnell. **A Programming Logic with an Introduction to the PL/CV Verifier**. Cambridge, Mass.: Winthrop, 1978.

(Conway 1963)
M. E. Conway. "Design of Separable Transition-Diagram Compiler." **Comm. ACM 6** 7 (July 1963): 396–408.

(Conway 1978)
R. Conway. **A Primer on Disciplined Programming**. Cambridge, Mass.: Winthrop, 1978.

(Conway and Gries 1979)
R. Conway and D. Gries. **An Introduction to Programming—A Structured Approach Using PL/I and PL/C.** 3rd edition. Cambridge, Mass.: Winthrop, 1979.

(Conway et al. 1977)
R. Conway, D. Gries, and D. B. Wortman. **Introduction to Structured Programming Using PL/I and SP/k**. Cambridge, Mass.: Winthrop, 1977.

(Conway et al. 1979)
R. Conway, D. Gries, M. Fay, and C. Bass. **Introduction to Microprocessor Programming Using PLZ**. Cambridge, Mass.: Winthrop, 1979.

(Crespi-Reghizzi et al. 1980)
S. Crespi-Reghizzi, P. Corti, and A. Daprá. "A Survey of Microprocessor Languages." **Computer 13** 1 (Jan. 1980): 48–66.

(Dahl and Hoare 1972)
See (Dahl et al. 1972).

(Dahl and Myhrhaug 1969)
O.-J. Dahl and B. Myhrhaug. "SIMULA 67 Implementation Guide." **Publication N. S-9**. Oslo: Norwegian Computing Center, June 1969.

(Dahl et al. 1970)
O.-J. Dahl, B. Myhrhaug, and K. Nygaard. "SIMULA 67 Common Base Language." **Publication N. S-22**. Oslo: Norwegian Computing Center, Oct. 1970.

(Dahl et al. 1972)
O.-J. Dahl, E. W. Dijkstra, and C. A. R. Hoare. **Structured Programming**. New York: Academic Press, 1972.

(Darlington and Burstall 1976)
J. Darlington and R. M. Burstall. "A System Which Automatically Improves Programs." **Acta Informatica 6** 1 (1976): 41–60.

(Demers and Donahue 1980a)
A. Demers and J. Donahue. "Data Types, Parameters and Type Checking." **Conference Record of the 7th Annual ACM Symp. on Principles of Programming Languages** (Jan. 1980): 12–23.

(Demers and Donahue 1980b)
A. Demers and J. Donahue. "Type Completeness as a Language Principle." **Conference Record of the 7th Annual ACM Symp. on Principles of Programming Languages**. (Jan. 1980): 234–244.

(DeMillo et al. 1979)
R. A. DeMillo, R. J. Lipton, and A. J. Perlis. "Social Processes and Proofs of Theorems and Programs." **Comm. ACM 22** 5 (May 1979): 271–280.

(DeRemer and Kron 1976)
    F. DeRemer and H. Kron. "Programming-in-the-Large Versus Programming-in-the-Small." **IEEE Transactions on Software Engineering SE-2** (June 1976): 80–86.

(Deutsch and Bobrow 1976)
    L. P. Deutsch and D. G. Bobrow. "An Efficient Incremental Automatic Garbage Collector." **Comm. ACM 19** 9 (Sept. 1976): 522–526.

(Dijkstra 1962)
    E. W. Dijkstra. **A Primer of ALGOL 60 Programming**. New York: Academic Press, 1962.

(Dijkstra 1968**a**)
    E. W. Dijkstra. "Goto Statement Considered Harmful." **Comm. ACM 11** 3 (March 1968): 147–149.

(Dijkstra 1968**b**)
    E. W. Dijkstra. "Cooperating Sequential Processes." In **Programming Languages**, ed. F. Genuys. New York: Academic Press, 1968.

(Dijkstra 1968**c**)
    E. W. Dijkstra. "The Structure of The Multiprogramming System." **Comm. ACM 11** 5 (May 1968): 341–346.

(Dijkstra 1972)
    See (Dahl et al. 1972).

(Dijkstra 1976)
    E. W. Dijkstra. **A Discipline of Programming**. Englewood Cliffs, N.J.: Prentice-Hall, 1976.

(Dijkstra et al. 1978)
    E. W. Dijkstra, L. Lamport, A. J. Martin, C. S. Scholten, and E. F. M. Steffens. "On-the-Fly Garbage Collection: An Exercise in Cooperation." **Comm. ACM 21** 11 (Nov. 1978): 966–975.

(DOD 1977)
    United States Department of Defense. **Requirements for High Order Computer Programming Languages, Revised "Ironman." SIGPLAN Notices 12** 12 (Dec. 1977): 39–54.

(DOD 1978)
    United States Department of Defense. **Requirements for High Order Computer Programming Languages, "Steelman."** June 1978.

(DOD 1980**a**)
United States Department of Defense. **"Stoneman": Requirements for Ada Programming Support Environment**. Feb. 1980.

(DOD 1980**b**)
United States Department of Defense. **Reference Manual for the Ada Programming Language**. Proposed standard document. July 1980.

(Elliott and Barnard 1978)
W. D. Elliott and D. T. Barnard, eds. "Notes on Euclid." **SIGPLAN Notices 13** 3 (March 1978): 34–89.

(Elson 1973)
M. Elson. **Concepts of Programming Languages**. Chicago: SRA, 1973.

(Falkoff and Iverson 1978)
See (ACM-SIGPLAN 1978).

(Findlay and Watt 1978)
W. Findlay and D. A. Watt. **Pascal: An Introduction to Methodical Programming**. Potomac, Md.: Computer Science Press, 1978.

(Fischer and LeBlanc 1980)
C. N. Fischer and R. J. LeBlanc. "The Implementation of Run-Time Diagnostics in Pascal." **IEEE Transactions on Software Engineering SE-6** 4 (July 1980): 313–319.

(Floyd 1967)
R. W. Floyd. "Assigning Meanings to Programs." Proc. Symp. Appl. Math. In **Mathematical Aspects of Computer Science**, ed. J. T. Schwartz. Providence, R.I.: American Mathematical Society, 1967.

(Fosdick and Osterweil 1976)
L. D. Fosdick and L. J. Osterweil. "Data Flow Analysis in Software Reliability." **Computing Surveys 8** 3 (Oct. 1976): 305–330.

(Foxall et al. 1979)
D. G. Foxall, M. L. Filiat, R. F. Kamel, and J. J. Miceli. "PROTEL: A High Level Language for Telephony." **Proc. 3rd International Computer Software and Applications Conf.** (Nov. 1979): 193–197.

(Francez 1977)
N. Francez. "Another Advantage of Keyword Notation for Parameter Communication with Subprograms." **Comm. ACM 20** 8 (Aug. 1977): 604–605.

(Gannon 1977)
J. D. Gannon. "An Experimental Evaluation of Data Type Conventions." **Comm. ACM 8** 20 (Aug. 1977): 584–595.

(Gannon and Horning 1975)
J. D. Gannon and J. J. Horning. "Language Design for Programming Reliability." **IEEE Transactions on Software Engineering SE-1** 2 (1975): 179–191.

(Geschke and Mitchell 1975)
C. Geschke and J. Mitchell. "On the Problem of Uniform References to Data Structures." **IEEE Transactions on Software Engineering SE-1** 2 (June 1975): 207–219.

(Geschke et al. 1977)
C. M. Geschke; J. H. Morris, Jr.; E. H. Satterthwaite. "Early Experience with Mesa." **Comm. ACM 20** 8 (Aug. 1977): 540–553.

(Goguen et al. 1978)
See (Yeh 1978).

(Good 1977)
D. I. Good, ed. **Constructing Verifiably Reliable and Secure Communications Processing Systems.** Univ. of Texas at Austin, ICSCA-CMP-6 (Jan. 1977).

(Good et al. 1978)
D. I. Good, R. M. Cohen, and L. W. Hunter. "A Report on the Development of Gypsy." **Proceedings ACM National Conference** 1 (Dec. 1978): 116–122.

(Goodenough 1975)
J. B. Goodenough. "Exception Handling: Issues and a Proposed Notation." **Comm. ACM 16** 12 (Dec. 1975): 683–696.

(Goodenough)
See (Wegner 1979).

(Gordon 1979)
R. Gordon. **The Denotational Description of Programming Languages,** New York: Springer Verlag, 1979.

(Gries 1971)
D. Gries. **Compiler Construction for Digital Computers.** New York: J. Wiley, 1971.

(Gries and Gehani 1977)
D. Gries and N. Gehani. "Some Ideas on Data Types in High-Level Languages." **Comm. ACM 20** 6 (June 1977): 414–420.

(Griswold 1972)
R. E. Griswold. **The Macro Implementation of SNOBOL4**. San Francisco: W. H. Freeman, 1972.

(Griswold 1978)
See (ACM-SIGPLAN 1978).

(Griswold and Griswold 1973)
R. E. Griswold and M. T. Griswold. **A SNOBOL4 Primer**. Englewood Cliffs, N.J.: Prentice-Hall, 1973.

(Griswold et al. 1971)
R. E. Griswold, J. F. Poage, and I. P. Polonsky. **The SNOBOL4 Programming Language,** (2nd edition). Englewood Cliffs, N.J.: Prentice-Hall, 1971.

(Guarino 1978)
L. R. Guarino. "The Evolution of Abstraction in Programming Languages." Carnegie-Mellon Univ. Dept. of Computer Science **Report CMU-CS-78-120** (May 1978).

(Guttag 1977)
J. V. Guttag. "Abstract Data Types and the Development of Data Structures." **Comm. ACM 20** 6 (June 1977): 396–404.

(Guttag et al. 1978)
See (Yeh 1978).

(Habermann 1973)
A. N. Habermann. "Critical Comments on the Programming Language Pascal." **Acta Informatica 3** (1973): 47–57.

(Habermann 1975)
A. N. Habermann. **Introduction to Operating System Design.** Chicago: SRA, 1976.

(Habermann 1979)
A. N. Habermann. "An Overview of the Gandalf Project." **Carnegie Mellon University—Computer Science Research Review 1978–79.** 1979.

(Hartmann 1977)
A. C. Hartmann. **A Concurrent Pascal Compiler for Minicomputers.** Lecture Notes in Computer Science 50, New York: Springer Verlag, 1977.

(Hecht 1977)
M. S. Hecht. **Flow Analysis of Computer Programs.** New York: Elsevier North-Holland, 1977.

(Henderson 1980)

P. Henderson. **Functional Programming: Application and Implementation.** Englewood Cliffs, N.J.: Prentice-Hall, 1980.

(Hill 1976)

See (Bauer and Eickel 1976).

(Hoare 1969)

C. A. R. Hoare. ''An Axiomatic Basis of Computer Programming.'' **Comm. ACM 12** 10 (Oct. 1969): 576–580.

(Hoare 1972**a**)

See (Dahl et al. 1972).

(Hoare 1972**b**)

C. A. R. Hoare. ''Proof of Correctness of Data Representations.'' **Acta Informatica 1** (1972): 271–281.

(Hoare 1973)

C. A. R. Hoare. ''Hints on Programming Language Design.'' Keynote address given at the ACM SIGACT/SIGPLAN Conference on Principles of Programming Language. Boston: Oct. 1973. See also Stanford Univ. Computer Science Dept. Tech. of Rep. **STAN-CS-74-403.**

(Hoare 1974)

C. A. R. Hoare. ''Monitors: An Operating System Structuring Concept.'' **Comm. ACM 17** 10 (Oct. 1974): 549–557.

Hoare 1975**a**)

C. A. R. Hoare. ''Data Reliability.'' **Proceedings Intl. Conf. on Reliable Software—SIGPLAN Notices 10** 6 (June 1975): 528–533.

(Hoare 1975**b**)

C. A. R. Hoare. ''Recursive Data Structures.'' **Int. Journal of Comp. and Inf. Sciences 4** 2 (1975): 105–132.

(Hoare 1978)

C. A. R. Hoare. ''Communicating Sequential Processes.'' **Comm. ACM 21** 8 (Aug. 1978): 666–677.

(Hoare and Wirth 1973)

C. A. R. Hoare and N. Wirth. ''An Axiomatic Definition of the Programming Language Pascal.'' **Acta Informatica 2** (1973): 335–355.

(Holt et al. 1978**a**)

R. C. Holt, G. S. Graham, E. D. Lazowska, and M. A. Scott. **Structured Con-**

current Programming with Operating System Applications. Reading, Mass.: Addison-Wesley, 1978.

(Holt et al. 1978**b**)
R. C. Holt, D. B. Wortman, J. R. Cordy, D. R. Crowe. "The Euclid Language: A Progress Report." **Proceedings of the ACM National Conference** 1 (Dec. 1978): 111–115.

(Horowitz 1975)
E. Horowitz, ed. **Practical Strategies for Developing Large Software Systems.** Reading, Mass.: Addison-Wesley, 1975.

(Howard 1976**a**)
J. H. Howard. "Proving Monitors." **Comm. ACM 19** 5 (May 1976): 273–79.

(Howard 1976**b**)
J. H. Howard "Signaling in Monitors." **Proceedings of the 2nd Intl. Conference on Software Engineering.** IEEE cat. no. 76CH1125-4C (San Francisco, Oct. 1976): 47–52.

(Ichbiah and Morse 1972)
J. D. Ichbiah and S. P. Morse. "General Concepts of the SIMULA 67 Programming Language." **Annual Review of Automatic Programming** I (1972): 65–95.

(Ichbiah et al. 1979)
See (ACM-SIGPLAN 1979).

(Ingalls 1978)
D. H. Ingalls. "The Smalltalk-76 Programming System Design and Implementation." **Conference Record of the 5th Annual ACM Symp. on Principles of Programming Languages** (Jan. 1978): 9–16.

(Iverson 1962)
K. E. Iverson **A Programming Language**. New York: J. Wiley, 1962.

(Iverson 1979)
K. E. Iverson. "Operators." **ACM Transactions on Programming Languages and Systems 1** 2 (Oct. 1979): 161–176.

(Iverson 1980)
K. E. Iverson. "Notation as a Tool of Thought." **Comm. ACM 23** 8 (Aug. 1980): 444–465.

(Jackson 1975)
M. A. Jackson. **Principles of Program Design.** New York: Academic Press, 1975.

(Jensen and Wirth 1975)
  K. Jensen and N. Wirth. **Pascal User Manual and Report.** New York: Springer Verlag, 1975.

(Johnson 1978)
  S. C. Johnson. ''A Portable Compiler: Theory and Practice.'' **Conf. Record of 5th Annual ACM Symp. on Principles of Programming Languages** (Jan. 1978): 97–104.

(Johnston 1971)
  J. Johnston. ''The Contour Model of Block-Structured Processes.'' **Proceedings Symp. Data Structures in Programming Languages—SIGPLAN Notices 6** 2 (Feb. 1971): 55–82.

(Kahn et al. 1980)
  G. Kahn, V. Donzeau-Gouge, B. Lang. ''Formal Definition of the Ada Programming Language.'' Honeywell-Bull INRIA Report. (Nov. 1980).

(Kennedy and Schwartz 1975)
  K. Kennedy and J. Schwartz. ''An Introduction to the Set Theoretical Language SETL.'' **Journal Computer and Math. with Applications** 1 (1975): 97–119.

(Kernighan and Mashey 1979)
  B. W. Kernighan and J. R. Mashey. ''The UNIX Programming Environment.'' **Software—Practice and Experience 9** 1 (1979): 1–16.

(Kernighan and Plauger 1976)
  B. W. Kernighan and P. J. Plauger. **Software Tools.** Reading, Mass.: Addison-Wesley, 1976.

(Kernighan and Ritchie 1978)
  B. W. Kernighan and D. M. Ritchie. **The C Programming Language.** Englewood Cliffs, N.J.: Prentice-Hall, 1978.

(Kieburtz 1976)
  See (ACM-SIGPLAN 1976).

(Kieburtz et al. 1978)
  R. B. Kieburtz, W. Barabash, and S. R. Hill. ''A Type-Checking Program Linkage System for Pascal.'' **Proceedings 3rd Int. Conf. on Software Eng.** Atlanta, Ga.: May 10–12, 1978.

(King 1976)
  J. C. King. ''Symbolic Execution and Program Testing.'' **Comm. ACM 19** 7 (July 1976): 385–394.

(Knuth 1967)
D. E. Knuth. ''The Remaining Trouble Spots in ALGOL 60.'' **Comm. ACM 10** 10 (Oct. 1967): 611–617.

(Knuth 1973)
D. E. Knuth. **The Art of Computer Programming.** Vol. 1: **Fundamental Algorithms,** 2nd ed. Reading, Mass.: Addison-Wesley, 1973.

(Knuth 1974)
D. E. Knuth ''Structured Programming with GOTO Statements.'' **ACM Computing Surveys 6** 4 (Dec. 1974): 261–301.

(Lampson et al. 1974)
B. Lampson, J. Mitchell, and E. Satterthwaite. ''On the Transfer of Control between Contexts.'' **Lecture Notes in Computer Science 19:** 181–203. New York: Springer Verlag, 1974.

(Lampson et al. 1977)
B. W. Lampson, J. J. Horning, R. L. London, J. G. Mitchell, and G. J. Popek. ''Report on the Programming Language Euclid.'' **SIGPLAN Notices 12** 2 (Feb. 1977). (Revised Report, XEROX PARC Tech. Rep. CSL78-2.)

(Landin 1966)
P. J. Landin. ''The Next 700 Programming Languages.'' **Comm. ACM 9** 3 (March 1966): 157–164.

(Lasker 1979)
D. M. Lasker. ''Module Structure in an Evolving Family of Real Time Systems.'' **Proc. 4th Intl. Conf. Software Engineering** IEEE cat. no. 79 CH1479-SC (Munich 1979) (Sept. 1979): 22–28.

(Lauer and Satterthwaite 1979)
H. C. Lauer and E. H. Satterthwaite. ''The Impact of Mesa on System Design.'' **Proc. 4th Intl. Conf. Software Engineering.** IEEE cat. no. 79CH1479-5C (Munich 1979): 174–182.

(LeBlanc and Fischer 1979)
R. J. LeBlanc and C. N. Fisher. ''On Implementing Separate Compilation in Block-Structured Languages.'' **Proceedings SIGPLAN Symp. on Compiler Construction—SIGPLAN Notices 14** 8 (Aug. 1979): 133–143.

(Lecarme and Desjardins 1975)
O. Lecarme and P. Desjardins. ''More Comments on the Programming Language Pascal.'' **Acta Informatica 4** (1975): 231–243.

(Ledgard 1981)

H. Ledgard. **Ada: An Introduction** (Part 1) **Ada Reference Manual—July 1980** (part 2), New York, N.Y.: Springer Verlag, 1981.

(Levin 1977)

R. Levin. **Program Structures for Exceptional Condition Handling.** Ph.D. dissertation. Carnegie-Mellon Univ. Dept. of Computer Science, June 1977.

(Lindsey 1972)

C. H. Lindsey, ''ALGOL 68 with Fewer Tears.'' **Computer Journal 15** (1972): 176–188.

(Lindsey and van der Meulen 1977)

C. H. Lindsey and S. G. van der Meulen. **Informal Introduction to ALGOL 68,** rev. ed. Amsterdam: North-Holland, 1977.

(Liskov 1974)

B. H. Liskov. ''A Note on CLU.'' **Computation Structures Group Memo 112.** Cambridge, Mass.: MIT Project MAC, Nov. 1974.

(Liskov and Snyder 1979)

B. H. Liskov and A. Snyder. ''Exception Handling in CLU.'' **IEEE Trans. on Software Engineering 5** 6 (Nov. 1979): 547–558.

(Liskov and Zilles 1974)

B. H. Liskov and S. N. Zilles. ''Programming with Abstract Data Types.'' **SIGPLAN Symp. on Very High Level Languages—SIGPLAN Notices 9** 4 (Apr. 1974): 50–59.

(Liskov and Zilles 1975)

B. H. Liskov and S. N. Zilles. ''Specification Techniques for Data Abstractions.'' **IEEE Trans. on Software Engineering SE-1** 1 (1975): 7–19.

(Liskov et al. 1977)

B. H. Liskov, A. Snyder, R. Atkinson, and C. Schaffert. ''Abstraction Mechanisms in CLU.'' **Comm. ACM 20** 8 (Aug. 1977): 564–576.

(Liskov et al. 1978)

B. Liskov, E. Moss, C. Schaffert, R. Scheiffer, and A. Snyder. ''CLU Reference Manual.'' In **Computation Structures Group Memo 161.** Cambridge, Mass.: Massachusetts Institute of Technology Laboratory for Computer Science, July 1978.

(London 1979)

See (Wegner 1979).

(London et al. 1978)
R. L. London, J. V. Guttag, J. J. Horning, B. W. Lampson, J. G. Mitchell, and G. J. Popek. "Proof Rules for the Programming Language Euclid." **Acta Informatica 10** (1978): 1–26.

(Lucas and Walk 1969)
P. Lucas and K. Walk. "On the Formal Description of PL/I." **Annual Review of Automatic Programming 6** 3 (1969): 105–182.

(MacLaren 1977)
D. M. MacLaren. "Exception Handling in PL/I." **Proceedings Conference on Language Design for Reliable Software—SIGPLAN Notices 12** 3 (March 1977): 101–104.

(Magó 1980)
G. A. Magó. "A Network of Microprocessors to Execute Reduction Languages." **Int. J. Computer and Information Sci.** 1980.

(Manna 1973)
Z. Manna. **The Mathematical Theory of Computation.** New York: McGraw-Hill, 1973.

(Marlin 1980)
C. D. Marlin. **Coroutines.** Lecture Notes in Computer Science 95. New York: Springer Verlag, 1980.

(McCarthy 1960)
J. McCarthy. "Recursive Functions of Symbolic Expressions and Their Computation by Machine." **Comm. ACM 3** 4 (April 1960): 184–195.

(McCarthy 1963**a**)
J. McCarthy. "A Basis for a Mathematical Theory of Computation." In **Computer Programming and Formal Systems,** eds. P. Braffort and D. Hirschberg: 33–37. Amsterdam: North-Holland, 1963.

(McCarthy 1963**b**)
J. McCarthy. "Towards a Mathematical Science of Computation." Proceedings of IFIP Congress (Munich): 21–28. Amsterdam: North-Holland, 1963.

(McCarthy et al. 1965)
J. McCarthy, P. W. Abrahams, D. J. Edwards, T. P. Hart, and M. I. Levin. **LISP 1.5 Programmer's Manual.** 2nd edition. Cambridge, Mass.: The MIT Press, 1965.

(McCarthy 1978)
See (ACM-SIGPLAN 1978).

(Metzger 1973)
P. W. Metzger. **Managing a Programming Project.** Englewood Cliffs, N.J.: Prentice-Hall, 1973.

(Mitchell et al. 1979)
J. G. Mitchell, W. Maybury, and R. Sweet. **Mesa Language Manual (Version 5.0)** Xerox Research Center, Palo Alto, Cal.: CSL-79-3 (Apr. 1979).

(Moon 1974)
D. A. Moon. **MACLISP Reference Manual.** Project MAC Technical Report. Cambridge, Mass.: Massachusetts Institute of Technology, 1974.

(Myers 1975)
G. J. Myers. **Reliable Software through Composite Design**. New York: Petrocelli/ Charter, 1975.

(Myers 1976)
G. J. Myers. **Software Reliability: Principles and Practices**. New York: J. Wiley, 1976.

(Myers 1978)
G. J. Myers. **Composite/Structured Design**. New York: Van Nostrand Reinhold, 1978.

(Myers 1979)
G. J. Myers. **The Art of Software Testing**. New York: J. Wiley, 1979.

(Naur 1963)
P. Naur, ed. "Revised Report on the Algorithms Language ALGOL 60." **Comm ACM 6** 1 (Jan. 1963): 1–17. See also (Rosen 1967).

(Naur 1978)
See (ACM-SIGPLAN 1978).

(Nori et al. 1976)
K. V. Nori, U. Ammann, K. Jensen, H. H. Nageli, and Ch. Jacobi. **The Pascal "P" Compiler: Implementation Notes**, rev. Edition. Berichte Nr. 10. Zurich: Institut fur Informatik, Eidgenossische Technische Hochschule, 1976.

(Nygaard and Dahl 1978)
See (ACM-SIGPLAN 1978).

(Organick et al. 1978)
E. I. Organick, A. I. Forsythe, and R. P. Plummer. **Programming Language Structures**. New York: Academic Press, 1978.

(Pagan 1976)
F. P. Pagan. **Practical Guide to ALGOL 68**. New York: J. Wiley, 1976.

(Parnas 1972**a**)
D. L. Parnas. "A Technique for Module Specification with Examples." **Comm. ACM 15** 5 (May 1972): 330–336.

(Parnas 1972**b**)
D. L. Parnas. "On the Criteria to Be Used in Decomposing Systems into Modules." **Comm. ACM 15** 12 (Dec. 1972): 1053–1058.

(Parnas 1975)
D. L. Parnas. "On the Design and Development of Program Families." **IEEE Transactions on Software Engineering SE-2** 1 (March 1975): 1–9.

(Parnas 1977)
See (Yeh 1977).

(Parnas and Würges 1976)
D. L. Parnas and H. Würges. "Response to Undesired Events in Software Systems." **Proceedings 2nd Intl. Conference on Software Engineering**. IEEE cat. no. 76CH1125-4C: 437–446 (San Francisco, Cal., 13–15 Oct., 1976).

(Peck 1970)
J. E. L. Peck, ed. **ALGOL 68 Implementation**. Amsterdam: North-Holland, 1970.

(Perlis 1978)
See (ACM-SIGPLAN 1978).

(Polivka and Pakin 1975)
R. P. Polivka and S. Pakin. **APL: The Language and Its Usage**. Englewood Cliffs, N.J.: Prentice-Hall, 1975.

(Popek et al. 1977)
G. J. Popek, J. J. Horning, B. W. Lampson, J. G. Mitchell, and R. L. London. "Notes on the Design of Euclid." **Proceedings ACM Conference on Language Design for Reliable Software—SIGPLAN Notices 12** 3 (March 1977): 11–18.

(Pozefsky 1977)
M. Pozefsky. "Programming in Reduction Languages." Ph.D. dissertation. Univ. of North Carolina Computer Science Dept., 1977.

(Pratt 1975)
T. W. Pratt. **Programming Languages: Design and Implementation**, Englewood Cliffs, N.J.: Prentice-Hall, 1975.

(Pyle 1981)

I. C. Pyle. **The Ada Programming Language.** Englewood Cliffs, N.J.: Prentice-Hall, 1981.

(Radin 1978)

See (ACM-SIGPLAN 1978).

(Randell 1975)

B. Randell. "System Structure for Software Fault Tolerance." **IEEE Transactions on Software Engineering SE-1** 2 (June 1975): 220–232.

(Randell and Russell 1964)

B. Randell and L. Russell. **ALGOL 60 Implementation**. New York: Academic Press, 1964.

(Reynolds 1970)

J. C. Reynolds. "GEDANKEN—A Simple Typeless Language Based on the Principle of Completeness and the Reference Concept." **Comm. ACM 13** 5 (May 1970): 305–319.

(Reynolds 1979)

J. C. Reynolds. "Syntactic Control of Interference." **Proc. Fifth Annual ACM Symp. on Principles of Programming Languages**. Tucson, Ariz.: Jan. 23–25, 1979.

(Richard and Ledgard 1977)

F. Richard and H. F. Ledgard. "A Reminder for Language Designers." **SIGPLAN Notices 12** 12 (Dec. 1977): 73–82.

(Richards 1969)

M. Richards. "BCPL: A Tool for Compiler and System Writing." **Spring Joint Comp. Conference** (1969): 557–566.

(Ritchie and Thompson 1974)

D. Ritchie and K. Thompson. "The UNIX Time-Sharing System." **Comm. ACM 17** 7 (July 1974): 365–375.

(Rosen 1967)

S. Rosen. **Programming Systems and Languages**. New York: McGraw-Hill, 1967.

(Sammet 1969)

J. E. Sammet. **Programming Languages: History and Fundamentals**. Englewood Cliffs, N.J.: Prentice-Hall, 1969.

(Sammet 1978)
   See (ACM-SIGPLAN 1978).

(Sandewall 1978)
   E. Sandewall. "Programming in the Interactive Environment: The LISP Experience." **ACM Computing Surveys 10** 1 (March 1978): 35–71.

(Schorr and Waite 1967)
   H. Schorr and W. Waite. "An Efficient Machine Independent Procedure for Garbage Collection in Various List Structures." **Comm. ACM 10** 8 (Aug. 1967): 501–506.

(Schwartz 1974)
   J. T. Schwartz. **On Programming: An Interim Report on the SETL Project**. New York: Courant Inst. Math. Sci. of New York Univ., 1974.

(Schwartz 1978**a**)
   R. L. Schwartz. "Parallel Compilation: A Design and Its Application to SIMULA 67." **Journal of Computer Languages 3** (1978): 75–94.

(Schwartz 1978**b**)
   R. L. Schwartz. "An Axiomatic Semantic Definition of ALGOL 68." Ph.D. dissertation. Univ. of Calif. at Los Angeles Computer Science Dept. Rep. no. UCLA-ENG-7838, July 1978.

(Shaw et al. 1977)
   M. Shaw, W. A. Wulf, and R. L. London. "Abstraction and Verification in Alphard: Defining and Specifying Iteration and Generation." **Comm. ACM 20** 8 (Aug. 1977): 553–564.

(Siklóssy 1976)
   L. Siklóssy. **Let's Talk LISP**. Englewood Cliffs, N.J.: Prentice-Hall, 1976.

(Snook et al. 1978)
   T. Snook, C. Bass, J. Roberts, A. Nahapetian, and M. Fay. **Report on the Programming Language PLZ/SYS**. New York: Springer Verlag, 1978.

(Steele 1975)
   G. L. Steele. "Multiprocessing Compactifying Garbage Collection." **Comm. ACM 18** 9 (Sept. 1975): 495–508.

(Steele and Sussman 1980)
   G. L. Steele and G. J. Sussman. "Design of a LISP-Based Microprocessor." **Comm. ACM 23** 11 (Nov. 1980): 628–645.

(Tai 1980)
   K.-C. Tai. "Program Testing Complexity and Test Criteria." **IEEE Transactions on Software Engineering SE-6** 6 (Nov. 1980): 531–538.

(Tanenbaum 1976)
   A. S. Tanenbaum. "A Tutorial on ALGOL 68." **ACM Computing Surveys 8** 2 (June 1976): 155–190.

(Tanenbaum 1978)
   A. S. Tanenbaum. "A Comparison of Pascal and ALGOL 68." **Computer Journal 21** (1978): 316–323.

(Tausworthe 1977)
   R. C. Tausworthe. **Standardized Development of Computer Software**. Englewood Cliffs, N.J.: Prentice-Hall, 1977.

(Teichrow and Hershey 1977)
   D. Teichrow and E. A. Hershey III. "PSL/PSA: A Computer-Aided Technique for Structured Documentation and Analysis of Information Processing." **IEEE Transactions on Software Engineering SE-3** 1 (Jan. 1977): 41–48.

(Teitelman 1975)
   W. Teitelman. **INTERLISP Reference Manual**. Palo Alto, Cal.: Xerox Research Center Technical Report, 1975.

(Teitelman and Masinter 1981)
   W. Teitelman and L. Masinter. "The INTERLISP Programming Environment." **IEEE Computer 14** 4 (April 1981): 25–33.

(Tennent 1973)
   R. D. Tennent. "Mathematical Semantics of SNOBOL4." **Proceedings ACM Symp. on Principles of Programming Languages**. (Boston, 1973): 95–107.

(Tennent 1976)
   R. D. Tennent. "The Denotational Semantics of Programming Languages." **Comm. ACM 19** 8 (Aug. 1976): 437–453.

(Tennent 1978)
   R. D. Tennent. "Another Look at Type Compatibility in Pascal." **Software— Practice and Experience 8** (1978): 429–437.

(Tichy 1979)
   W. F. Tichy. "Software Development Based on System Structure Description." **Proceedings 4th Intl. Conference on Software Engineering**. IEEE cat. no. 79CH1479-5C (Munich, Sept. 1979): 29–41.

(Valentine 1974)
S. H. Valentine. "Comparative Notes on ALGOL 68 and PL/I." **Computer Journal 17** (1974): 325–331.

(van der Poel and Maarsen 1974)
W. L. van der Poel and L. A. Maarsen, eds. **Machine Oriented Higher Level Languages**. Amsterdam: North-Holland, 1974.

(van Wijngaarden et al. 1976)
A. van Wijngaarden, B. J. Mailloux, J. E. L. Peck, C. H. A. Koster, M. Sintzoff, C. H. Lindsey, L. G. L. T. Meertens, and R. G. Fisker. **Revised Report on the Algorithmic Language ALGOL 68**. New York: Springer-Verlag, 1976.

(Walker et al. 1980)
B. J. Walker, R. A. Kemmerer, and G. J. Popek. "Specification and Verification of the UCLA UNIX Security Kernel." **Comm ACM 23** 2 (Feb. 1980): 118–131.

(Wegbreit 1974**a**)
B. Wegbreit. "The ECL Programming System." **Fall Joint Comp. Conf.** (1974): 253–262.

(Wegbreit 1974**b**)
B. Wegbreit. "The Treatment of Data Types in EL1." **Comm. ACM 17** 5 (May 1974): 251–264.

(Wegbreit and Spitzen 1977)
B. Wegbreit and J. Spitzen. "Proving Properties of Complex Data Structures." **Journal ACM 23** 2 (April 1976): 389–396.

(Wegner 1968)
P. Wegner. **Programming Languages, Information Structures, and Machine Organization**. New York: McGraw-Hill, 1968.

(Wegner 1972)
P. Wegner. "The Vienna Definition Language." **ACM Computing Surveys 4** 1 (1972): 5–63.

(Wegner 1976)
P. Wegner. "Programming Languages—The First 25 Years." **IEEE Transaction on Computers C-25** 12 (1976): 1207–1225.

(Wegner 1979)
P. Wegner, ed. **Research Directions in Software Technology**. Cambridge, Mass.: The MIT Press, 1979.

(Wegner 1980)
P. Wegner. **Programming with Ada: An Introduction by Means of Graduated Examples**. Englewood Cliffs, N.J.: Prentice-Hall, 1980.

(Weinberg 1971)
G. M. Weinberg. **The Psychology of Computer Programming**. New York: Van Nostrand Reinhold, 1971.

(Welsh et al. 1977)
J. Welsh, M. J. Sneeringer, and C. A. R. Hoare. "Ambiguities and Insecurities in Pascal." **Software—Practice and Experience 7** 6 (Nov. 1977): 685–696.

(Wichmann 1973)
B. A. Wichmann. **ALGOL 60 Compilation and Assessment**. London: Academic Press, 1973.

(Williams 1979)
G. Williams. "Program Checking." **Proceedings Symposium on Compiler Construction—SIGPLAN Notices 14** 8 (Aug. 1979).

(Winograd 1979)
T. Winograd. "Beyond Programming Languages." **Comm. ACM 22** 7 (1979): 391–401.

(Wirth 1968)
N. Wirth. "PL360, A Programming Language for the 360 Computers." **Journal of the ACM 15** 1 (Jan. 1968): 37–74.

(Wirth 1971**a**)
N. Wirth. "The Programming Language Pascal." **Acta Informatica 1** (1971): 35–63.

(Wirth 1971**b**)
N. Wirth. "Program Development by Stepwise Refinement." **Comm. ACM 14** 4 (April 1971): 221–227.

(Wirth 1971**c**)
N. Wirth. "The Design of a Pascal Compiler." **Software—Practice and Experience 1** (1971): 309–333.

(Wirth 1973)
N. Wirth. **Systematic Programming**. Englewood Cliffs, N.J.: Prentice-Hall, 1973.

(Wirth 1974)
N. Wirth. "On the Composition of Well-Structured Programs." **ACM Computing Surveys 6** 4 (Dec. 1974): 247–259.

(Wirth 1975**a**)

N. Wirth. ''On the Design of Programming Languages.'' In **Information Processing 74** (Proc. IFIP Congress 74). Amsterdam: North-Holland, 1975.

(Wirth 1975**b**)

N. Wirth. ''An Assessment of the Programming Language Pascal.'' **IEEE Transactions on Software Engineering SE-1** 2 (June 1975): 192–198.

(Wirth 1976**a**)

N. Wirth. **Algorithms + Data Structures = Programs**. Englewood Cliffs, N.J.: Prentice-Hall, 1976.

(Wirth 1976**b**)

N. Wirth. ''Modula: A Language for Modular Multi-programming.'' **Software—Practice and Experience 7** (1977): 3–35.

(Wirth 1976**c**)

N. Wirth. ''The Use of Modula.'' **Software—Practice and Experience 7** (1977): 37–65.

(Wirth 1976**d**)

N. Wirth. ''Design and Implementation of Modula.'' **Software—Practice and Experience 7** (1977): 67–84.

(Wirth 1977)

N. Wirth. ''Toward a Discipline of Real-Time Programming.'' **Comm. ACM 20** 8 (Aug. 1977): 577–583.

(Wirth 1978)

N. Wirth. ''Modula-2.'' Tech. Report 27. Zurich: Institut fur Informatik, ETH, Dec. 1978.

(Wirth 1979)

N. Wirth. ''The Module: A System Structuring Facility in High-Level Programming Languages.'' Internal Tech. Report. Zurich: Institut fur Informatik, ETH, Sept. 1979.

(Wortman 1979)

D. B. Wortman. ''On Legality Assertions in Euclid.'' **IEEE Transactions on Software Engineering SE-5** 4 (1979): 359–367.

(Wulf 1977)

See (Yeh 1977).

(Wulf and Shaw 1973)

W. A. Wulf and M. Shaw. ''Global Variables Considered Harmful.'' **SIGPLAN Notices 8** 2 (Feb. 1973): 80–86.

(Wulf et al. 1971)
W. A. Wulf, D. B. Russell, and A. N. Habermann. "BLISS: A Language for Systems Programming." **Comm. ACM 1** 12 (Dec. 1971): 780–790.

(Wulf et al. 1972)
W. A. Wulf, et al. **BLISS-11 Programmer's Manual**. Maynard, Mass.: Digital Equipment Corp., 1972.

(Wulf, et al. 1975)
W. A. Wulf, R. K. Johnsson, C. B. Weinstock, S. O. Hobbs, and C. M. Geschke. **The Design of An Optimizing Compiler**. New York: American Elsevier, 1975.

(Wulf et al. 1976)
W. A. Wulf, R. L. London, and M. Shaw. "An Introduction to the Construction and Verification of Alphard Programs." **IEEE Transactions on Software Engineering SE-2** (Dec. 1976): 253–265.

(Yeh 1977**a**)
R. T. Yeh, ed. **Current Trends in Programming Methodology**. Vol. 1, **Software Specification and Design**. Englewood Cliffs, N.J.: Prentice-Hall, 1977.

(Yeh 1977**b**)
R. T. Yeh, ed. **Current Trends in Programming Methodology**. Vol. 2, **Program Validation**. Englewood Cliffs, N.J.: Prentice-Hall, 1977.

(Yeh 1978)
R. T. Yeh, ed. **Current Trends in Programming Methodology**. Vol. 4, **Data Structuring**. Englewood Cliffs, N.J.: Prentice-Hall, 1978.

(Yourdon 1975)
E. Yourdon. **Techniques of Program Structure and Design**. Englewood Cliffs, N.J.: Prentice-Hall, 1975.

(Zahn 1974)
C. T. Zahn. "A Control Statement for Natural Top-Down Structured Programming." **Symp. on Programming Languages**. Paris, 1974.

(Zahn 1979)
C. T. Zahn. **C Notes—A Guide to the C Programming Language**. New York: Yourdon Press, 1979.

(Zelkowitz et al. 1979)
M. V. Zelkowitz, A. C. Shaw, and J. D. Gannon. **Principles of Software Engineering and Design**. Englewood Cliffs, N.J.: Prentice-Hall, 1979.

INDEX